PUBLIC POLICY STUDIES IN AMERICAN GOVERNMENT

Edgar Litt, General Editor

POLITICAL SOCIALIZATION AND EDUCATIONAL CLIMATES

A Study of Two School Districts

POLITICAL SOCIALIZATION AND EDUCATIONAL CLIMATES
A Study of Two School Districts

RICHARD M. MERELMAN
University of Wisconsin

HOLT, RINEHART AND WINSTON, INC.

*New York   Chicago   San Francisco   Atlanta
Dallas   Montreal   Toronto   London   Sydney*

Copyright © 1971 by Holt, Rinehart and Winston, Inc.
All rights reserved
Library of Congress Catalog Card Number: 78-142827
SBN: 03-078655-X
Printed in the United States of America
1234 68 987654321

To the educators,
   especially R. D. M. and the late M. E. M.

Foreword to the Series

A series devoted to the consequences of American public policy ought, at the outset, to indicate why it came into being. What has been lacking in the scholarly literature is overt analysis of the political consequences of policy on human institutions and on the life style of human beings themselves. A review of the literature convinced the editor, and his colleagues who are to contribute to the series, that the vast analytical skills of political scientists have for too long been directed at the "input" side of politics, the ways in which policy is fashioned or administered out of the mélange of groups competing for public favor. Scholars have studied the behavior of organized interest groups, the calculations of administrative and policy experts, and the meaning of concrete policies for the totality of the political system itself. Yet, in an era where federal policies themselves are major sources of impact and of innovations on society, it is crucial that the scope of our inquiries not be restricted.

The scholar's responsibility extends to an evaluation of policy-forming agencies in terms of clear and realistic values and to an evaluation of the impact of policy "outputs" on the social system. Such responsibility has been asserted by one critical voice in the present epoch in this way:

> Of basic importance is the modern redefinition of "politics." No longer does the term refer to the promotion of justice or the search for the best organization of social life. The term now refers to "who gets what, when, how" or to some similar concept, which focuses not on justice but on power. This focus makes political science more quantifiable and political scientists more pliable and useful for the powers that be. At the same time it severs the study of politics from any direct bearing on the task of developing institutions and organizations in the service of human needs.[1]

The volumes in this series will raise this issue for the distribution of power in the American society, the civil liberties of the individual in times of immense governmental control, the quality of personal and political education received by black and white Americans, and the distribution of housing and other social goods in our urban centers. In our view, this perspective best accounts for the processes and quality of our political life. Moreover, these studies build on the intellectual tradition of public policy exploration that has importantly contributed to the maturation of the field of political science itself.

Storrs, Connecticut   E. L.

---

[1] Christian Bay, "The Cheerful Science of Dismal Politics," in Theodore Roszak (ed.), *The Dissenting Academy* (New York: Pantheon, 1967), p. 3.

Preface

This is a study of political socialization as it proceeds in two California school districts. It is an attempt to investigate how one public service—education—affects the attitudes and behavior of future citizens. No claim is made that the results reported here are completely representative, but they are indicative.

Education is a service that brings together constituencies of students, teachers, administrators, and lay citizens. The effectiveness of this service depends upon the behavior of its constituents: the ability and desire of students to learn, of teachers to teach, of administrators to recruit and protect good teachers, and of citizens to support good education. These are the issues we investigate.

Methodologically and theoretically, this study falls into the genre of policy analysis now known as impact research. Until recently, most policy analysis focused on the outputs of political decisions rather than on the social effects of these outputs. By contrast, this analysis places impact at the center of its concerns.

The difficulties in assessing impact are many; this study has at least confronted them all.

Every author has many helpers, but I doubt that any needed more than I. My enduring thanks go to: the staff of the UCLA Computing Center and Harold Hayward, Peter Lenz, and Terry Jackson, for their help in the data analysis; Douglas Madsen, who aided in the analysis of the teacher material; Margaret Coe, Isaac Winegart, Perry Hirsch, and Harriet Stillman for their precise and rapid coding; the UCLA Survey Research Center, particularly Dr. Michael Walton and Ruth Glucksman, for their supervision of the teacher interviews; and my colleague at UCLA, Carl Hensler, whose reading of Chapter 3 improved it materially.

I owe much to Katherine Ann Goldstein, who served as my research assistant in the early phases of the study. I am particularly indebted to William Broadbent, my research assistant for the bulk of the project. Bill's knowledge, enthusiasm, and dedication combined to provide me a resource any investigator would envy. The administrators and teachers of my two districts were patient and cooperative. I have come away from this study with much admiration for their efforts to provide education to an often uncongenial public. I hope some of my respect for them reveals itself in the pages to follow.

This research was supported by the UCLA Civic Education Committee, Professor Richard Longaker, Chairman; the University of California; and the Department of Health, Education, and Welfare, Office of Education, under Grant #OEG-9-8-081104-0123 (010). I am grateful to all parties.

My wife and son have had sizeable portions of their lives disrupted by the demands of this research. Each has responded graciously. Both have looked forward to the day when this project would not haunt us. Praise be, that day is here.

Madison, Wisconsin   R. M. M.
December 1970

Contents

POLITICAL SOCIALIZATION AND EDUCATIONAL CLIMATES
A Study of Two School Districts

Chapter 1
The Schools and Political Learning

This book has a number of interwoven purposes, but what holds them together—the seam of this inquiry, as it were—is the public school; the study revolves around the public school as the planets circle the sun. The following questions arise: Why should we pay special attention to the schools? What reason is there to start with the schools if we want to explore the way children become citizens? Don't we already know how limited a role the schools play in the political socialization of the young?

THE SCHOOL AS AN OBJECT OF INQUIRY

Although these questions are powerful, there seem to be several ways in which they might be answered. First, generations of Americans have nourished the belief that the way to the good American life leads through a common public-school experience, which, if successfully mastered, provides children with the social skills, intellectual competence, and business credentials necessary for success in a competitive society. Having come to this conclusion, Americans have adopted the public school as an article of faith in the national life. They have sheltered it from the winds of politics the best they could, have contributed untold billions of dollars to its development, and have, through widespread local control, kept it close to themselves and their purposes.

Some observers claim that Americans have miscalculated the actual character of the public school. This charge, though perhaps true, is of less importance than the fact that the relationship between the public school and the American people has been unique. While other countries are making more or less successful efforts to nationalize their educational systems, Americans are still attempting to keep their public schools responsive to "the grass roots." As a consequence, public schooling remains one of the last important American governmental services to have most of its finances, control, and character lodged in truly local districts.[1] Housing, economic planning, city structures, transportation, and even agriculture —all are now subject to national control. Why then have Americans clung so tenaciously to local dominance over the public school? Perhaps if we can answer this question, we can begin to justify this study's special interest in the schools.

Few would argue that the peculiar American preoccupation with public education derives from solicitude for the intellectual life. On the contrary, as Richard Hofstader has pointed out, Americans often make intellectuals their first targets when political ills are widespread.[2]

It seems more likely that the character of public education in the United States is rooted in the national origins. Americans are all immigrants, and although some studies indicate that the marks of immigration are now slowly fading as an influence on our politics, for generations the ethnic identities in America shaped

[1] Approximately 60 percent of public school costs are paid from local taxes. For details, see Jesse Burkhead, *State and Local Taxes for Public Education* (Syracuse, N.Y.: Syracuse University Press, 1963), pp. 5–6.

[2] Richard Hofstader, *Anti-Intellectualism in American Life* (New York: Alfred A. Knopf, Inc., 1963).

its political and social life.[3] Many immigrants had fled from countries that denied them a share in the national life. The badge of inferiority in such societies was either a child's inability to attend school at all or the inferior character of the schooling provided him. Although education remained an avenue of mobility in those societies, mobility proceeded, in Turner's phrase, by "sponsorship" rather than by "contest."[4] Most children had no sponsors.

Therefore, it should be clear why an open public-school system that provided avenues of ascent for all was especially attractive to Americans.[5] Such an educational system gradually came to be seen as a right to which all Americans were entitled, and massive pressures were brought to secure the right. The Black Revolution only reminds us of the depths of these sentiments. As the black man objects to the inequality and inferiority of his schooling, he speaks for all his disadvantaged predecessors who also saw in an open public-school system the first hope for their own rise.

The public school, therefore, held a special place for the immigrant. But the school was equally important for those who already occupied secure positions in the American scene. Although many native Americans feared the hordes of immigrants and some actually urged the end of immigration, others felt that the immigrants could be assimilated, but only if the public schools inculcated in them an appreciation of American values. Thus, reluctantly, many native Americans came to the financial and political support of public education. More important, only the wives and daughters of native Americans possessed the skills to teach the immigrants. Therefore, a combination of self-interest and personal

[3] For an important general consideration of this topic, see Oscar Handlin, *The Uprooted* (New York: Grosset and Dunlap, Inc., 1951). For details on the continued importance of ethnic identities in the politics of a northeastern state, see Edgar Litt, *The Political Cultures of Massachusetts* (Cambridge, Mass.: The MIT Press, 1965). See also Robert A. Dahl, *Who Governs?* (New Haven, Conn.: Yale University Press, 1961), for an account of ethnic differences in New Haven politics.

[4] Ralph Turner, "Sponsored and Contest Mobility in the Public School System," *American Sociological Review*, 25, No. 6 (December 1960), pp. 855–867.

[5] Some immigrants, of course, also realized that the public school was a device to take the child away from his parents and funnel him into the mainstream of American life.

involvement welded native Americans to the public schools, and it seems fair to say that the dialectic of immigration helps to explain the unique character of public education in the United States.

But another major influence on the American public school had made its appearance centuries before the tide of immigration. The New England Puritans saw the school as an important agency of moral training for children, who, without it, might well fall prey to the devil.[6] It was the Puritans who were responsible for the tie between religion and education in America, a tie that is more visible today at the college level than at the primary-school or secondary-school levels. Most of the major universities in the East and a great many elsewhere originated as arms of a church. The place of the public school in moral education continues to vex the nation, as indicated by the widespread unease when the Supreme Court restricts prayer in the schools or when a college does not seem to live up to its role *in loco parentis*.

The public school is thus uniquely important to Americans as a symbol of citizenship, as a channel through which moral and political values can be inculcated, and as a link to the religious life. Perhaps it is for these reasons that Gladys A. Wiggin believes "the school is the most important instrument of cultural transmission in American society."[7] Today, of course, the school is important for a last, more compelling reason. Technological change has placed a premium on the development of talent. Even so, as John Porter points out, industrial needs and technological innovation are rapidly exhausting the current pool of competence. "It is becoming apparent that all large-scale industrial societies are failing to produce the full range of highly qualified manpower that is necessary for them to maintain themselves and to develop further their industrial potential and economic growth."[8] In large measure, it is the educational system that absorbs the blame for society's failure to exploit its resources of talent.

The situation looms especially bleak for the disadvantaged minorities in American society. Just as they begin to emerge from the nether world to which America's laws have confined them,

[6] Dahl, *Who Governs?*, pp. 141–142.
[7] Gladys A. Wiggin, *Education and Nationalism: An Historical Interpretation of American Education* (New York: McGraw-Hill, Inc., 1962), p. 34.
[8] John Porter, "The Future of Upward Mobility," *American Sociological Review*, 33, No. 1 (February 1968), p. 5.

America's industrial system seems on the verge of stealing from them the success they had envisaged. Our economy's demands outstrip their current capacities. Hardly less frustrating is the dilemma faced by the middle-class American parent, forced to threaten his son with financial hardship and loss of love if he does not work hard enough in school. Increasingly, the requirements of our highly diversified economy and the concern of parents for the success of their children combine to focus attention upon the schools. School administrators pass on these pressures to their communities in programs for more innovative curricula, higher-salaried teachers, and more and improved school facilities. These programs, because they strain community tax resources, threaten the autonomy of the local school board. Thus, both history and contemporary developments justify an interest in the public school at a time when the school faces perhaps its most severe crisis.

DIVERGENT VIEWS OF THE SCHOOL AS A SOCIALIZATION AGENT

The optimism that Wiggin voices about the centrality of the schools in conveying the national heritage has increasingly received criticism. As inquiry succeeds inquiry, it becomes difficult to believe that *any* formal agencies of political socialization can compete effectively with informal sources of political learning. The issue is complex, however.

For example, Friedenburg has written that those who derogate the schools for their bland, noncontroversial approach to the teaching of political values misunderstand the place of the school in socialization.[9] The school attempts to generate support for the political system by inculcating the most inclusive values espoused by the system. Educators do not want to divide students against one another. They believe quite rightly that consensus, not conflict, supports the political regime. Yet, it is undeniable that the school's emphasis upon the general, the ideal, and the consensual allows other socialization agencies to focus on the particular, the practical, and the divisive. The tense political world that many children ex-

[9] Edgar Z. Friedenburg, *Coming of Age in America: Growth and Acquiescence* (New York: Random House, Vintage, 1967), pp. 221–226.

perience may be far removed from the political world their teacher attempts to convey. This gap undoubtedly limits the influence of the school.

Certainly no one need doubt the pervasiveness of extraschool forces in political socialization. There is already evidence that many a child inherits through his family political values that endure for a lifetime.[10] Studies also indicate that children from different social classes react differently to politics. The middle-class child rapidly develops confidence in his ability to influence the political process. The lower-class child, however, learns early that he and his parents do not have much power in the political system.[11] We can also document the early political interests of boys and the simultaneous loss of political interest among girls. Political sex roles are apparently adopted at a tender age.[12]

As if these findings were not themselves enough to cast doubt on the school's importance in political socialization, there is even evidence that classwork in civics and political science has little effect on students. Langton and Jennings, in their study of twelfth-grade students throughout the nation, report only a slight relationship between the number of civics courses a student has taken and the nature of his political beliefs.[13] Sigmund Diamond concurs, arguing that the quantity of work done in social studies has no bearing on the acquisition of democratic political attitudes. According to Diamond, the morale and spirit of a school and the structure of the community in which pupils live determine attitudes

[10] For reviews of the literature, see Herbert Hyman, *Political Socialization* (New York: The Free Press, 1959), chap. 4; and Richard E. Dawson and Kenneth Prewitt, *Political Socialization* (Boston: Little, Brown and Company, 1968), chap. 7.

[11] For useful hints on the educational origins of this class difference, see Robert D. Hess and Judith Torney, *The Development of Political Attitudes in Childhood* (Chicago: Aldine Publishing Co., 1967), p. 149. Coleman and his associates found that the lack of a feeling of power on the part of lower-class children was closely associated with the inability to achieve well in school. See James S. Coleman *et al., Equality of Educational Opportunity* (Washington, D.C.: Government Printing Office, 1966), p. 23.

[12] Fred I. Greenstein, *Children and Politics* (New Haven, Conn.: Yale University Press, 1965), chap. 6.

[13] Kenneth P. Langton and M. Kent Jennings, "Political Socialization and the High School Civics Curriculum," *American Political Science Review*, 62, No. 3 (September 1968), pp. 852–868.

more completely than does the finest instruction.[14] Even in college, where we would expect teaching to have its greatest impact, variations in the structure of introductory political-science courses apparently exert no influence on student attitudes toward political participation.[15]

The school seems to be lagging behind other socialization agencies in the race to inculcate political values. But if the matter is so clear-cut, how can different authors come to such divergent conclusions? Hess and Torney state that *"the public school is the most important and effective instrument of political socialization in the United States."*[16] Herbert Hyman, however, claims that most political values of any importance are passed on from generation to generation. He reports a high correlation between parent and child political party identification,[17] and Jennings and Niemi place this correlation at .47.[18] Yet Hess and Torney argue that "children's attitudes towards partisan commitment appear to be most completely socialized by the school. . . ."[19] In addition, according to Martin Levin, "the climate of political opinion in the high school community appears to be exerting influence on all the students within the community to choose the political party that had already been chosen by the majority of the adult members, regardless of the party preferences of their own parents."[20]

There is also disagreement about the age structure of political socialization as it intersects the school. Hess and Easton claim that by the time high-school teachers begin their attempt to transmit

[14] Sigmund Diamond, "Studies and Projects in Citizenship Education," in Franklin Patterson (ed.), *The Adolescent Citizen* (New York: The Free Press, 1960), pp. 72–73.

[15] Albert Somit *et al.*, "The Effect of the Introductory Political Science Course on Student Attitudes towards Personal Political Participation," *American Political Science Review*, 52, No. 4 (December 1958), pp. 1129–1132.

[16] Hess and Torney, *The Development of Political Attitudes in Children*, p. 200. Italics theirs.

[17] Hyman, *Political Socialization*, pp. 69–74.

[18] M. Kent Jennings and Richard G. Niemi, "The Transmission of Political Values from Parent to Child," *American Political Science Review*, 62, No. 1 (March 1968), pp. 169–185.

[19] Hess and Torney, *The Development of Political Attitudes in Children*, p. 365.

[20] Martin L. Levin, "Social Climates and Political Socialization," *Public Opinion Quarterly*, 25, No. 4 (Winter 1961), p. 601.

political attitudes, the child is already well-socialized politically.[21] Litt, however, shows that differing high-school civics courses can have substantial effects.[22] And Maccoby *et al.* apparently concur, suggesting that public education encourages political change by forcing students to reconsider the political predispositions they bring with them from home.[23] Student self-examination is more likely to occur in the intellectually demanding milieu of the high school than in the custodial atmosphere of the elementary school.

The confusion that we have documented has several sources. The student populations observed and the methodologies employed have varied. In some cases, different investigators began with different preconceptions or pursued divergent goals. While our study attempts in part to restudy the questions these investigators have raised, we have deliberately limited ourselves to only a few of those facets of the school setting that might affect political socialization. These facets bear most directly on the political position of the school in the community. We have asked ourselves whether the aspects of education that occupy most of the community attention, such as the quality of instruction and the character of the teaching staff, have effects on the political socialization of students. We could have studied other, perhaps more promising, educational variables. Here we refer, of course, to the social structure of the school—its informal organizations and cliques.[24] We have not investigated these informal mechanisms because we have been primarily concerned to know if those aspects of the school setting most under the influence of the educational policy maker bear any relation to political socialization. Do the elements of schooling that occupy the center of policy-making debate and that, therefore, are the most amenable to policy innovation or change

[21] Robert D. Hess and David Easton, "The Role of the Elementary School in Political Socialization," *The School Review*, 70, No. 3 (Autumn 1962), pp. 257–267.

[22] Edgar Litt, "Civic Education, Community Norms, and Political Indoctrination," *American Sociological Review*, 28, No. 1 (February 1965), pp. 69–75.

[23] Eleanor E. Maccoby, Richard E. Matthews, and Anton S. Morton, "Youth and Political Change," *Public Opinion Quarterly*, 18, No. 1 (Fall 1954), pp. 23–39.

[24] For one of the best studies of this aspect of the problem, see James S. Coleman, *The Adolescent Society* (New York: The Free Press, 1961). See also H. O. Dahlke, *Values in Culture and Classroom: A Study in the Society of the School* (New York: Harper and Row, Publishers, 1958).

touch the process of political socialization? If they do, then policy makers can, by their decisions, shape political socialization. If they do not, then the public, the policy makers, the teachers, and the students are not really playing the same game. Whatever the outcome of our inquiry, we should be able to focus on forces critical to the school in its attempt at political socialization. We should also be able to buttress prescriptive arguments with empirical data.

AN APPROACH TO THE STUDY OF THE SCHOOL
AS AN AGENT OF SOCIALIZATION

Americans spend billions of dollars each year in an attempt to purchase quality public education for their children. They hope that the money they spend will somehow be transformed into programs capable of spurring their children's cognitive growth. They believe that good schools will recruit able teachers, who can communicate effectively the democratic values espoused by the American political system. It is the public's expectation of a relationship between school quality and democratic socialization that we wish to investigate.

We have already described the doubt surrounding the effects of social-studies course work on political values, but our concern goes beyond this question. After all, school quality encompasses much more than the social-studies curriculum.

We also focus on the school district as a whole, not on the individual school. The school district is the political unit that channels the educational aspirations of a community and the decisions of policy makers. Therefore, if we wish to propose or to evaluate educational policies as they affect political socialization, we must focus on the entire school district, for it is the political agency of political socialization in the schools. This emphasis also involves a methodological premise of some import.

The "behavioral" revolution thrust a wedge into the discipline of political science. Traditional political scientists thought wrong the behavioralists' concentration on attitudinal and extragovernmental sources of political behavior. Such an orientation, they felt, ignored the impact of the institutional and organizational structure of the political system itself. Worse, it ignored policy—the substance of political life. Behavioralists, however, believed that the traditionalists' focus on formal organizations provided only a superficial look at the actual nature of political conduct. The resulting chasm has until recently not been bridged. This study is another step in the bridging process.[25]

We are attempting to describe a relationship between quality education—an output of a governmental structure—and political socialization. In so doing, we try to link the traditionalist's concern with policy making in such governmental organizations as the school district with the behavioralist's attention to attitudes and values. Our goal is to offer several supported propositions relating attitudinal and institutional variables to each other.

Why should we suspect there to be any relationship at all between educational quality and democratic socialization? Milbrath[26] cites many studies that demonstrate a correlation between the amount of education and the belief in such democratic values as political efficacy and civic obligation. We know that students who proceed to higher education normally develop more democratic attitudes than do those students left behind. But Milbrath does not consider the possibility that it is educational quality that might be responsible for *both* student educational success and support for democratic values.

There is another more plausible possibility, however. A process of self-selection may be operating. Perhaps students who come from homes that convey democratic values perform well in school and go to the best schools, thereby winning the right to higher education. The actual effect, either of amount or quality of education, may be minimal.

Our task is complicated even further because the majority of successful university students come from relatively affluent families and communities. Most studies also suggest a strong relationship between educational quality and the class structure of a school district.[27] Consequently, it is difficult to disentangle the effects of

[25] An essay that carefully considers prospects for a *rapprochement* is Douglas Price, "Micro- and Macro-Politics: Notes on Research Strategy," in Oliver Garceau (ed.), *Political Research and Political Theory* (Cambridge, Mass.: Harvard University Press, 1968), pp. 102–140.

[26] Lester Milbrath, *Political Participation* (Skokie, Ill.: Rand McNally and Company, 1965), pp. 57, 63.

[27] William D. Firman, "The Relationship of Cost to Quality in Education," *Long-Range Planning in School Finance*, Proceedings of the 6th National School Finance Conference (Washington, D.C.: National Education Association, 1963), pp. 101–110.

social background from the effects of quality education. Nonetheless, there is still reason to believe that educational quality is implicated in the relationship between the amount of education and the support of democracy.

The methodological problems discussed can be minimized if we measure school quality primarily with reference to educational input, rather than with reference to data on individual students. Such measurements of student attainment as scores on achievement tests, the number of students attending college, and the number of students dropping out are so heavily influenced by the socioeconomic background of the school district as to confound our task enormously; these data are useful only in a secondary capacity. In this study, therefore, we have defined school-district educational quality mainly in terms of the money spent per child and its associated program components.

There are two major advantages to this approach. First, we can take advantage of a great range of information provided by the districts. Second, and more important, the financial measure of input has already been employed in many studies of education and has been found to be a relatively reliable index of program quality.[28]

Although our efforts are thus simplified methodologically, they still remain problematic. Indeed, our survey of the literature on educational quality leads us to very mixed conclusion. Consider, for example, the fullest and most publicized recent investigation of public education, the Coleman report. Summing up his exhaustive study of a national high-school sample, Coleman writes, "it appears that differences between schools account for only a small fraction of differences in pupil achievement."[29] According to Coleman, all school-input measures combined explain only approximately 10 percent of the variance in student achievement.[30] The bulk of the variance may be traced to social and personal factors that the school seems generally unable to modify.

---

[28] For a sophisticated study in this tradition, see Jesse Burkhead, *Input and Output in Large-City High Schools* (Syracuse, N.Y.: Syracuse University Press, 1967).

[29] Coleman *et al., Equality of Educational Opportunity*, p. 21.

[30] Coleman *et al., Equality of Educational Opportunity*, p. 21. For a critique and reconsideration of Coleman's conclusions, see Henry S. Dyer, "School Factors and Equal Educational Opportunity," *Harvard Education Review*, 3, No. 1 (Winter 1968), pp. 38–56.

Yet the effectiveness of education may not be as limited as the Coleman report implies. There are some indications that the school *can* have considerable impact on the achievement of students no matter what their social background. Mollenkopf and Melville, for example, who studied one hundred high schools, discovered that instructional support per pupil was closely correlated with student achievement levels.[31] Another investigation, which controlled for background factors, traced a relatively high correlation of .27 between expenditure levels and student achievement.[32] Paul Mort not only confirms the high correlation between expenditures per student and measures of achievement, but suggests that program adaptability, or the sloughing off of outmoded educational practices, is closely related to expenditure per child.[33] Shaycoft concludes from her reanalysis of the data compiled in Project TALENT, a ten-year study of educational achievement, that much variance in student performance can be explained not by community influences but by differences between schools.[34] Shaycoft believes that the school makes its impact felt mainly in curriculum-related subjects. Finally, Firman argues that the school budget is an excellent measure both of aggregate inputs to education and of educational quality. He writes that good schools spend almost 25 percent, or approximately $125 per pupil, more than poor schools.[35] Thus, it appears that both our emphasis on expenditures and on program inputs has support in the literature; it cannot be said, however, that we will be examining a set of hypotheses that gives obvious and easy hope of validation.

These considerations give us reason to believe that the quality of education is somehow related to the acquisition of democratic attitudes. People who go to good schools are relatively democratic,

[31] William G. Mollenkopf and S. Donald Melville, "A Study of Secondary School Characteristics as Related to Test Scores" (Princeton, N.J.: Educational Testing Service, 1956), unpublished.

[32] Samuel M. Goodman, *The Assessment of School Quality* (Albany, N.Y.: New York State Education Department, 1959), p. 49.

[33] Paul Mort and Orlando F. Furno, *Theory and Synthesis of a Sequential Simplex: A Model for Assessing the Effectiveness of Administrative Policies* (New York: Columbia University Press, 1960).

[34] Marion F. Shaycoft, *The High School Years: Growth in Cognitive Skills* (Pittsburgh, Pa.: American Institute for Research and School of Education, University of Pittsburgh, 1967), pp. 7–12.

[35] Firman, "The Relationship of Cost to Quality in Education," pp. 101–110.

and good schools contribute to high achievement, one element of which may be the acquisition of democratic attitudes. So far, however, we have ignored a crucial component of educational quality as it might influence political socialization: the teachers.

EDUCATIONAL CLIMATE AND TEACHER RECRUITMENT

Teachers are the link between the policies adopted by school boards and the outcomes of the educational process. Teachers thus reflect the views of education that prevail in their districts, but they are also relevant to this study for another, more prosaic reason. Most districts spend the bulk of their budget on the instructional staff.[36] For these two reasons, therefore, we must include teachers in our study. Ultimately the characteristics and capacities of its teachers determine the educational quality of the district.

What is the relationship between a district's budgetary decisions and the quality of its teaching staff? Answers to this question are not as self-evident as they at first appear. After all, even high salaries may not lure superior teachers to ghetto schools.

It is apparent that any investigation of the relationship between salary levels and teacher quality confronts several problems. The first is the absence of criteria by which to assign teachers quality ratings. It is true that teachers normally are subject to tenure decisions a few years after entering a district, at which time superiors judge their efforts. But, aside from their interest in good teaching, those who make tenure decisions have no guides in common.[37] Worse yet, there are different standards for different groups of teachers. For example, the ability to maintain class discipline may be counted more heavily as evidence of teaching ability in the elementary school than in the high school. Nor do some often-used criteria seem to bear much intuitive relationship to effective teaching. For instance, is there really much reason to believe that a teacher who disciplines well encourages learning?

[36] William W. Brickman, *Educational Systems in the United States* (New York: Center for Applied Research in Education, 1964), p. 54.
[37] Hazel Davis, "Evolution of Current Practices in Evaluating Teacher Competence," in Bruce S. Biddle and William J. Ellena (eds.), *Contemporary Research on Teacher Effectiveness* (New York: Holt, Rinehart and Winston, Inc., 1964), pp. 41–67.

There is a relationship between salary levels in a district and the number of applicants for teaching positions: districts that reward teachers generously expand their recruitment pool. Such districts purchase the opportunity to choose among a greater number of recruits whose credentials give evidence of teaching potential. But the closeness of relationship between teacher background and teacher quality is not clear.[38]

There is at least one undeniable link between salary levels and teacher characteristics, however. It is no secret that the teaching career contains a distinctive circulation process. As Becker points out,[39] young and inexperienced teachers are usually assigned to the least desirable schools within a district. These novices find themselves facing children whose motivation for learning is low, whose behavior may be disruptive, and whose parents are often uncooperative or unavailable. The new teacher may also find herself part of an instructional staff that has by and large reconciled itself to its own lack of influence on these discouraging conditions. It is only natural, therefore, that many young teachers who are ambitious and anxious to convey learning seek a transfer to schools in better areas or in better districts. Those districts that can lure the ambitious teacher with promising students can usually also offer the additional incentive of good salaries.

Thus, school districts that offer the twin incentives of good students and good salaries usually attract the most motivated and, probably, the best-qualified teachers. But the process is not automatic. Other influences affect the job choices of many teachers, particularly teachers at the elementary-school level. Women, who constitute a majority of elementary-school teachers, are often restricted in their choice of job by the preferences of their husbands. The husband's desire to live near his place of work may limit the job mobility of female teachers. In addition, some teachers choose their districts for idiosyncratic, purely personal reasons. Finally, many a teacher, having grown up in the community in which he teaches, is attached to it for sentimental and familial reasons.[40]

---

[38] Peter H. Rossi, "Social Factors in Academic Achievement: A Brief Review," in A. H. Halsey, Jean Flond, and C. Arnold Anderson (eds.), *Education, Economy, and Society* (New York: The Free Press, 1961), pp. 269–272.
[39] Howard S. Becker, "The Career of the Chicago Public Schoolteacher," *American Journal of Sociology*, 57, No. 5 (March 1952), pp. 470–477.
[40] Ward S. Mason, *The Beginning Teacher* (Washington, D.C.: U.S. Department of Health, Education, and Welfare, 1961), p. 54.

There are even some teachers who do not want highly moti-vated students. For some teachers, good students are more difficult than enjoyable. Student alertness, when combined with parental overconcern about the child's educational success, may create unpleasant pressure for the teacher. Pressures such as these have convinced some teachers that the good student is likely to be a potential troublemaker or the overprivileged child of objectionable parents. There is, in other words, a host of factors that reduce the relationship between educational finance and teacher quality. Still, we can at least predict a moderate correlation and proceed accord-ingly.

The relationship between teacher quality, teacher character-istics, and the inculcation of political attitudes is not simple or well understood. We can hypothesize, however, that the impact of teachers on political socialization depends partly upon the nature of teacher recruitment, the motivation and intellectual skills of teachers, and the constraints, both administrative and political, within which teaching proceeds. Let us examine each of these factors.

Before we can speculate intelligently about the nature of teacher recruitment, it is necessary to discuss a major paradox in the general position of teaching in American society. America has not rewarded its teachers in proportion to the value it places upon education.[41] Therefore, many gifted potential teachers can find more lucrative and less anxious employment in nonteaching careers. Because our society has relegated teaching to the dedicated and the mediocre, it has weakened the education it so desires for its children.

Whatever the reason for this paradox, the results are marked. Teaching has attracted mainly two social groups: the sons of the working class and the daughters of the middle and upper class.[42] There are many reasons for this pattern of recruitment, but most involve either the financial rewards of teaching or the social mean-ing of teaching as an occupation.

The middle-class boy of average intelligence can usually aspire to a more remunerative career than that of public-school teaching. Indeed, if such a boy chooses to teach, it may be taken as a sign

---

[41] Mason, *The Beginning Teacher*, chap. 7.

[42] Harmon Zeigler, *The Political Life of American Teachers* (Englewood Cliffs, N.J.: Prentice-Hall, Inc., 1967), p. 32.

of inadequate ambition or intellectual failure. Therefore, the middle-class boy's absence opens teaching to the ambitious son of the working class.

Working-class boys find teaching a convenient and attractive mobility channel to the white-collar world. Teaching offers moblity without requiring the shrinkage of those family bonds that are particularly important in the working class. Other occupations with marginal middle-class status, such as being a salesman, may demand much traveling and long hours away from home. In addition, the prevalence and inexpensiveness of state teacher colleges have made it possible for sons of the working class to qualify as teachers without having to expend inordinate sums. The conjunction of these circumstances allows the working-class boy to purchase status cheaply through teaching. Nor should we ignore the fact that some politicians have dispensed patronage to working-class constituencies through the educational system.

The sons of the working class are attracted to teaching for their own reasons; the daughters of the middle and upper classes have quite different motives for entering teaching. Most of these motives stem from discrimination against female participation in other occupations and from the dependent position of the young married woman. Although barriers against female entrance into a wide variety of occupations are rapidly falling, many women still find the social and personal costs attached to full participation greater than they can bear. Teaching therefore remains a major source of full-time employment for women. In addition, the respectability that teaching conveys recommends it strongly to the middle-class girl. Even today, the woman in teaching conveys an image of gentility and refinement that most middle- and upper-class families embrace. Among the reasons for such an image, none is more important than the seemingly selfless character of the teaching enterprise. Partly as cause and partly as consequence of low teaching salaries, the public has expected enough moral commitment from the teacher to make virtue its own reward. The apparent selflessness of teaching fits our ideal of the woman more closely than does the materialistic, hard-driving and selfish world of business. In addition, the moral commitment of teaching seems a natural extension of the maternal childrearing role.

Of course, teaching does have some appeals to self-interest. Many single middle-class girls whose major preoccupation is marriage enjoy the quick, certain monetary rewards and the relatively noncompetitive environment of teaching. Teaching permits such girls to save the risk capital they will need to help finance the first years of marriage. In addition, many young wives teach in order to send their husbands through advanced graduate or professional training. Another attraction is that, once obtained, the teaching credential ensures a virtual lifetime of job security. A woman may leave to raise a family and return without an appreciable loss of teaching status. There is no other occupation open to women that is so receptive to lateral career movement.

Given these divergent origins and motivations, it is no surprise that men and women have different conceptions of their place in teaching. Male teachers feel distinctly less happy about their jobs than do female teachers.[43] Zeigler believes that male teachers form a pool of dissatisfaction ready to boil into protest, union activity, or political militance.[44] Women, however, are by and large pleased with teaching; indeed, their high level of satisfaction helps explain their conservatism within the teaching profession.[45] The female-dominated National Education Association has been a bulwark of political moderation, while the male-controlled American Federation of Teachers has attracted large numbers of disgruntled male teachers who wish to change the structure of the educational system.

The situation described is in flux. For one thing, resistance to female participation in nonteaching occupations is disintegrating, with unpredictable effects on recruitment to teaching. Because they need no longer feel restricted to teaching as a career, talented women may leave the profession to their less gifted sisters. The rise of teacher militance should also be considered. The activism of teachers may raise salaries, thus attracting higher-status teachers to the profession. Teacher unions may also profoundly alter the public's image of teaching. Finally, the urban crisis, with its close ties to educational inequalities and school segregation, may have a major impact on the structure of the teaching profession. In some places, teachers have already demanded greater control over their courses and are now attempting to change educational priorities.

---

[43] Zeigler, *The Political Life of American Teachers*, pp. 29–30. See also Mason, *The Beginning Teacher*, p. 81.

[44] Zeigler, *The Political Life of American Teachers*.

[45] Zeigler, *The Political Life of American Teachers*, chap. 3.

While their demands are usually made in the name of the disadvantaged, the same teachers, in an effort to maintain their job security, have also fought the disadvantaged.[46] Such inconsistencies can only emphasize the fluidity of the current situation.

THE TEACHER AND SOCIALIZATION

Strangely, debate about the changing role of the teacher in society has proceeded in virtual ignorance about any effects teachers might have on their students. No one really knows what consequences new circumstances of teaching will produce for students. Indeed, no one really knows what effects current practices have. Thus, although it is difficult to postulate a relationship between teacher quality and district salary levels, it is even more problematic to attempt to establish a connection between salaries, teacher quality, and educational outcomes. When we reflect on the vast research into education, it seems incredible that we should be so unsure about the effects of teaching.

One reason for the perplexity is the sparsity of productive research on this particular subject, a fact which seems absurd in view of the size and wealth of the teacher colleges, the state education departments, and the Federal Office of Education. All these agencies have direct interests, it would seem, in identifying the factors that produce good teaching and in demonstrating the relationship between those factors and student achievement. So far, however, the research sponsored by these agencies has provided us only scattered hints.[47]

A second reason for our lack of knowledge is the diversity of goals in public education. Should the schools encourage life adjustment or the uses of the intellect? Should they emphasize the acquisition of factual knowledge or the ability to manipulate ideas

[46] The most notable case is the now infamous Ocean Hill-Brownsville controversy. See Marilyn Gittel and Alan G. Hevesi (eds.), *The Politics of Urban Education* (New York: Frederick A. Praeger, Inc., 1968), chap. 5, pp. 23–25.

[47] However, see David G. Ryans, *Characteristics of Teachers* (Washington, D.C.: American Council on Education, 1960); and Paul O. Flanders, "Some Relationships among Teacher Influence, Pupil Attitudes, and Achievement," in Biddle and Ellena, *Contemporary Research on Teaching Effectiveness*, pp. 196–232.

creatively? Should they prepare students for college or for vocations? Because these and other debates about teaching goals remain unresolved, there exist no accepted criteria of effectiveness against which the efforts of teachers can be compared.

Many teachers would undoubtedly argue that their effectiveness is partly a function of student motivation. Some students are stimulating; others are inhibiting or downright discouraging. Some teachers perform brilliantly with bright students, but are mediocre with the less talented. The same teacher may behave differently in different districts. And, of course, teachers apply some techniques better than others. In short, teaching quality is anything but a uniform characteristic. For all these reasons, therefore, the sparseness of productive findings about teacher quality is less surprising than it first appears.

What do we know from those few useful studies that have been done? Rossi sums up the findings well when he writes that "the teacher's contributions to his students' achievement, in the short run, are minimal, i.e., the indexes of teaching experience correlate with student achievement around .2 at the maximum and are often zero or slightly negative. . . ."[48]

If existing studies of teaching effectiveness are discouraging, even more unsettling is Mayer's conclusion about social-studies teaching in particular. Mayer claims that social-studies teachers have among the lowest IQ scores of all teachers.[49] If Mayer is correct, social-studies teachers may be even less effective than are most other teachers.

But the picture is not entirely bleak. There is evidence that the higher the proportion of tenured teachers in a school, the more successful students are in achievement tests.[50] Furthermore, Dandes reports that such teacher personality characteristics as warmth, absence of authoritarianism, openness of belief systems, and liberalism of educational viewpoint aid students in their development of both democratic attitudes and critical skills.[51] In addition, Hess and Torney present evidence that teachers are effective in imbuing their

[48] Rossi, "Social Factors in Academic Achievement," p. 270.
[49] Martin Mayer, *Social Studies in American Schools* (New York: Harper and Row, Publishers, 1962), p. 20.
[50] Firman, "The Relationship of Cost to Quality in Education."
[51] Herbert M. Dandes, "Psychological Health and Teaching Effectiveness," *Journal of Teacher Education*, 17, No. 3 (Fall 1966), pp. 301–306.

students with a belief in the desirability of independent voting behavior.[52] We are therefore encouraged enough to hypothesize a relationship between school-district financial effort, teacher quality, and student achievement. We expect all these factors to aid in the growth of democratic attitudes among students.

There are, of course, environmental and social factors that can inhibit a closer link between teacher quality and pupil achievement. For example, some teachers may fear that uninhibited innovation on their part would elicit the hostility of conservative political groups and skeptical parents. Similar considerations may prevent such teachers from pursuing controversial topics. In short, community resistance may prevent good teachers from being effective.

The quality of social-studies teaching is perhaps especially sensitive to community pressures. The vulnerability of teachers to community opposition has undoubtedly had a disproportionate impact on social-studies instruction, because the social studies seem often to involve mere matters of opinion. Thus, it is not surprising to find that only a small group of teachers is committed to classroom discussion of controversial political questions.[53] Of course, the public is also split, with perhaps a majority believing that the treatment of political values should be left to the family. It is hard to see how the reluctance of teachers to confront political controversy in the classroom can help but convince the student that the school is irrelevant to the understanding of politics.

The reluctance of teachers to deal with controversial problems apparently is not wholly the result of community pressure. Withdrawal from political disputation seems to be built into the teaching career. According to Zeigler, teachers believe "that the proper place for the expression of political opinions is away from the impressionable minds of the children."[54] Carson, Goldhammer, and Pellegrin report that their sample of Oregon teachers not only takes a minimal part in political affairs outside the classroom but also feels that any greater political activity would be illegitimate.[55]

[52] Hess and Torney, *The Development of Political Attitudes in Children*, pp. 213–214.
[53] Zeigler, *The Political Life of American Teachers*, pp. 98–99.
[54] Zeigler, *The Political Life of American Teachers*, pp. 98–99.
[55] Robert B. Carson, Keith Goldhammer, and Roland Pellegrin, *Teacher Participation in the Community* (Eugene, Ore.: University of Oregon, Center for Advanced Study in Educational Administration, 1967), pp. 21–32.

Zeigler presents evidence indicating a positive relationship between teaching experience and political conservatism. Conservative teachers are also less likely than liberal teachers to express their political values in class or to confront controversial problems.[56] It thus follows that the teacher's experience is negatively related to political disputation in the classroom.

It appears that the impact of teacher quality on political socialization is complex and indirect. But the data are sufficiently scattered and unclear that we can still predict a positive, though complicated relationship between district financial support for education, teacher quality, and the development of democratic values in students. Estimating the extent and character of that relationship, however, will not be an easy task, and the connection between these variables may turn out to be weak and diffuse.

THE COMMUNITY ENVIRONMENT OF EDUCATION

The quality of education depends upon community educational values as well as upon teacher qualifications. The community must pay the substantial costs of good teachers, and a district must also elect school-board members who are committed both to innovation and to the recruitment of good teachers. In addition, we must not overlook the importance of dedicated and flexible administrators. It is true, as Gross says, that "the important factors . . . are more often the attitudes, interests, motives, social skills and values of people . . . than they are the factual conditions describing the communities in which they live."[57]

In this chapter we will only sketch the political and organizational environment of public education. In Chapter 2, where we describe in detail the two school districts that this study examines, we will be more precise. However, we ought to present at least short profiles of educational administrators, school-board members, and school constituencies.

Callahan writes that "as a result of their graduate training administrators have developed a kind of protective coloration that

---

[56] Zeigler, *The Political Life of American Teachers*, p. 102.

[57] Neal Gross, *Who Runs Our Schools?* (New York: John Wiley and Sons, Inc., 1958), p. 69.

has enabled them to keep their jobs. . . ."[58] It is easy to understand the origins of administrative defensiveness. The administrator plays the classic bureaucratic role of middleman. He must be flexible when community protest erupts against the school, but he must at the same time maintain the confidence of his teachers. In so doing, he finds himself representing his teachers to the community and the community to his teachers. A few skillful superintendents may be able to isolate their teaching staffs from public pressures, but most are constantly on the alert to pick up danger signals in the community.[59] Therefore, it is no surprise that administrators think of themselves as possessing little freedom of maneuver, and that the education of administrators reinforces such perceptions.

It is not the administrator, however, but the board of education that speaks for the public to the schools directly. The board also sets salary schedules and working conditions, shapes curricula, and oversees the physical facilities of the district. Unfortunately, we can say more about the formal powers than the actual behavior of school boards, but several useful items may be extracted from our small store of knowledge.

Counts demonstrated years ago that the recruitment of school-board members is highly selective.[60] Today, businessmen, officials, and managers still compose the bulk of board membership. Member incomes are commensurately high, especially when compared to the median for citizens in the district. Only recently have representatives of the working class and of the disadvantaged minorities pushed their way onto school boards in any numbers. Not surprisingly, most school boards generally reflect the conservative fiscal policies associated with the Republican party.[61]

Cunningham believes that most aspirants to the school board

[58] Raymond E. Callahan, *Education and the Cult of Efficiency* (Chicago: University of Chicago Press, 1962), p. 255.

[59] For a pathbreaking examination of the superintendent's management of such pressures, see Neal Gross *et al.*, *Explorations in Role Analysis* (New York: John Wiley and Sons, Inc., 1958).

[60] Roald F. Campbell *et al.*, *The Organization and Control of American Schools* (Columbus, Ohio: Charles E. Merrill Books, Inc., 1965), p. 173.

[61] For an article that reports the facts of school-board composition, but disputes our imputation of fiscal conservatism, see Donald G. Nugent, "Are Local Control and Lay Boards Obsolete?" in Harold Full (ed.), *Controversy in American Education* (New York: Crowell-Collier and Macmillan, Inc., 1967), pp. 290–293.

are selfishly motivated. "They openly acknowledged that member-ship would help them achieve highly personal goals or special interest group goals."[62] Gross agrees and presents evidence indi-cating that avowedly political motives are the most common among school-board members in industrial districts.[63] These findings are useful correctives to the commonly held nonpolitical image of the school board. Apparently, many board members wish either to legislate their partisan views of education or to use their board membership as a springboard to higher political positions.

Relatively few board members attain their positions by work-ing through established community political organizations. Rarely do cohesive political parties or community organizations control school-board selection. Three major consequences emerge from this organizational vacuum. First, there are few mechanisms by which the visibility of right-wing extremists, dedicated to attacking "com-munist" influences in the schools, can be reduced. Second, school-board elections rarely get organizational involvement sufficient to stir much community interest. Third, the lack of structural controls makes it difficult to ensure continuity in board policy.[64]

As already suggested, the usual attitude of the public toward the school is apathy. Rarely does voter turnout in school-board elections rise much above 30 percent of the eligible.[65] There also appears to be an inverse relationship between voter turnout and support for school tax overrides and bond issues.[66] As Goldstein

[62] Luvern L. Cunningham, "Community Power: Implications for Education," in Robert S. Cahill and Stephen P. Hencley (eds.), The Politics of Education in the Local Community (Danville, Ill.: The Interstate Press, 1964), pp. 41–42.

[63] Gross, Who Runs Our Schools?, p. 84.

[64] But, according to Minar, in wealthy suburban school districts informal caucuses choose school-board candidates, thereby reducing friction in the community and ensuring policy continuity. See David Minar, "The Com-munity Basis of Conflict in School Politics," American Sociological Review, 31, No. 6 (December 1966), pp. 832–835. Cunningham finds that most school boards enforce a decision-making norm of unanimity, thereby limit-ing debate over policy and further encouraging continuity. See Luvern L. Cunningham, "Decision-Making Behavior of School Boards," The American School Board Journal, 144 (February 1962), pp. 13–16.

[65] Richard Carter and John Sutthoff, Communities and Their Schools (Stan-ford, Calif.: Stanford University School of Education, 1960), p. III.

[66] For an examination of a similar phenomenon with regard to fluoridation decisions, see Robert L. Crain, Elihu Katz, and Donald B. Rosenthal, The Politics of Community Conflict (Indianapolis: The Bobbs-Merrill Company, Inc., 1969).

and Cahill put it, there is "a body of citizens who are unwilling to accept proposals put to them by the city fathers. These citizens form a large proportion, maybe even the majority, but are composed of the least involved, least articulate, and least active citizens, whose negative outlook usually comes to naught because . . . their low rate of participation leaves the field to the highly participant groups which drafted the proposal in the first place."[67] Thus, although the public is potentially hostile, it is generally ignorant of the school.

To sum up the discussion: The public-school climate is usually characterized by administrator vulnerability and caution, school-board fiscal and educational conservatism, and public apathy. Some administrators and many board members, fearing community hostility to the spending increases that accompany reform, normally resist innovation. Occasionally, community dissatisfaction with the schools erupts, not only over fiscal matters, but also over teaching methods, sex education, the school's treatment of political values, and "communist" influences. Thus, one can only conclude that the political and organizational context of the school normally inhibits the development or expansion of innovative curricula, particularly in the social studies.

Our research proceeds from our data about student and teacher attitudes in the sample districts to a speculative discussion of the social and educational context of the school. Finally, we hope to offer supported propositions about those contextual arrangements that do or do not facilitate democratic socialization.

SEQUENCE AND STRUCTURE IN POLITICAL SOCIALIZATION

One final problem that our study investigates remains. Easton claims that the school's formal teaching of political values occurs after the child is well on the way toward political maturity.[68] In addition, Piaget's work suggests that there may be a sequential

[67] Marshall N. Goldstein and Robert S. Cahill, "Mass Media and Community Politics," in Cahill and Hencley, *The Politics of Education in the Local Community*, p. 171.
[68] See also Gloria Cammarota, "Children, Politics, and Elementary Social Studies," *Social Education*, 27, No. 4 (April 1963), pp. 205–208.

development of political attitudes, which, because it proceeds largely as a function of age alone,[69] is untouched by education. Our task, therefore, is not only to describe the changing political orientations of schoolchildren, but also to identify the effects, if any, of educational experiences on these orientations.

We will employ two methods in attacking this problem. The first is a factor analysis to uncover the structure of political cognitions among students of the sixth, ninth, and twelfth grades in our two districts. As Freyberg has shown, there is a major shift toward more sophisticated thinking around ages eleven and twelve.[70] We therefore expect the political cognitions of sixth-graders to be relatively unstructured, but considerable cognitive organization to occur between the sixth and ninth grades. We also expect relatively little change in the structure of democratic cognitions between the ninth and twelfth grades. Our factor analysis will for the first time portray accurately the child's own organization of democratic attitudes, and we will thereby be able to ascertain the degree to which the child's conception of democratic values resembles democratic theory itself.[71]

We will next construct indices of democratic values from our test battery. By carefully comparing the scores of children in the two districts, we will estimate the independent effect of school-district quality on support for democracy.

There are several advantages to this approach. The factors analysis will enable us to assess the correspondence between "textbook democracy" and the child's own conception of democracy.

[69] For a review and synthesis of Piaget's work as it bears on political socialization, see Richard M. Merelman, "The Development of Political Ideology: A Framework for the Analysis of Political Socialization," *American Political Science Review*, 63, No. 3 (September 1969), pp. 750–767. For a review of the research that stems from Piaget's work, coupled with an incisive critique, see Eleanor E. Maccoby, "The Development of Moral Values and Behavior in Childhood," in John Clausen (ed.), *Socialization and Society* (Boston: Little, Brown and Company, 1968), pp. 227–269.

[70] P. S. Freyberg, "Concept Development in Piagetian Terms in Relation to School Attainment," *Journal of Educational Psychology*, 57 (June 1966), pp. 164–168. For Piaget's own formulation of the relationship between maturation and components of democratic thought, see Jean Piaget, *The Moral Judgment of the Child*, trans. Marjorie Graham (New York: The Free Press, 1965), pt. 3.

[71] Greenstein argues that the young child simply has no coherent organization to his political thought. Greenstein, *Children and Politics*, pp. 67–71.

In addition, not only will our findings unite psychological learning theory with curriculum planning, but we will also suggest some social-studies curriculum reorganization. We will also be able to judge whether Piaget's theory of cognitive stages can be applied usefully to the study of political socialization. The comparison of sixth-, ninth-, and twelfth-graders will test whether political socialization is completed as early as Easton and others believe it to be. Finally, the comparisons among teachers and students will enable us to delineate the relationship of educational climates to political socialization.

SUMMARY

This chapter has touched on a host of problems that are germane to the focus of this study—the school's role in inculcating democratic values. It seems best, at this point, to bring the themes of the chapter together by setting forth some of the hypotheses this study will investigate.

A. *Hypotheses about educational quality and political socialization*
1. A school district that provides quality education will be relatively successful in socializing its students to the support of democratic values. Specifically:
   a. A school district that provides quality education will accelerate its students quickly to an appreciation of democratic values between the sixth and twelfth grades.
   b. A school district that provides quality education will convey relatively large amounts of political information to its students between the sixth and twelfth grades.
   c. A school district that provides quality education will motivate its students to political participation between the sixth and twelfth grades.
   d. A school district that provides quality education will be successful in conveying support for the current party system. By the twelfth grade relatively few students in such a district will be unable to choose a partisan identification.

B. *Hypotheses about educational quality and teachers*

2. A school district that supports education financially will recruit teachers whose characteristics make it likely that they will succeed in their job of inculcating democratic values and imparting political information and motivation. It is the teaching staff that links the school board's commitment to quality education and the political socialization of children. The teaching staff is responsible for the successful inculcation of democratic values in good school districts. Specifically:

a. The teachers in such a district will manifest democratic values.

b. The teachers in such a district will possess high levels of morale.

c. The teachers in such a district will participate in politics relatively frequently.

d. The teachers in such a district will be willing to discuss controversial political issues in the classroom.

e. The teachers in such a district will be well-qualified. They will be experienced, will have attended good schools, will possess many advanced degrees, and will have cosmopolitan backgrounds. They will also have performed well in school.

f. The teachers in such a district will enjoy a sense of *esprit de corps*. They will have many friends among their fellow teachers and will feel relatively content in the district.

C. *Hypotheses about extraschool influences on political socialization*

3. Age, sex, social status, and intelligence will have a major impact on the political socialization of students. Some of these extraschool factors will be more influential than school quality in the process of political socialization, while others will be less influential. Specifically:

a. The most important determinant of the political information, motivation, and democratic support levels of students will be their age. The older the child, the more democratic, politically motivated, and informed he will become.

b. However, age has differential effects. Some democratic attitudes change greatly with age, while others change little. In addition, young children will impose little cognitive structure on democratic attitudes, while older children will impose more.[72]

c. Children from lower social-class backgrounds will possess less political information, will be less motivated politically, and will support democracy less fully than will other children.

d. Girls will possess less political information, will be less motivated politically, and will support democracy less fully than boys.

e. Good students will possess more political information, will be more motivated to participate in politics, and will manifest greater support for democracy than poor students.

f. The acquired partisan identifications of children will be related to their knowledge about politics, political motivation, and support for democracy.

These hypotheses constitute only a generous sample of the questions we will investigate. Broadly put, we will examine the effects of social class, age, intelligence, school-district quality, sex, and party identification on levels of political information, political motivation, and democratic support among students of the sixth, ninth, and twelfth grades. We will also inquire into the role of teachers as they attempt to socialize their students to democratic values. We will concentrate on describing the connection between support for education in a school district, teacher characteristics, and political socialization. In short, we will attempt to estimate the relationship between political socialization and educational climates. We will present further details of the study in the next chapter and in Appendix A.

---

[72] Our notion of cognitive structure relies heavily on Converse's discussion of constraints. See Philip E. Converse, "The Nature of Belief Systems in Mass Publics," in David E. Apter (ed.), *Ideology and Discontent* (New York: The Free Press, 1964), pp. 206–262.

Chapter 2
The School Districts

Los Angeles County contains thirty-eight unified school districts, numerous elementary-school and secondary-school districts, and a sizable number of junior-college districts.[1] School administrators and citizens in these districts have had to struggle to keep pace with the expanding educational needs of their children. Indeed, education is one of Southern California's major businesses.

Those involved with education have encountered three major barriers to their efforts. The first is the unprecedented population explosion that the Los Angeles metropolitan area has experienced.[2]

[1] William Broadbent gathered much of the background information and interview material used in this chapter. I am most grateful for his energies and accomplishments in my behalf.

[2] Between 1950 and 1960 the population of Los Angeles County increased 45 percent, as compared with a national growth rate of only 18 percent. Winston W. Crouch, "Los Angeles," in W. Robson and D. E. Regan (eds.), *Great Cities of the World* (London: George Allen and Unwin, Ltd., forthcoming), p. 2.

The explosion began with World War II and the emergence of Los Angeles as an important military supplier and assembler; it continues today, with no end in sight. The accessibility of freeways and the lure of cheaper housing is now subjecting adjacent Orange County to a similar, but even more spectacular, spurt of development than that of Los Angeles.[3] Most of the immigrants to Southern California have been relatively young, and many have brought with them children of school age. Consequently, the area has been hard pressed to meet the increasing demand for education.

A second barrier to the provision of public education is the extreme decentralization of the Los Angeles metropolitan area. Flexible state laws governing the incorporation, zoning, and governmental structure of localities have encouraged massive political fragmentation.[4] Cities in the Los Angeles metropolitan area range in population from 2,000,000 in the city of Los Angeles to minicities of only a few hundred.[5] This diffusion and multiplicity of governmental patterns has had grave, but uneven effects upon school organization. Some communities, having no schools of their own, send their children to schools in adjacent areas. Other communities run only primary or secondary schools. Increasingly, however, the problems of decentralization have encouraged cities to form unified school districts.

These difficulties have in turn raised a third barrier to education. Most school funds must still come from the property tax, but the willingness of the property owner to support educational expansion has deteriorated under the pressures we have described. Consequently, in 1965 a widespread taxpayer revolt began against California schools. Though statewide, the revolt was most intense in Southern California. Voters have rejected increasing percentages of school tax override and bond-issue proposals. The sources of hostility have, of course, been many. Some people believe that the expense of their homes and of their way of life no longer permits increased support for schools. Already California boasts one of the

---

[3] Crouch, "Los Angeles," p. 2.
[4] Crouch, "Los Angeles," p. 8.
[5] Thus, for example, the City of Industry is a community virtually without residents; it functions as a tax haven for industries that wish to escape high property taxes. The city's population in January 1969 was 704. *Los Angeles County Census Tract Report No. 29* (January 1, 1969), p. 13.

highest bankruptcy rates of any American state.[6] Other people object to what they believe to be the unwillingness of schools to teach "fundamentals." Still others resent the seeming prodigality of school administrators who are all too eager to spend tax funds on "frills." Early manifestations of these voter attitudes aided the politically and educationally conservative Max Rafferty in his successful 1962 campaign to become State Superintendent of Public Education.

The revolt persists. In April 1969, voters in the city of Los Angeles decisively rejected a crucial school bond issue and tax-override initiative. Consequently, the educational program of the Los Angeles schools, already acknowledged as deficient, had to be reduced even further. Opponents of increased school funding have now added the weapon of widespread student unrest to their battery of arguments. It is against this complex background that we can best view the two communities of this study and their schools.

THE COMMUNITIES

Almost directly west of downtown Los Angeles, in the heart of a major industrial-residential complex, is the community of Chalmers. Despite its being surrounded by parts of the city of Los Angeles, Chalmers maintains its governmental and educational autonomy. In addition, because of its proximity to the downtown area, Chalmers experienced an earlier population boom than did the outlying suburbs of Los Angeles. Thus, while between 1950 and 1960 its population expanded 63.1 percent, from 1960 to 1966 the rise was only 4.2 percent.[7] Chalmers' population in 1966 was approximately 33,500.

[6] Administrative Office of the United States Courts, *Tables of Bankruptcy Statistics* (Washington, D.C.: Government Printing Office, April 22, 1969), Table F-1.

[7] Figures based on U.S. Bureau of the Census, *U.S. Censuses of Population and Housing: 1960. Census Tracts.* Final Report PHC (1)-82 (Washington, D.C.: Government Printing Office, 1962), p. 26; and recent information gained from the Chalmers Chamber of Commerce. Hereafter, we will refer to this publication simply as *Census.* It should be recognized that the names of the two communities and other pertinent identification marks, such as the identities of educators, have been changed.

The late 1940s and early 1950s constituted the formative period of Chalmers' development. At that time the commercial foundations of the city were completed. Today the city relies on a financial base composed largely of two products: aircraft and movies. A major movie studio and several minor companies have made Chalmers their home for many years. In addition, the Hughes Tool Company now has a major plant in the community. Not only does Hughes provide employment to many people in Chalmers, but the company's real-estate holdings, including an airport, are substantial. The recently developed relocation plans of the largest film company, combined with new state legislation reducing the tax liabilities of movie studios, have placed the Chalmers Unified School District in financial jeopardy.

Most of the major industries in the area actually date from the late 1920s and early 1930s, when the center of town was built. Viewed today, the Chalmers downtown has few esthetic features to recommend it. Railroad tracks, a relic of the days when the Chalmers station was still in use, cut through the business district. The buildings are old and dingy. Indeed, the entire commercial core suffers from an evident lack of planning. Only recently the city council formed a commission whose job it is to plan the reconstruction of downtown Chalmers.

Moss City, on the other hand, has had a different history. Founded in 1911 by a real-estate developer, Moss City lies well to the southwest of downtown Los Angeles, below the harbor area. Because of its greater distance from the city, its period of growth came more recently than did that of Chalmers. The population of Moss City grew approximately 350 percent between 1950 and 1960; by 1968 the community had become the fourth-largest city in Los Angeles County, with a population of 133,000.[8] Although it was originally envisioned as a wholly industrial community, which would house machine-tool companies and iron works, the city today is a highly diversified residential-commercial area. Its major industries include electrical components, aircraft and related systems development corporations, and petroleum. A good part of Moss City is given over to a large industrial park, within which reside many of the community's major industries; these include Harvey Aluminum, Dow Chemical, and Mobil Petroleum.

[8] *Moss City Clarion*, June 26, 1968.

Both the rapidity of its growth and its lack of a natural center have led to several shopping districts in Moss City, none of which constitutes a downtown in the strict sense of the term. The oldest section of the community, the Pueblo area in the northeast, is now populated largely by Mexican-Americans and includes the bulk of Moss City's substandard housing. The quality of housing improves as one moves south and west through the city, and at the southwestern boundary of the community one enters some of the most prized residential areas in Los Angeles County. Adjacent to Moss City on the south are the city of Rolling Hills and the Palos Verdes Peninsula, both of which are luxurious and scenic. Not surprisingly, the Riviera section of Moss City, generally considered the most desirable residential area in the community, is in the southwest corner of town. Although it was the commercial hub of Moss City in the early days, the Pueblo has now been supplanted by the Del Amo Financial Center, a modern commercial development including banks and many other business enterprises. Compared with the older, somewhat faded community of Chalmers, Moss City appears even more typical than it actually is of the prosperous, burgeoning suburban cities of Southern California.

In Chapter 1 we outlined the difficulties in trying to assess the effects of educational quality on student achievement. Problems arise chiefly because of the high correlation of socioeconomic background factors with educational inputs and outputs. No method of evaluation can eliminate this problem. Even when we are able to control for relevant socioeconomic variables to examine educational factors directly, we still have no way of estimating community differences in regard to the value placed on education. Still, we can minimize these problems somewhat by comparing those few school districts, which, though similar in socioeconomic background, differ in the quality of education they provide. The effects of education will become more visible and reliable by such a comparison. Pursuit of this strategy has led us to Moss City and Chalmers.

From the description so far, it should have been easy to predict that Moss City would possess a higher proportion of well-educated, relatively affluent people than Chalmers. Moss City's attractiveness, its distance from the decaying core of Los Angeles, and the newness of its residential areas are particularly appealing to young, upwardly mobile families. Thus, in 1960 the Moss City median family income was $8050, more than $1000 above the county median.[9] In addition, whereas 12.6 percent of the families in Los Angeles County earned less than $3000 in 1960, only 5.5 percent of the families in Moss City were similarly deprived. At the other end of the financial scale, 29.3 percent of Moss City's families enjoyed incomes above $10,000 per year; the comparable figure for the county as a whole was only 24.6 percent.[10]

Moss City incomes are closely related to the educational structure of the community. In Los Angeles County, 25.9 percent of the residents aged twenty-five or older had less than a grade-school education in 1960, but the same was true of only 15.8 percent of the comparable Moss City residents. At the other extreme, 11.1 percent of Moss City residents aged twenty-five years or older had earned college degrees by 1960. The county figure was only 9.8 percent.[11] Note that, unlike the income comparison, the percentage of well-educated Moss City people differs little from that in Los Angeles County as a whole. This observation leads us to believe that many Moss City residents may now be enjoying a better standard of living than that which their educational qualifications might have afforded them in the East or the Midwest. Such people are direct beneficiaries of the California boom in aerospace and defense-related industries.

Moss City seems to be a prosperous community of predominantly upper middle-class people. But two things should be kept in mind. The Moss City income figures may cover many families in which both parents work. We cannot ascertain the incidence of this practice in Moss City, but the pattern is common in Southern California; indeed, sometimes it is virtually dictated by the high cost of residential property and the need for families to maintain two automobiles. Therefore, high family incomes may not reflect an entirely comfortable style of life. In addition, as we have seen, Moss City is a highly mobile area. We must, therefore, be reserved in conclusions from census data compiled in 1960, but used for this study in 1967.[12] Despite these caveats, we still believe the 1960

[9] *Census*, p. 28.
[10] *Census*, pp. 25, 28.
[11] *Census*, pp. 25, 28.
[12] The problem of data availability for small cities is serious. During our investigation, we approached the planning departments of both cities, in addition to numerous other possible sources of information. None was able to do much more for us than point us to the appropriate census material,

census comparisions of Moss City and Chalmers to be generally reflective of the situation in 1967.

In Chalmers, 7.5 percent of the families made incomes below $3000 in 1960, while 30 percent reported incomes of $10,000 or more. Thus, it would appear that Chalmers is more heterogeneous economically than Moss City. Most of Chalmers' wealthy families live in the eastern part of the city, the Baldwin Hills area; however, the extreme western part of the community is now experiencing an influx of impoverished Mexican-Americans. The important point for our purposes is that Chalmers, with its 1960 median income of $7862, is somewhat poorer than Moss City.[13]

These socioeconomic differences between Moss City and Chalmers aid us considerably in comparing their school districts. Let us remember that Moss City grew much more rapidly during the same period, 1950 to 1966, than did Chalmers. This fact would lead us to predict a more youthful population in Moss City than in Chalmers, a hunch which can be verified. The median age of Moss City residents in 1960 was 25.7 years, whereas the comparable figure in Chalmers was 31.4.[14] Only 36.7 percent of the

---

which we had already surveyed. The fact is that public officials in small cities such as Moss City and Chalmers have little reliable information about the character of their communities. It is difficult to see how local politicians can plan for their community's future without such information, but, at least in our experience, there is little commitment to gather appropriate data. Such problems are obviously exacerbated in a growing community, such as Moss City. If it is true that much of the action of American politics in the years to come will occur at the local level, communities will have to commit themselves to the gathering of pertinent socioeconomic data—a commitment that, in turn, bears upon the desire to support local planning efforts. In fact, the lack of availability of data is not only traceable to the intellectual and political weakness of local planning departments, but also to the unwillingness of local politicians to recognize the importance of forecasting the future for their communities. Those investigators who have concentrated on social forecasting at the national level would do well to think about the important problems of data gathering at the local level. See Raymond Bauer *et al., Social Indicators* (Cambridge, Mass.: The MIT Press, 1966).

This problem does not cripple our study, however. The educational differences between the two districts began some years before our study, when the census data were more accurate; nor is there evidence that the *composition* of the two populations shifted fundamentally during the 1960s. The major differences merely involve growth rates.

[13] *Census*, p. 26.
[14] *Census*, pp. 26, 28.

1960 population was of school age in Chalmers, while in Moss City, fully 47.5 percent of the population was of school age.[15] The youthfulness of Moss City has placed the community's school system under a strain far greater than that experienced in Chalmers.

Furthermore, its unusual commercial structure, resting largely on movies, gives Chalmers a tax base superior to that which would be expected from a knowledge of its income characteristics alone. There is not a sufficient tax base in Moss City, however, to ease appreciably that community's educational dilemma. In sum, despite its high income level, the age and tax structure of Moss City combine to exert a greater strain on education than that felt in Chalmers.

Like many communities in Southern California, both Moss City and Chalmers have been heavily influenced by local business and real-estate groups. That these interests are powerful comes as no surprise; after all, Los Angeles is an area of rapid and recent expansion. One can discover the impact of real estate and business elites in the permissive and haphazard zoning generally characteristic of Los Angeles, as well as in the propensity of communities to incorporate.[16] Home ownership is, of course, a major preoccupation. The value placed upon such ownership became clear in 1964 when the voters repealed open-housing legislation. Even more indicative was the Watson Amendment of 1968, which, had it been adopted by the voters, would have ended the use of the property tax for such programs as schools and welfare.[17]

The importance of property becomes particularly visible in Moss City, where the mayor is one of the largest property owners in the area, and the influential former president of the school board is a major local realtor. Real-estate development has, of course, been a major force in the Del Amo Center and in the rapid growth of Moss City residentially.

Although the influence of real-estate leadership in Chalmers is perhaps less obtrusive, businessmen have been quite active. The Chamber of Commerce has become a focus for community initia-

---

[15] *Census*, pp. 26, 28.

[16] Crouch, "Los Angeles," p. 8.

[17] However, the Watson Amendment was defeated by a comfortable margin. The final vote tallies were Yes 1,056,365 and No 1,403,077 for Los Angeles County; and Yes 2,146,010 and No 4,570,097 (32 percent Yes and 68 percent No) statewide.

tive and planning, particularly in regard to the downtown. At the same time developers, who are replacing older homes with cheaply built, multiple-unit dwellings, have endangered the single-family character of Chalmers. Indeed, the entire position of developers in Chalmers has now erupted into a major community political issue.[18]

Racially, the cities resemble each other: neither contains many Negroes. Recently, some white residents of an adjacent Los Angeles city neighborhood, viewing Chalmers as a kind of haven, even contemplated trying to annex themselves to that city in order to avoid having Negro children bussed to their schools. It is clear that some residents have been attracted to Chalmers and Moss City because of the seeming immunity to minority-group influx that these districts enjoy. For example, many recent arrivals in Moss City apparently fled from a community directly to the north, Inglewood, which has been experiencing considerable Negro immigration in its northeastern section. However, not only are there small populations of Japanese- and Chinese-Americans in Moss City and Chalmers, but both communities also contain sizable concentrations of Mexican-Americans, who now constitute a majority of the student body in one of the new Chalmers elementary schools.[19] Not surprisingly, student achievement levels in this school are below those of others in the district. The racial comparability of the two communities is important for this study, for the differences in value patterns, educational achievements, and political attitudes of whites and Negroes are well known.[20] We could not have even attempted

---

[18] The issue is complicated, however. It is bound up with concern about the availability of public recreational facilities, which, it is alleged, developers have little interest in maintaining.

[19] Census data for 1960 place the Spanish surname population of Chalmers at approximately 6 percent and of Moss City at 5 percent. However, since 1960, the Mexican-American population of Chalmers has undoubtedly increased in percentile terms. As of 1968, the combined minority group proportion of the school population in Chalmers and Moss City, respectively, was 12.2 percent and 8.0 percent. *Los Angeles Times*, February 23, 1968.

[20] See Gerhard Lenski, *The Religious Factor* (New York: Doubleday and Company, Inc., 1961), chaps. 3, 5. Dwaine Marvick, "The Political Socialization of the American Negro," *The Annals*, 361 (September 1965), pp. 12–28. Arthur R. Jensen, "How Much Can We Boost IQ and Scholastic Achievement?" *Harvard Educational Review*, 39, No. 1 (Winter 1969), pp. 1–123.

a reasonable comparative study without utilizing districts that were both relatively homogeneous and similar racially.

Politically, the cities differ somewhat. Although registration in both communities favors the Democrats, 66.3 percent of the qualified voters in Chalmers listed themselves Democrats in 1964 to only 56.2 percent in Moss City.[21] The discrepancy between these two figures initially might be explained by the higher socioeconomic level of Moss City. The registration figures, however, are not guides to the actual voting behavior of the two communities. It is a rule of Southern California politics that Republicans normally do much better than their registration would indicate; neither Moss City nor Chalmers violates this rule. Ronald Reagan, the Republican, won 56 percent of the vote in Chalmers when he ran against the Democratic incumbent, Governor Edmund Brown, in 1966. Reagan did even better in Moss City, where he won fully 69 percent of the vote.[22] Still, it is hard to interpret prevailing political attitudes in the two communities solely by knowing their electoral behavior. We can tell a little more, however, by examining their response to Proposition 16 in 1966, which was a highly controversial ballot initiative designed to curb alleged pornography that some felt had become a major business in Los Angeles County. Although the initiative was soundly defeated in the state, it still won 50 percent of the Moss City voters. Not quite as many, 46 percent, of the voters in Chalmers preferred it.[23] These indications suggest that Moss City is, by and large, somewhat more conservative than Chalmers.

Local politics affords further evidence of Moss City's conservative temper. Citizens reacted sharply when the city fathers attempted to enforce the local housing code, thereby paving the way toward urban renewal in the northeastern part of the city. Irate voters turned three incumbent councilmen out of office in

[21] These figures were aggregated by census tract. The raw data are provided in the University of California at Los Angeles POLCEN print-out, available in the Statistical Laboratory of the Department of Political Science, UCLA. POLCEN combines pertinent socioeconomic data with census-tract political information for the Los Angeles area.

[22] Frank M. Jordan, Secretary of State (comp.), *California Statement of Vote and Supplement: November 8, 1966, Election,* (Sacramento: n. p., n. d.), p. 72.

[23] Jordan, *California Statement of Vote and Supplement,* p. 86.

the 1968 election; to ensure no repetition of code enforcement, the community voted the code out of existence. As the local paper described it, "If the new City Council can take one lesson from Tuesday's balloting, it probably should be that the people do not want urban renewal in Moss City."[24]

Hostility to code enforcement and community development is centered in the northern part of town, where many working-class families live. The same section of the city recently and vociferously opposed a regional recreation complex to be financed with federal money. Citizens in the area have also organized a local vigilante police force; the Moss City police authorities, although clearly unhappy about this last development, can do little to prevent it.

Before concluding unequivocally that Moss City is more conservative than Chalmers, let us remember that Chalmers is not even contemplating a major urban renewal project. There is no way of predicting community reaction to any such proposal. Still, on balance, Moss City does appear the more conservative of the two communities.

The extent to which these political differences contaminate our study is uncertain. It would be almost impossible to find two school districts that were absolutely identical except for the quality of education they provide. We have had to content ourselves with two communities sufficiently similiar to permit prudent comparisons. There is certainly no evidence that the liberal edge in Chalmers produces any special disposition in that community to support the schools financially. Tax-override measures failed in February 1966 and again in April 1969. Indeed, the latter defeat, coming over a year after we completed the field work for our study, has seriously jeopardized the future of public education in Chalmers.

Both cities are served by local papers owned and published by the staunchly conservative Copley Press. The *Los Angeles Times* also is an important influence in both cities, as it is throughout Southern California. In addition, a regional newspaper covers Moss City and several surrounding communities. Possibly because of the larger city it serves, Moss City's Copley paper boasts more sophistication, better writing, and more information than does its counterpart in Chalmers. Moreover, the Moss City paper also offers more

[24] Moss City *Clarion*, April 10, 1968.

news about school affairs than does the Chalmers paper. Judging only by the editorials and the letters to the editor of both Copley papers, one would conclude that political conservatives and religious fundamentalists are the sole inhabitants of Moss City and Chalmers, but of course this is not the case.

It is difficult to estimate the impact that their community newspapers have on Chalmers and Moss City. Similar neighborhood and small-city papers blanket the Los Angeles area; such papers may knit communities together, conveying some sort of local identity in the fragmented metropolis. If so, they would conform to the model that Janowitz postulates for the community press in Chicago.[25]

We have not been able to assess accurately the religious composition of the two communities. There is no reliable religious census for either city, and school authorities in Moss City prevented us from ascertaining the religious preferences of their students. We can, however, hazard some guesses. There is reason to believe that Jews compose as much as 30 percent of the Chalmers population, for Chalmers lies at the southern end of a section of Los Angeles heavily populated by middle-class Jews. Indeed, at the time of our study, four of the five members of the Chalmers school board were Jewish. An impressionistic survey also uncovers a wide variety of Protestant churches in Chalmers, including as many as twenty Southern Baptist and other lower-status denominations.[26] Indeed, fundamentalist Protestantism seems to be the religious core of the community.

The religious composition of Moss City apparently differs from that of Chalmers in two respects. First, there are undoubtedly far fewer Jews. Still, at the time of our study, two members of the five-man school board were Jewish, and the mayor is also a Jew. There is also reason to believe that the affluent southern part of Moss City contains a relatively high proportion of Jews. Second, there are many Lutheran churches and Churches of Christ in the

[25] Morris Janowitz, *The Community Press in an Urban Setting*, 2d ed. (Chicago: University of Chicago Press, 1967), pp. 120–129.

[26] Again, it suffices to refer to the limited information available on small cities. In making these estimates, we have relied upon local religious leaders and religious writers for the local papers. The lack of census material on religion constitutes a major barrier to the use of the religious variable in studies of the kind we are pursuing.

city, indicating a high proportion of immigrants from the Midwest and perhaps the Southwest.

Our inability to control for religion in this study is not only regrettable, but potentially damaging, for the effects of religious affiliation on political attitudes are substantial.[27] Some of our conclusions would perhaps have required modification had we been able to examine religion separately. Of course, there is no reason to believe that differences in the religious composition of the two communities are marked enough to invalidate our findings.

THE SCHOOL DISTRICTS

Although neither school district is coterminous with its community, the boundary differences are insignificant for this study. As one would expect, school-enrollment figures reflect the population and age disparities of Moss City and Chalmers. In the 1967–1968 school year, Moss City's schools had an enrollment of 33,993, while the Chalmers schools enrolled 7083.[28]

The districts organize their schools slightly differently. Moss City operates its schools on an 8-4 pattern, while Chalmers inserts a junior high between elementary and high school. Its scheme, therefore, becomes 6-3-3. So far as we can determine, such organizational differences are unrelated to educational outcomes.

Moss City's large size dictates a need for four high schools. The two newest and best equipped of these are in the southern and western parts of the district. In order to accommodate its heavy population of primary-age youngsters, the city also operates twenty-nine elementary schools. By contrast, in Chalmers there is a single combination junior-senior high school located in the center of the district. This complex is large enough to service students coming from the district's eight elementary schools.

Although we feared that the size disparity between the two districts would prevent fruitful comparison, we are persuaded that these fears are groundless. Both districts lie in the core of a single

[27] Lenski, *The Religious Factor*, chap. 4. See also Lucy Dawidowicz and Leon S. Goldstein, *Politics in a Pluralist Democracy* (New York: Institute of Human Relations Press, 1963).
[28] The sources for these figures were the Chalmers and Moss City Unified School Districts.

metropolitan area, which constitutes a common cultural context of education. In addition, the literature indicates that disparities in district size bear on educational outcomes mainly in very small rural districts.[29] Finally, although the size of individual schools may have an effect on the learning process,[30] school sizes are comparable in the two communities.

Both districts emerged in the late 1940s, each by breaking away from the Los Angeles city school system. Not only are the districts similar in origins, they also resemble each other in their supervisory structures. At the time of the study, there was only one important administrative difference: this difference involved the continuity of leadership. The Moss City schools have had the same superintendent since the district was founded, whereas the Chalmers schools have had three superintendents.

Doctor Fritz Harder has shepherded the Moss City schools from their small beginnings to their contemporary size. He took his Ph.D. at the University of Southern California, the college that has had the greatest impact on Southern California education. Harder's general approach to education has been characterized as moderately progressive in the style of Dewey; this commitment persists. In a recent newspaper interview Harder mused, "There is excessive pressure on children to achieve. The world would be better off if children had a chance to live a little as they go along. The climate is often too tense for good learning."[31] These sentiments clearly seem to be those of an educator steeped in the philosophy of encouraging students to learn by doing. Further clues to the superintendent's educational outlook may be found both in the district's emphasis on reading readiness and in its development of a nondepartmental integrated curriculum. Indeed, Harder once even attempted to abolish grades in elementary schools. However, a hostile majority on the board of education, which originally took office in 1962, has either modified or obliterated many of his programs. Today the Moss City curriculum contains few traces of innovation.

[29] It is for this reason that Conant is such a strong proponent of district unification in rural areas. See James B. Conant, *The American High School Today* (New York: McGraw-Hill, Inc., 1959), pp. 77–85.

[30] Robert E. Stephens and John Spiess, "What does Research Say about the Size of a Local School District?" *Journal of State School Systems Development*, 1, No. 3 (Fall 1967), pp. 182–90.

[31] Moss City *Clarion*, December 27, 1967.

Harder's administrative style apparently does not reflect his commitment to a permissive school environment, for observers describe him as paternalistic and domineering. He encourages bureaucratization and, according to some, breeds distrust among his administrative staff. He carefully reviews most of the major decisions of his subordinates and rarely delegates authority. Brief contacts with the author convinced the latter of Harder's keen sense for the difficult political position of the superintendent, his skepticism about social research, and his somewhat cavalier attitude toward teachers. It is true, however, that Harder's long tenure has permitted him to shape much of the administrative structure and educational substance of the district in his own image. By so doing, he has produced a measure of educational continuity in Moss City.

In contrast, the Chalmers Unified School District has had two superintendents, David Player and Boyd Pace. The district has just now chosen a third. Player held office until 1962, at which time disgruntled teachers, dissatisfied board members, and the local Committee for Basic Education joined hands to oust him. Many complained that Player seemed more interested in school buildings and finance than in education. It is true that he maintained close and fruitful relations with the Chalmers business community; he even held stock in two local banks and was for a time president of the Lions Club. Still, despite the legitimate objections by his opponents to these activities, one cannot deny that Player's rapport with the business community produced much financial and attitudinal support for the expanding school district.

Player's successor, Boyd Pace, had quite a different orientation. Chalmers could lure him away from his previous superintendency of the Champaign, Illinois, schools only by paying him a salary of $25,000, substantially above the national average for superintendents. Pace came to Chalmers with a national reputation as an educational innovator, heavily committed to research and experimentation. This reputation proved accurate. In Chalmers, Pace pioneered such innovations as the nongraded elementary school and team teaching.[32] Many teachers in the district undertook special training in these subjects at the UCLA Experimental Ele-

---

[32] Thus, Dr. Madeline Hunter of the UCLA Elementary School described Chalmers as "the only district that has, in a way that would be condoned by learning theorists, gone into learning." She went on to describe the contributions of Pace to team teaching and nongraded schooling in Chalmers. Chalmers *Bugle*, April 20, 1968.

mentary School. By September 1968, two elementary schools in Chalmers were operating entirely on the nongraded principle.

Like Harder of Moss City, Pace was thought to have an autocratic style of administration. To some, his hiring and firing procedures appeared arbitrary, while others found him personally inaccessible and impulsive. Pace conventionally ended his tenure interviews with a teacher by reminding her that tenure was revocable and by suggesting that she would do well to keep him informed of matters that might be of direct interest to him. It is undeniable, however, that his innovations restructured education in Chalmers, but eventually members of the school board became concerned about the cost of innovation. As one member remarked when reviewing an ambitious reading program for kindergarten children, "Let's not get involved in every experimental project that comes before us. Let's have another school district have a chance to experiment for a change."[33] The financial burden of innovation undoubtedly contributed to the failure of the tax override in April 1969. The consequent constriction of funds for innovation must certainly have encouraged Pace suddenly to accept an attractive offer to become superintendent of the Springfield, Illinois, schools. At this writing, the district has only just chosen a new superintendent.

Both districts are served by five-man boards of education elected at large. The Chalmers board, at the time of our study, was composed of an optometrist, two attorneys, and two housewives who had come up through the Parent-Teachers Association. In Moss City, both the president and the most recent addition to the board were real-estate men of substantial wealth and influence; other members were the wife of a professional sailmaker and two aerospace engineers. The disparity in the composition of the two boards reflects well the differences in the economy, life style, and income between the two communities.

The two boards have diverged markedly in their willingness to spend money for education. During the 1967–1968 school year, teachers in Moss City objected strongly to what they felt to be a poor salary schedule. Though they complained bitterly, the board proved resistant. The teachers then resorted to some minor picketing, after which the board reluctantly agreed to a sharp salary rise.

[33] Chalmers *Bugle*, May 24, 1968.

No such strains have existed between teachers and the Chalmers board, which, in fact, has willingly rewarded teachers far beyond the state average. A recent study places the salary schedule in Chalmers among the top five in the state.[34] When, in 1968, the district became strapped financially, the board did contemplate withholding from teachers the usual cost of living increment, but the ensuing teacher criticism induced the board to abandon the idea before a serious breach occurred.

Moss City is one of the few California school districts that has never attempted to tax up to its legal capacity. Either because of timidity or principled frugality, the board has consistently maintained a tax rate below the maximum that the voters themselves have granted it. In 1968, when the people agreed to an extension of the current tax ceiling, the board and its supporters were careful to point out that a Yes vote meant not a rise in taxes, but only the maintenance of existing levels. Still more anomalous is the fact that the district's financial surplus, both in absolute and percentile terms, is actually greater than that of most other districts, yet the surplus is not used. By contrast, the Chalmers board over the years has not only spent up to its legal limit, but now finds itself in serious financial difficulties.

The response of Moss City voters to school bond and tax initiatives has rarely given the board cause for concern. Only one such proposal failed—in 1967. When an authorization for the construction of swimming pools was removed from it, the proposal passed easily. Resubmission of the current tax ceiling in 1968 won 75 percent of the vote. Thus, there is little evidence that a taxpayer revolt is responsible for the board's frugality, although, of course, the law of anticipated reactions may be operating.[35] The board may submit to the electorate only those proposals that it believes the voters will accept. Whatever the reason, the tax rate in Moss City is surprisingly low.

[34] The survey was conducted by the California Teacher Association and was reported in the Chalmers *Bugle*, January 22, 1969. It was also reported in the *Los Angeles Times* on approximately the same date.

[35] On the concept of anticipated reactions, see Carl J. Friedrich, *Man and His Government* (New York: McGraw-Hill, Inc., 1968), chap. 3. See also Robert A. Dahl, "Power," in David L. Sills (ed.), *International Encyclopedia of the Social Sciences*, 12 (New York: Crowell-Collier and Macmillan, Inc., 1968), pp. 405–415.

By contrast, the residents of Chalmers have resisted their board's proposals to spend money. A bond initiative for the repair of two elementary schools failed in 1965. Though the bond issue finally squeaked through the next year, a tax-override measure lost at the same time. In 1968, with another override election in the offing, prospects looked bleak. As the local paper observed, "Persons involved in the probable upcoming school tax-override proposition in Chalmers are facing an uphill battle. . . ."[36] The paper was all too correct. Despite the apparent absence of organized opposition, the crucial tax override was overwhelmingly defeated in April 1969.

It is difficult to understand why a community that is fairly liberal, moderately Jewish, and generally open to innovation manifests such resistance to voting money for schools. There are two possible explanations. First, the community's large blue-collar population may be mobilized against educational spending. A number of studies indicates a direct relationship between the proportion of working-class people in a community and the lack of support for education.[37] Second, when compared with similar districts, Chalmers by 1967–1968 was already spending at a high rate. Voter disaffection in Chalmers may therefore be explained simply by reference to the disparity between community resources and school-expenditure levels.

Our description of the two districts reveals a paradox: Moss City has a low tax rate and a budget surplus. The result is that it spends comparatively little on education despite its voters always having supported education proposals. Chalmers taxes at a relatively high tax rate, but is now in a budgetary crisis. It spends a great deal on education, despite its voters having been quite resistant to spending proposals. We shall return to this paradox shortly.

More evidence of conservative politics in Moss City involves the attempts of right-wing extremists to influence the schools. The John Birch Society has not been particularly active in either district, but administrators and board members in both areas are sensitive to the possibility of right-wing agitation. There appears

---

[36] Chalmers *Bugle*, November 8, 1968.

[37] For example, see R. V. Smith *et al.*, *Community Organization and Support for the Schools* (Ypsilanti, Mich.: January 31, 1964), Cooperative Research Project No. 1828, Office of Education, U.S. Department of Health, Education, and Welfare, pp. 37–40.

to be no current right-wing agitation in Chalmers, but some right-wing groups have made their presence felt in Moss City. Such groups not only protested Moss City's acceptance of federal aid, but also expressed dismay when elementary schools in the district persisted in using a phonograph record entitled "Itsy Bitsy Spider," which allegedly contained communist propaganda. Members of the Birch Society attend every meeting of the Moss City school board and observe activities carefully. Amounts of right-wing sentiment in the two communities can perhaps be gauged by comparing levels of electoral support for George Wallace in 1968. Wallace received 7.5 percent of the vote in Moss City and 5.4 percent in Chalmers.[38]

Teachers organize themselves somewhat differently in the two communities. From their professional affiliations, Moss City teachers appear to be less militant than teachers in Chalmers. At the time of this study only nineteen Moss City teachers belonged to the local branch of the activist American Federation of Teachers. By contrast, the AFT chapter in Chalmers boasted a membership of sixty-five and cooperated closely with the local California Democratic Council club. This comparison takes on greater significance when we recall that, because of the size differences of the districts, there are many more teachers in Moss City than in Chalmers. The figures may be deceptive, however, for some observers believe that the AFT membership in Moss City is actually larger than has been reported. Furthermore, the Moss City chapter of the National Education Association has become increasingly militant in its salary negotiations with the board. Indeed, the chapter recently hired its first full-time organizer-negotiator. Moss City teachers, therefore, may not need the AFT to articulate their grievances. The Chalmers Education Association, on the other hand, is generally considered ineffectual and seems completely unable to compete effectively with the AFT for the support of local teachers.

The future of both districts is shadowy. It is true that the voters' acceptance of current tax ceilings in Moss City augurs well for the district. In addition, there is every reason to believe that the Moss City population will become more affluent, although a sudden cutback in defense contracts or in government support for the aerospace industry could damage the economy of the area.

[38] Percentages were calculated from information secured from the Los Angeles County Registrar of Voters.

There appear to be two other unknowns in the district's immediate future. The first is the appointment of a new superintendent when Dr. Harder's current and final term ends. The second, and more important, is the willingness of both community and board to spend money to secure quality education.

The future of the Chalmers schools appears especially problematic. A number of interrelated and convergent problems face the district. The tax base is shrinking because the movie studios are moving to the less congested San Fernando Valley. The consequent tax loss will be substantial, and, although there are plans to replace the movie complex with an industrial park, the financial future remains dim.

Recently the district experienced three additional shocks to its fiscal viability. First, a state law exempted movie studios from a unique school tax applied to them by cities such as Chalmers. Second, the regular assessment of taxable property in the school district added less to the tax base than had been anticipated. As a consequence, the board was obliged to make preliminary cutbacks in school programs.[39] Third, the tax override, which was to raise enough revenue to compensate for these other setbacks, lost badly in April 1969. Under pressure from teachers who boycotted classes for a day, the board scheduled another election, but the voters seem in no mood to support their schools. In the midst of these disappointments, Dr. Pace resigned, leaving Chalmers education leaderless at a crucial time. Finally, looming over all else is the fear that the Negro ghetto, slowly expanding westward through Los Angeles, may soon reach Chalmers.[40]

EDUCATIONAL QUALITY IN THE TWO DISTRICTS

Let us now consider the major independent variable. Which of these districts provides superior education? We must recognize

[39] A concise summary of the problem may be found in the editorial of the Chalmers *Bugle*, May 10, 1968.

[40] Some residents have finally recognized the need to provide an acceptable integration climate in Chalmers. These citizens have united to form the Chalmers Neighbors, an organization modeled on the Crenshaw Neighbors group, which operates in a nearby section of Los Angeles. The goal of both organizations is the prevention of white exodus from newly desegregated areas and the establishment of stable, multiracial communities.

that, in view of the many controversies about what constitutes quality education, any answer to this question can only be tentative. To us, quality education combines three components: substantial community inputs, favorable school characteristics (which are only partly independent of community effort), and superior educational payoffs. Of these three components, the first and second are, for reasons already stated in Chapter 1, the most important.

Community Effort

Chalmers clearly makes a greater financial effort in the area of education than does Moss City. This judgment is based on a number of considerations. For example, during the 1966–1967 school year, the ratio of taxable assessed valuation per kindergarten through eighth-grade student in Moss City was only $12,500. The comparable figure for Chalmers was $25,000.[41] Thus, the financial strain of education struck Moss City twice as badly as it did Chalmers. The important fact, however, is that Chalmers taxed itself for schools at a stiffer rate than did Moss City; yet, if Moss City were to compensate for its unfavorable position, the reverse should have been the case. The 1966–1967 general-fund tax rate in Chalmers was 3.5045 mills, while the figure for Moss City was only 3.3728.[42] Even in comparison with districts having similarly favorable assessment ratios, Chalmers taxes at a high rate. Moss City's tax rate, however, is considerably lower than that of other districts with comparably discouraging assessment-student ratios.[43]

[41] Los Angeles County Superintendent of Schools, Business Advisory Services, *Rank Order Arrangement of Data for All Unified School Districts of Los Angeles County, 1966–1967*, p. 58. The figures for finance and assessed valuation that we shall report are relatively stable over the period 1964–1968. Thus, the expenditure and salary differentials between the districts are long-standing and reflect community inputs over a considerable period. It is this cumulative effect over some years of community effort that we are examining; the data we are reporting are merely illustrative of these cumulative differences.

[42] Los Angeles County Superintendent of Schools, *Rank Order Arrangement of Data . . . of Los Angeles County, 1966–1967*, p. 61.

[43] Los Angeles County Superintendent of Schools, *Rank Order Arrangement of Data . . . of Los Angeles County, 1966–1967*, pp. 54–55. For a consideration of alternative measures of community tax effort in support of the schools, see Warner Bloomberg, Jr., and Morris Sunshine, *Suburban Power*

The result, therefore, is that Chalmers has consistently made a greater attempt to educate its students than has Moss City. Evidence for this assertion comes from an examination of the money spent per school child in the districts. This figure, by expressing the linkage between tax effort and student needs, summarizes the educational effort each district is making. The combined effects of high valuation per schoolchild and high taxes placed Chalmers, with its 1967–1968 expenditure rate of $774.19 per child, fifth in expenditures among the thirty-eight unified school districts in Los Angeles County. By contrast, the combination of its poor assessment ratio and its low tax rate saddled Moss City with a total expenditure rate of only $617.21 per child, which relegated it to twenty-sixth among the districts in the county.[44]

Let us remember that socioeconomically, Moss City actually ranks higher than Chalmers. Usually there is a direct relationship between district wealth and support for education, but in this instance we have two deviant cases. What accounts for the paradox? One explanation is the large proportion of Chalmers tax money that comes not from citizens of the district, but rather from local industries, particularly the movie studios. Another explanation is the peculiarity of Moss City residents, who simply do not conform to normal expectations about districts with assessment problems. Indeed, many of the districts that have assessment ratios as low as Moss City are predominantly Negro or Mexican-American. Yet, most such districts, though populated by groups that can afford to pay far less for education than can the residents of Moss City, actually tax themselves more for schools.[45]

Not surprisingly, the tax effort in Chalmers produces a superior teacher salary schedule. The average teacher's salary per student in Chalmers during the 1967–1968 school year was $744.19. The comparable figure in Moss City was only $582.76.[46] These figures take on more meaning when converted into absolute num-

Structures and Public Education (Syracuse, N.Y.: Syracuse University Press, 1963), pp. 44–50. See also H. Thomas James, J. Allen Thomas, and Harold J. Dyck, *Wealth, Expenditure and Decision-making for Education* (U.S. Office of Education, Cooperative Research Report No. 1241, Stanford University: School of Education, 1963).

[44] Los Angeles County Superintendent of Schools, *Rank Order Arrangement of Data . . of Los Angeles County, 1967–1968*, p. 84.

[45] See Chapter 2, fn. 42; see also *Los Angeles Times*, February 23, 1968.

[46] Los Angeles County Superintendent of Schools, *Rank Order Arrangement of Data . . . of Los Angeles County, 1967–1968*, pp. 54–55.

bers. In the early stages of their career, teachers in Chalmers average only a few hundred dollars more than teachers in Moss City; disparities become greater, however, among the more qualified and experienced teachers. Thus, some experienced Chalmers teachers earn $1000 per year more than their Moss City counterparts.[47]

School Characteristics

The deficient salary structure of the Moss City schools decreases the district's ability to retain experienced teachers. At the time of this study, almost one-half of Moss City teachers had experience of three years or less.[48] By contrast, Chalmers has succeeded in building a core of experienced teachers strongly committed to the district. Studies that indicate a relationship between teacher experience and educational quality therefore work to the advantage of Chalmers.[49] The recent salary raise in Moss City, coupled with the financial difficulties in Chalmers, may redress the balance between the districts in future years. Still, at the time of this study, inexperienced teachers were responsible for much of Moss City education.

Generous expenditures have not only helped Chalmers to recruit and hold an experienced faculty, but have also permitted most of the Chalmers faculty to teach small classes. In 1967–1968, the ratio of Chalmers teachers to students in grades 1–3 was 27.4 to 1. The comparable figure in Moss City was 28.9 to 1. A sharper disparity becomes noticeable in grades 4–8, with the ratios for Chalmers and Moss City being 24.3 to 1 and 31.0 to 1, respectively. The figures move in favor of Moss City beyond the eighth-grade level, however, from 27 to 1 to 29 to 1.[50] Though they

[47] This comparison is based on information provided by the two districts.
[48] The figure was calculated from responses to "How long have you been teaching in this district?" (item 15) in our Teacher Interview Schedule.
[49] William G. Mollenkopf and S. Donald Melville, "A Study of Secondary School Characteristics as Related to Test Scores" (Princeton, N.J.: Educational Testing Service, 1956), p. 21. See also Samuel M. Goodman, *The Assessment of School Quality* (Albany, N.Y.: New York State Education Department, 1959).
[50] The first two sets of figures are reported in Los Angeles County Superintendent of Schools, *Rank Order Arrangement of Data . . . of Los Angeles County, 1967–1968*, pp. 54–55. The last set was secured in personal correspondence with the districts themselves, dated, in the case of Moss City, June 11, 1968, and, undated from Chalmers.

differ about the scale of impact, most educators agree that small classes contribute to educational quality.[51]

Mollenkopf and Melville argue that another variable that successfully predicts program quality is spending on incidental instructional methods.[52] This relatively small figure indexes efforts to enrich a curriculum beyond the normal course offerings. For 1967–1968, the incidental instructional expenditure rates for Chalmers and Moss City, respectively, were $33.19 and $24.67 per student.[53]

Another important component of the school's program is the availability of administrators. Included within an administrator-student ratio is the school's attention to guidance counseling, which a number of researchers have found a useful index of quality education. Again, the expenditure levels show superiority in Chalmers. The ratio of students to administrators in Moss City during 1967–1968 was 363 to 1, while the comparable figure for Chalmers was 310 to 1.[54]

The amount of reading material available to students is another crucial part of an effective educational program. Usually educators employ a student-book ratio as a measure of reading availability, but, unfortunately, we could apply no such precise index in this study. Moss City's lack of libraries for its elementary schools poses a problem to which administrators in the district are sensitive and for which they plan remedies in the future. Nevertheless, at the time of the study, only the Moss City high schools possessed self-contained libraries. The situation was only slightly better in Chalmers. Like Moss City, Chalmers had a single centralized library system staffed by qualified personnel. The two newest Chalmers elementary schools, however, which became operational in September 1968, were designed especially for educational experimentation and do contain their own libraries. The

---

[51] As James B. Conant puts it, *"If one is seeking any one single criterion to use as the basis for a first approximation to a judgment as to the adequacy of the offerings of a medium-size widely comprehensive school the certified professional staff-student ratio is to be recommended."* (Italics his.) James B. Conant, *The Comprehensive High School* (New York: McGraw-Hill, Inc., 1967), p. 18.

[52] Mollenkopf and Melville, "A Study of Secondary School Characteristics as Related to Test Scores," pp. 29–35.

[53] Los Angeles County Superintendent of Schools, *Rank Order Arrangement of Data . . . of Los Angeles County, 1967–1968*, p. 72.

[54] Personal correspondence from the districts.

high schools in both districts, of course, have their own libraries. The picture becomes even cloudier when we realize that one of Moss City's finest educational plants is its enormous materials center, located directly across from the district administration headquarters. Its ability to coordinate and distribute a wide range of reading material to teachers has made the materials center the envy of many surrounding districts. Thus, although Chalmers ranks third in the county and Moss City fourteenth in textbook expenditures per child, the order is reversed for expenditures on nontextbooks. Here Moss City places second and Chalmers sixteenth.[55] In view of these complexities, we should probably classify the reading-availability comparison of the districts a standoff.

An aspect that distinguishes more clearly between the districts is educational innovation. We have already mentioned Superintendent Pace's introduction of nongraded schools to Chalmers. In addition, the district has pioneered in the establishment of reading programs for kindergarten children. And, of course, most teaching in the nongraded schools proceeds via the team approach. Therefore, if experimentation is related to quality education, Chalmers certainly ought to rank high.[56]

Finally, any relationship between student political participation in the school and the development of democratic attitudes[57] would also favor Chalmers, which has added to the usual elections and activities of class and school officers two experimental programs. First, during the 1967–1968 school year, students joined with parents and teachers at Chalmers High School to form one of the first California Parent-Student-Teacher Associations. Students were also accorded consultation rights in the determination of certain of the organization's policies.[58] In 1967–1968, Chalmers High sponsored a forum entitled "Youth Speaks Out," which discussed such sensitive political problems as the death penalty, the

---

[55] Los Angeles County Superintendent of Schools, *Rank Order Arrangement of Data . . . of Los Angeles County, 1967–1968*, p. 72.

[56] Experimentation is one of the variables used by Clark in his evaluation of educational quality. See Harold F. Clark, *Cost and Quality in Education* (Syracuse, N.Y.: Syracuse University Press, 1963), chap. 5.

[57] Such a relationship seems at best, indirect. See David Ziblatt, "High School Extracurricular Activities and Political Socialization," *Annals*, 361 (September 1965), pp. 20–31.

[58] The innovation was of sufficient importance that the Los Angeles *Times* paid heed. See *Los Angeles Times*, December 17, 1967.

voting age, and the role of police in the community. No such programs appear in the Moss City schools.

To sum up, on seven of our measures of program quality, Chalmers seems superior to Moss City; on one—the availability of books—the districts are equal.

Educational Outputs

For reasons discussed in Chapter 1, it is difficult to consider outcomes as pure measures of educational quality. Nevertheless, we would like to have some general indication of the effectiveness with which the districts have employed their resources. A knowledge of student achievement in the districts is helpful in estimating the impact of financial resources on students; but as we shall see, Moss City and Chalmers are difficult to distinguish in student achievement.

We will examine four major outcomes of the educational process: achievement on standardized tests, IQ scores, dropout rates, and college attendance and performance records. Performance in each of these domains, while closely related to extraschool influences, is partly the product of school programs.

Because the state of California requires a standardized testing program of all its districts, it becomes possible to make some comparisons between Moss City and Chalmers, though the findings are anything but conclusive. The 1967–1968 Chalmers' first-, third-, sixth- and tenth-grade mean percentile scores on the Stanford Reading Test were 66, 64, 59, and 57. Although these scores are all above the norm, the district gradually loses the favorable position from which its first-graders begin. Moss City scores for the same grades were 57, 58, 56, and 53.[59] The students in Moss City never equal the students in Chalmers, but the Moss City students slip less over time.

The Stanford Reading scores are useful summary output measures, but they do not cover skills in the social studies. A glimpse of the latter comes from comparing the districts' performance on the social-studies battery of the Iowa Test of Educational

[59] *Los Angeles Times*, February 23, 1968. The 1968–1969 scores were virtually identical to those of 1967–1968, as indicated by data that the districts provided us.

Development. Unfortunately, our scores come from grade 10 in Moss City and grade 11 in Chalmers. Still, since scores are computed against a state norm, the performances do admit comparison. The Basic Social Concepts mean percentile score equaled 56 percent in Moss City and 61 percent in Chalmers. Moss City students could read social-studies material at a 54 percent mean, while Chalmers students scored 56 percent. In both cases, the differences, though marginal, do favor Chalmers. The composite Iowa test scores, including social studies, natural sciences, quantitative thinking, literary material, and general vocabulary, were 58 percent in Moss City and 59 percent in Chalmers.[60]

Scores for IQ are available for the sixth-graders of both districts. Although educators once thought IQ measured innate ability, most now believe that school experience can have a substantial impact on IQ. Thus, our sixth-grade IQ scores may reflect some educational differences between the districts. Scores for sixth-graders in Moss City and Chalmers averaged 101.6 and 105.2, respectively.[61]

The scores of students in the two districts differ little; students of both districts excel in some areas and not in others. But students in Moss City are clearly superior in two other ways: they drop out of school less and attend college more than do their counterparts in Chalmers.

The annual dropout rates in Moss City and Chalmers average around 1.6 percent and 2.5 percent, respectively.[62] The significance to be attached to this disparity, however, is not as clear as are the figures themselves. For some students, dropping out may be a response to economic necessity, not to educational deficiency or disinterest. Let us recall that not only is the average income level lower in Chalmers than in Moss City, but also that the latter has the smaller minority population (12.2 percent to 8.0 percent).[63] Impoverished students or those possessing only a rudimentary knowledge of English are disproportionately likely to drop out of school.

[60] The Moss City data are provided in a report to the superintendent, dated May 20, 1968. The Chalmers data are provided in Chalmers Schools, *Annual Report of Pupil Personnel Services*, 1966–1967, pp. 99–108.

[61] *Los Angeles Times*, February 23, 1968.

[62] Personal correspondence with the two districts.

[63] *Los Angeles Times*, February 23, 1968.

More of Moss City's than of Chalmers' high-school graduates move on to higher education. Approximately 67 percent of the Moss City graduates enter either a two- or four-year college, but only 55 percent continue from Chalmers. By contrast, 22 percent of Chalmers' graduates enter a four-year college directly, while only 20 percent of Moss City's graduates do the same.[64] Again it is difficult to interpret these data. Economic differences no doubt explain some of the disparity between the districts, as may geographical accessibility to colleges and universities.[65]

Perhaps we can approach the problem more successfully by focusing on the experience of those high-school graduates who do enter college. Although we do not possess data on all these students, we can examine those who attended the University of California between 1963 and 1967. Graduates of the two districts perform almost identically. Between 1963 and 1966, 190 Moss City alumnae studied at the University of California. Their college grade-point averages fell below their high-school averages by 1.17 points, while the comparable figure for Chalmers graduates was 1.16. But the 1966–1967 entrants from the two districts differ from each other markedly. University of California freshmen from Chalmers dropped only .478 during that year, while graduates from the Moss City high school with the *lowest* high-school—college differential still declined .832.[66] Perhaps it is also significant that, although four times as many students graduate from Moss City as from Chalmers schools, less than twice as many later attend the University of California. This disparity can be explained partly by the higher Moss City income levels, which may allow many Moss City students to attend private universities. The disparity may also have something to do with the proximity of Moss City to a number of state and junior colleges. Nonetheless, the greater willingness of Chalmers students to attempt the difficult University of California system is noteworthy in its own right.

[64] Personal correspondence with the two districts.
[65] On this score, Moss City would appear to have the advantage. It is quite close to and has excellent relations with a nearby junior college.
[66] These data were secured with the cooperation of the superintendents of the two districts and with the help of Dr. Vern Robinson, Director, Relations with Schools, UCLA. I am most grateful for his cooperation.

CONCLUSION: THE SENSE OF THE RESEARCH

Let us now summarize the logic of this study. We have compared two school districts that, at the time of our inquiry, were deviant cases.[67] One district, though its citizens were not wealthy, provided good education, while the other district, though its residents were relatively affluent, supported education poorly. By choosing deviant cases for analysis we hoped to alleviate the contaminating effects of economic background on studies of educational quality. Our choice of districts had but one purpose: to allow us to attribute any superiority in Chalmers' conveyance of democratic attitudes primarily to the Chalmers educational system. Will our research permit us to make such a claim? We believe so. The educational superiority of Chalmers, though not great, is observable. The district provides a rich set of inputs to education, with the result that its students, many of whom come from unpromising socio-economic backgrounds, perform as well and in some cases better than students from the more promising backgrounds characteristic of Moss City.

It now remains to see what difference the quality of education in Chalmers makes to the acceptance of democracy, the assimilation of political knowledge, and the growth of political motivation among Chalmers students. It also remains to see whether the Chalmers teaching environment reflects the superior educational inputs that Chalmers as a district supports. Given what we now know about the districts, we may expect that the differences, though small, will favor Chalmers. Before advancing to the interdistrict comparisons, however, let us trace the development of democratic attitudes, the course of political motivation, and the acquisition of political information among all the students. Although focusing on the entire population of students after having distinguished between the two districts is awkward, placing the description of the two districts after a comprehensive consideration of all the students would have been even more awkward.

[67] The best statement of the logic of deviant case analysis may still be found in Paul F. Lazarsfeld and Morris Rosenberg (eds.), *The Language of Social Research* (New York: The Free Press, 1955), pp. 167–203. See especially Patricia L. Kendall and Katharine M. Wolf, "The Two Purposes of Deviant Case Analysis," pp. 167–170.

Chapter 3
The Growth
of Democratic
Attitudes

Political socialization is a gradual process. Experience with a culture is a prerequisite for assimilation or rejection of the culture, and aging, inasmuch as it indexes a person's exposure to cultural norms, should therefore be closely associated with shifts in political orientation. We propose that the ages of our students—or the age surrogate in this research, the grade level—will explain the greatest portion of student variance in democratic attitudes, political information, partisanship, and orientations related to participation.

We know little about the aging process and almost nothing about the place of political socialization in the life cycle.[1] Two

[1] For a useful general treatment of the life cycle from a quasi-psychoanalytic perspective, see Theodore Lidz, *The Person* (New York: Basic Books, Inc., 1969). One possible reason for the lack of interest in relating personal development to political socialization is the peripheral quality of politics among most Americans. Researchers may believe that this factor indicates only weak and primarily trivial links.

introductory questions come immediately to mind, however. First, at what ages do children acquire what kind of political orientations? Specifically, can we discern a uniform developmental sequence in political socialization to democracy? Second, what position in the maturation process does political socialization to democracy occupy? Of these two questions, the first has occupied more political scientists than the second.[2] This chapter will concentrate on both, tracing not only the course of political socialization to democracy, but also measuring the fit between democratic political socialization and general paradigms of child development.

Few students of political socialization have offered systematic theories about the development of political attitudes. Even fewer have drawn extensively on the child-development literature. To illustrate the point, let us glance briefly at two recent formulations before suggesting the relevance of a third. Dawson and Prewitt divide childhood political socialization into three stages. The young child acquires basic identifications with and orientations to the core political symbols of his culture. The older child gains some comprehension of the nation as a political unit and accumulates knowledge about the dimensions of nationality. The adolescent focuses upon specific, differentiated political objects and personalities.[3] In this paradigm, which is intended to encompass much of the current literature on political socialization, we see the child sloughing off undifferentiated, symbolic political associations and growing into a rationalizing, choosing, political animal.

This paradigm, however, although an undeniably useful summary of findings, is extremely sketchy. It says little about the actual content of the political learning process. Little Americans may be made early, but what about little Democrats or little authoritarians? More important, it does not identify the growth process in political socialization. It ignores the maturational forces that push the child from one set of political concerns to the next. Lacking a tie to the child-development literature, it becomes a static formulation.

Hess and Torney offer four models that are meant to "de-

[2] The recent full-scale study of political socialization that rekindled contemporary interest in the subject asked very much the same question. See Fred I. Greenstein, *Children and Politics* (New Haven, Conn.: Yale University Press, 1965), p. 1.

[3] Richard Dawson and Kenneth Prewitt, *Political Socialization* (Boston: Little, Brown and Company, 1968), pp. 43–45.

scribe in different ways the acquisition, change, and stabilization of political attitudes."[4] These models are accumulation, interpersonal transfer, cognitive development, and identification. Accumulation is the outcome of a teaching process during which formal agencies feed the child standardized bits of attitudes and information. Interpersonal transfer proceeds informally, as the child generalizes his nonpolitical experiences to politics. Imitation also occurs informally. The child simply assumes the political characteristics of adults or peers whom he admires. Finally, cognitive development appears to be an almost biological process, whereby the child's level of maturity determines the kinds of political stimuli to which he can respond.[5]

Hess and Torney believe that each of these forms of socialization takes precedence at a different stage in the life cycle,[6] but they never substantiate this contention. The hypothesis, not even particularly reasonable on its face, is never tested. In fact, Hess and Torney rarely place their actual findings within the theoretical context that they themselves have elaborated. As a result, their analysis gains most of its utility from its data rather than from its theory.

We will interpret the differences between our sixth-, ninth-, and twelfth-graders primarily by relying on a cognitive-development model. Political socialization in the United States may be viewed in many ways, of course, but we prefer to think of it as a process in which democratic ideology is transmitted more or less effectively. We believe that the capacity of children to understand and to accept this ideology depends more upon their level of cognitive development[7] than upon any other single factor.

The most exciting work on cognitive development is that stimulated by Jean Piaget. More important, Piaget's many studies

---

[4] Robert D. Hess and Judith Torney, *The Development of Political Attitudes in Childhood* (Chicago: Aldine Publishing Co., 1967), p. 191.

[5] Hess and Torney, *The Development of Political Attitudes in Childhood*, pp. 19–22.

[6] Hess and Torney, *The Development of Political Attitudes in Childhood*, p. 19.

[7] To some, our formulation may smack of teleology. It seems to imply that psychological maturity inevitably leads to an appreciation of democracy. We would support no such contention. We are maintaining, however, that cognitive development normally is necessary for appreciating the norms of a culture, in this case a democratic culture, but, perhaps in other contexts, a totalitarian culture.

of childhood concept attainment reveal an implicit model of democratic political socialization. We can therefore apply his theories both to existing studies of political socialization and to the data we shall report in this chapter.[8] According to Piaget, the child's increasing understanding of the world is characterized by a movement through several well-defined conceptual stages. The complexities of Piaget's stage model, though vast, need not deter us, and we need only describe those aspects of his theory that are germane to the considerations advanced in this chapter and elsewhere in the book.

Piaget portrays the young child as authoritarian, tradition-bound, arbitrary, unpredictable, primitive, and egocentric. Accumulating experience with peers and with adults other than his parents gradually removes from the child his undifferentiated, fear-oriented externalized view of the world. Slowly the child discovers that he must have reasons for his actions, that history and parental authority are sometimes fallible guides, and that the many doubtful aspects of living demand from him not only his own judgments but also his tolerance for the views of others. This brief résumé should make clear Piaget's disbelief in the capacity of the young child to be a democrat.[9]

Despite the many aspects of Piaget's work that are open to question, there is a striking resemblance of his description to much of what we know about political socialization. For example, though most investigators have agreed that the young child develops fundamental political orientations, no one contends that the sixth grader has much grasp of or sympathy for democracy. According to

[8] For an attempt to incorporate Piagetian theory into an analysis of political socialization, see Richard M. Merelman, "The Development of Political Ideology: A Framework for the Analysis of Political Socialization," *American Political Science Review*, 69, No. 3 (September 1969), pp. 750–767.
[9] Piaget's view comes through most clearly in his studies of moral development. See Jean Piaget, *The Moral Judgment of the Child*, trans. Marjorie Gabain (New York: The Free Press, 1965). For an overview of research in the Piagetian tradition, see Eleanor E. Maccoby, "The Development of Moral Values and Behavior in Childhood," in John Clausen (ed.), *Socialization and Society* (Boston: Little, Brown and Company, 1968), pp. 227–269. An important reformulation of Piaget is Lawrence Kohlberg, "Moral Development and Identification," in Harold Stevenson (ed.), *Child Psychology*, 62d Yearbook of the National Society for the Study of Education, pt. 1 (Chicago: University of Chicago Press, 1963), pp. 277–333.

Greenstein, the young child does not possess even the cognitive tools necessary to approve a political ideology, much less to understand it.[10]

Piaget's formulations suggest two specific hypotheses that this chapter will test. The first is that approval of democratic norms increases with age. Piaget's views suggest, for example, that because young children approve of arbitrary authority and are unable to tolerate ambiguity, they find it difficult to sympathize with minorities and to support freedom of speech, both of which are integral parts of the democratic creed. The second hypothesis is that the child's comprehension of democracy improves with age. The structuring of democratic ideology comes late because the young child cannot think in general terms. In addition, we suspect that the understanding of democracy always lags behind the acceptance of it.

But let us refine this discussion. Both Piaget and Weinstein remark that young children first cognize objects along an undifferentiated, unstructured good-bad dimension.[11] The child either accepts or rejects objects wholly. Thus, we hypothesize that our sixth graders will either give undiscriminating support to democracy or little support at all, with the balance being in the latter direction.

We suspect that the emergence of a differentiated structure to democratic attitudes occurs simultaneously with the increased acceptance of democratic norms. Thus, we must examine several different democratic values. Another reason for proceeding in this way, of course, is that democratic theory has many components, some of which are actually at odds with each other. For example, Dahl both exposes and explores the inconsistency between majority rule and minority rights.[12] There are also vexing areas of conflict between the freedom to speak and the freedom to be left alone. It is partly because democracy is so complex that certain democratic attitudes may be expected to be more labile than others. It would not be surprising to find, for example, that, although support for majority rule stands higher among younger children than does support for minority rights, support for the latter attitude

[10] Greenstein, *Children and Politics*, pp. 67–71.

[11] Piaget, *The Moral Judgment of the Child*, p. 135. E. A. Weinstein, "Development of the Concept of Flag and the Sense of National Identity," *Child Development*, 28, No. 1 (June 1957), pp. 166–174.

[12] Robert A. Dahl, *A Preface to Democratic Theory* (Chicago: University of Chicago Press, 1956), chaps. 1–2.

dimension grows more over the sixth- to the twelfth-grade period than does support for the former. We will therefore explore the data with an eye not only to ordering the components of democratic theory according to their levels of structure and their comparative levels of support, but also according to their volatility.

Summing up the major differences between Piaget's views of younger and older children, we can say that the younger the child, the more dominated he is by the past and by the agents and representatives of the past, especially his parents. The literature on political socialization, however, by supporting Piaget's assertion, leads us to another set of expectations.

No set of political attitudes reveals the influence of the past on the young child more completely than does partisanship. As Hyman first reported some time ago and as other investigators have subsequently confirmed, the child usually inherits his partisan affiliation from his parents.[13] Once established, partisanship can usually survive shocks of considerable magnitude[14]; indeed, partisan identification apparently conveys the same kind of anchoring symbolism to the child as does the family's name and religious affiliation. The inheritance of partisanship may no longer occur with the frequency or durability it once enjoyed, but inheritance remains the dominant process by which the individual becomes a partisan.[15]

If family and history exert their greatest influence on the young child, it follows that maturation encourages political self-assertion and the diminution of partisan ties. Hess and Torney present evidence to support this view, but their argument is marred by the use of data from a question that, instead of revealing individual self-identification, relies on the respondent's behavioral propensities. Consequently, their findings cannot be compared directly

[13] Herbert Hyman, *Political Socialization* (New York: The Free Press, 1959), chap. 4. Angus Campbell *et al., The American Voter* (New York: John Wiley and Sons, Inc., 1960), chap. 7. For more recent evidence, see M. Kent Jennings and Richard Niemi, "The Transmission of Political Values from Parent to Child," *American Political Science Review*, 62, No. 1 (March 1968), pp. 169–185. For a rigorous recent attempt to analyze the appeal of partisan identification, see Philip E. Converse, "Of Time and Partisan Stability" unpublished.

[14] Campbell *et al., The American Voter*, p. 148.

[15] For evidence on the deterioration of partisan inheritance, see Jennings and Niemi, "The Transmission of Political Values from Parent to Child," p. 173.

with those reported by other students of the subject.[16] We have corrected this deficiency by employing the standard Survey Research Center self-identification question. Assuming our maturational thesis is correct, we would expect to find higher rates of independence among older students. There should, in other words, be a markedly higher percentage of Independents among our twelfth- than among our sixth-graders.

The agencies of the past also impress themselves upon the child by sensitizing him differentially to political objects. For example, many elementary-school teachers and parents encourage the child to believe that political history revolves around extraordinary personages. This socialization process caters to the child's natural tendency to personalize complex social and political forces.[17] If Piaget is right, the young child is even incapable of assimilating information about institutions, much less about complex social processes. The child is thus prone to select political stimuli having to do with personalities. We already have confirmation of these tendencies. Easton and Hess found that young children reduce the concept of government to a benevolent president, a symbolic personage, rather than to a set of institutions. Older children, however, think of government in institutional terms.[18]

We shall approach this problem from a slightly different direction. We asked the students a number of information questions about political leaders and institutions; if Piaget's hypothesis is correct, we would predict that the proportion of correct answers to questions about political institutions will rise more sharply with age than will the proportion of correct answers to questions about political leaders.

Unfortunately, a confirmation of our hypothesis will not be definitive. We have already seen that young children are exposed

[16] Compare Hess and Torney's original report, "The Development of Basic Attitudes and Values toward Government and Citizenship during the Elementary Years," Cooperative Research Project No. 1078, U. S. Office of Education (Chicago: University of Chicago, 1965), p. 172; with, for example, Greenstein, *Children and Politics*, p. 73; and Eleanor E. Maccoby, Richard E. Matthews, and Anton S. Morton, "Youth and Political Change," *Public Opinion Quarterly*, 21, No. 1 (Fall 1954), pp. 23–39; Jennings and Niemi, "The Transmission of Political Values from Parent to Child," p. 173.
[17] For elucidation, see Merelman, "The Development of Political Ideology."
[18] Robert D. Hess and David Easton, "The Child's Changing Image of the President," *Public Opinion Quarterly*, 24, No. 4 (1960), pp. 632–644.

to more information about political personalities than institutions. Thus, differential rates of change may be explained not by maturational propensities, but by external manipulation. Our findings, therefore, can only suggest the sensitivity of students to different sorts of political stimuli at different ages.

Another important aspect of political maturation in a democracy involves the child's growing sense of his ability and obligation to assert himself politically. Piaget and others believe that the young child sees himself more as object than subject, more as the influenced than the influential.[19] Two attitudinal structures encompass these types of political thinking. One is the sense of citizen obligation to participate in politics, especially through voting. The other is the sense of political efficacy, the individual's belief that, should he attempt political influence, he would have a fair chance of success.

The structuring and approval of these two norms are crucial for a democracy,[20] which, both theoretically and empirically, relies heavily upon citizen participation in government. Not surprisingly, therefore, schools stress the obligation and capacity to participate. Consequently, we would expect these two dimensions to show considerable development between sixth and twelfth grades. Should we find that development does not occur, we would become more skeptical about the utility of Piaget's formulations.

Let us put the matter in slightly different terms. According to Hess and Torney, "children minimize conflict in viewing politics."[21] The child apparently resists the idea that political conflict

---

[19] For interesting experimental evidence on this subject, see Monique Laurendeau and Adrien Pinard, *Causal Thinking in the Child* (New York: International Universities Press, Inc., 1962), chaps. 1–4.

[20] Indeed, it could well be said that they underlie the attitudinal theory of democracy developed by Almond and Verba. The two dimensions seem particularly closely linked to Almond and Verba's notion of "competence." See Gabriel Almond and Sidney Verba, *The Civic Culture* (Boston: Little, Brown and Company, 1965), chaps. 6–7.

Psychologists have recently become interested in the individual's sense of competence, a dimension that may well be related to the concept of political efficacy. For a review of research on this topic, see M. Brewster Smith, "Competence and Socialization," in Clausen (ed.), *Socialization and Society*, pp. 270–321.

[21] Hess and Torney, *The Development of Political Attitudes in Childhood*, p. 152.

and personal commitment may often be prerequisities to the creation of social change. The assimilation of a tolerance for managed
conflict has many implications, the most important of which involve
the growth of political efficacy and citizen obligation. Children who
believe that the political system operates properly by itself have
little need for a sense of political efficacy or citizen obligation. Only
when the child recognizes that government does not serve him
automatically does he acquire a motive for political participation.
This discovery requires cognitive growth. Therefore, we expect the
development of citizen obligation and political efficacy to be especially marked between grade levels and to be interpretable in terms
of the general maturational paradigm we have outlined.

To sum up, in this chapter we will investigate the growth of
conceptualization about and support for democracy. We will also
focus on such related attitudes as partisanship and the desire to
participate in politics. Finally, we will assess the extent to which
socialization produces a politically informed citizen.

STRUCTURE IN DEMOCRATIC COGNITIONS

Let us first describe the structure of democratic attitudes among
the sixth-, ninth-, and twelfth-graders. We mean by "structure"
what Converse terms "constraint," namely, the degree to which
attitudes cluster together and intercorrelate in recognizable and
nameable sets.[22] From the several ways by which we might have
investigated the nature and extent of constraint in children's belief
systems, we chose the method of factor analysis.

We selected the attitudinal questions to be asked the subjects
in the following way. First, we decided to investigate nine democratic norms: (1) political efficacy, (2) opportunity for individuals
to enter politics, (3) rules of the game, (4) freedom of speech,
(5) majority rule, (6) importance of elections, (7) minority rights,
(8) support for the vote, and (9) sense of civic obligation.[23] We

[22] Philip E. Converse, "The Nature of Belief Systems in Mass Publics," in
David Apter (ed.), *Ideology and Discontent* (New York: The Free Press,
1964), pp. 206–263.
[23] For the con plete list of questions and the subjects tapped, see Appendix B. Generally, many of the questions will be familiar to readers of the
literature. Others, which were intended to probe areas previously not exam-

next designed questions to tap these norms. We added a series of items intended to uncover the student's liberal or conservative policy preferences on domestic problems.[24]

We sometimes asked three, but usually four, questions meant to tap each of the nine democratic norms. Some of the items will be familiar from previous studies. These at least possess the utility that time and frequent application have conferred upon them. Designing survey items for youngsters is a difficult and frustrating business, and using questions that have stood the test of time not only lightens the researcher's burdens but also permits comparison of his findings with those of other investigators. Of course, for some norms, such as majority rule, we could find no suitable questions and therefore formulated our own. We modified questions on the basis both of intuition and pretest results.[25]

But, even if we group the questions in our own categories, how would the students organize them? Would recognizable dimensions of democratic thought emerge from their responses? There are many studies of political thought in childhood, but none has described the way in which children cognize democracy. Certainly, given Converse's analysis of attitudinal fragmentation among adults,

---

ined, were formulated by the author. Unfortunately, the latter have neither the precision nor the reliability of the former. We treated each item as if it were part of a Likert scale. Mean scores within subject areas were accumulated simply by adding an individual's score on all the items in the area. For example, since there were four questions asked about majority rule, the individual could receive a score of 0–4. The higher his score, the more prodemocratic he was. Individual scores were then summed and divided by the relevant n to reach aggregate means for a classification.

[24] We do not view an individual's policy propensity as indicative of his views toward democracy. Instead, we included such questions for three reasons: (1) to see whether children had a cohesive view of the policy dimension, (2) to see whether views correlated with party preference, thereby forming a base for rational voting choice, and (3) to investigate the effect of our independent variables on policy preference, thereby adding richness to our analysis. Underlying all three of these concerns was our view that democracies, if they are functioning properly, should produce large numbers of individuals with formed policy preferences. In turn, such preferences permit rational participation in the political system. Thus, though an individual's policy preferences are not seen as a component of his belief in democracy, the quality of his policy views have a bearing on the viability of democracy.

[25] For further discussion of this phase of the research, the reader is referred to Appendix A.

we have no reason to expect more than the minimum structure to emerge from student responses.

We factor-analyzed the student findings by grade level, using the orthogonal rotation technique to maximize the distinctiveness of factors. Factor analysis is an extremely sensitive process, and conclusions based upon it should therefore be advanced and interpreted cautiously. These warnings apply particularly to our data, for we discovered little structure and that only by generous interpretation.

The criteria by which we chose the factors for inclusion in this discussion are the following: (1) we examined only the first six factors, for only they explained major portions of the variance, and (2) we named the factors and constructed scales from them by relying on those variables that loaded .40 or more on the factor. Relatively few variables met this criterion for each factor. Normally we characterized the factor by reference to its three highest loading variables. (3) Of the top six factors, we discuss only those that were recognizable in terms of democratic theory.

As we had expected, sixth-graders structure their democratic attitudes less completely than do older students. Only factors 1 and 2 are characterizable. We have tentatively labeled factor 1 diffuse anti-democracy. The variables that loaded .40 or more on this factor are as follows:

1. The whole government is run by a few big, powerful men, and they don't care about us ordinary people. (.710)
2. If the government would stay out of the way, private business would solve most of the country's problems. (.690)
3. It isn't important to vote when the man you like doesn't have a chance to win. (.478)
4. Sometimes elections should not be held, because they may divide our people and help our enemies. (.436)
5. Elections are silly, since most people don't know what they are voting for anyway. (.420)

These questions have little in common. Question 1 comes from the political efficacy group, question 2 from liberalism-conservatism, question 3 from citizen obligation to vote, and questions 4 and 5 from importance of elections. In fact, question 2, an index of domestic liberalism, is not even a measure of support for democracy.

We may interpret this factor in two ways. We first notice that the high loaders all have the same sign, positive. Does this similarity mean that the factor merely reflects the acquiescence set of young children, willing to agree to any positive assertion? Although we cannot rule out this possibility, we do not find it convincing. If the factor merely picked up response set, why did it not include some positive pro-democratic items? In fact, each item (other than item 2) aggressively takes an anti-democratic position. We thus feel justified in treating the factor as indicative of the diffuse anti-democratic tendencies of the young child. Our interpretation supports the developmental thesis that is the theme of this chapter, and we have already alluded to the way in which that thesis explains and predicts the child's rejection of democracy, a rejection that factor 1 portrays.

We have termed factor 2 "support for the vote." Three variables loaded .40 or more on this factor. They are as follows:

1. A country is not really free until every person can vote. (.766)
2. The government ought to make sure that all people can vote. (.714)
3. People in the government care about what people like my parents think. (.437)

Item 3, which comes from the political-efficacy group, adulterates the purity of this factor. Nonetheless, we are persuaded that the vote is central to the political thought of sixth-graders. The existence of a voting dimension among sixth-graders is inconsistent with the contentions of those investigators who believe that the young child lacks a sense of political participation and prefers passivity vis-à-vis government.[26] The sixth-grader's consciousness of the vote would not have been predicted by our developmental paradigm.

No other recognizable dimensions emerge from the political thought of sixth-graders. Most noteworthy is the absence of political efficacy. Dennis and Easton trace a marked and continuing increase in the child's sense of political efficacy from grades 3 to 8, but our findings suggest that political efficacy does not yet hold

[26] Hess and Torney, *The Development of Political Attitudes in Childhood*, pp. 110–112.

together as a concept for sixth-graders.[27] However vaguely effective they might feel, young children apparently possess no cohesive conceptual structure centered on political efficacy.

Not unexpectedly, ninth-graders differ more in the sophistication of their political thought from sixth-graders than from twelfth-graders. There is a richer structuring of attitudes among ninth- than among sixth-graders. Moreover, the factor analysis of ninth-grade attitudes reveals none of the severe interpretation problems we confronted among sixth-graders. Perhaps, while the sixth and twelfth grades are times of confusion and transition, the ninth grade is a temporary resting place in the political maturation process.[28]

The first major difference between the sixth and ninth grades lies in the disintegration of the diffuse negativism characteristic of the earlier period. Instead, political efficacy emerges to replace diffuse anti-democracy as factor 1 for ninth-graders. The three identifying variables of the political efficacy factor are as follows:

1. People in the government care about what people like my parents think. (.733)
2. The whole government is run by a few big, powerful men, and they don't care about us ordinary people. (—.618)
3. The real American way of life is dying so fast that we may have to use force to save it. (—.446)

Item 3 poses a problem of interpretation. We can only speculate about its unexpected appearance. Perhaps efficacious people believe that their sense of control over government obviates any need for them to use force in defending American values. More important, however, is that political efficacy emerges from an entirely unstructured position to a position of clear structure in only three years.

---

[27] Easton and Dennis find both cohesion and advancement in the child's appreciation of political efficacy. See David Easton and Jack Dennis, "The Child's Acquisition of Regime Norms: Political Efficacy," *American Political Science Review*, 61, No. 1 (March 1967), pp. 24–38.

[28] This formulation certainly does not conform to that of Sigel, however. See Roberta S. Sigel, "Image of a President: Some Insights into the Political Views of School Children," *American Political Science Review*, 62, No. 1 (March 1968), pp. 216–226.

Factor 2 for ninth-graders, support for the vote, is identical to that for sixth-graders. Not only is its placement the same, but so are two of the items that compose it.

1. A country is not really free until every person can vote. (.767)
2. The government ought to make sure that all people can vote. (.756)
3. If people are not allowed to vote, they may use force to get their way. Therefore, we must make sure they can vote. (.478)

The addition of item 3 to this set of variables gives the factor greater logical coherence than was evident in its sixth-grade form. The concept of the vote is now conceptually clean.

A third intelligible factor emerges for ninth-graders. The crystallization of this dimension not only distinguishes markedly between ninth-graders and their younger counterparts, but also has important theoretical implications of its own. Factor 3 is liberalism-conservatism and includes the following variables:

1. It is not up to the government to make sure that all Americans have jobs. (.737)
2. The government should see to it that every American has enough money to live on. (−.729)
3. The government ought to see to it that old and poor people get good medical care. (−.511)

This factor is not only one of our clearest, but also, to our surprise, reveals that by the ninth grade, children possess reasonably cohesive policy conceptions. By contrast, sixth-graders command neither the political information nor the cognitive tools necessary to interpret the behavior of governmental actors in ideological terms. Our finding contrasts with the views of the many observers who believe that children do not possess a clear conception of policy preferences.[29]

Political cognition among ninth-graders is markedly more sophisticated than that of sixth-graders. However, our picture becomes hazy once more when we turn to twelfth-graders. Still,

[29] See Greenstein, *Children and Politics*, pp. 67–71.

we can confirm one of our hypotheses: twelfth-graders differ less from ninth-graders than do the latter from sixth-graders. Beyond this rudimentary conclusion, the interpretation of our twelfth-grade findings leads to ambiguity.

Factors 1 and 2 remain stable for twelfth-graders. Factor 1 is again political efficacy, but now one of the three characterizing variables mars interpretation. The three highest loading items are the following:

1. People in the government care about what people like my parents think. (.739)
2. The whole government is run by a few big, powerful men, and they don't care about us ordinary people. (—.628)
3. The poor person should be helped to take part in politics, because he doesn't have as good a chance as the rich man. (—.546)

Although variables 1 and 2 are identical to those found in ninth-grade political efficacy, item 3 does not seem to fit. Perhaps efficacious students believe the political system to be so open that no special provision for the poor need be made. Or, perhaps those who are themselves efficacious project their feeling of efficacy onto all segments of society. Either way, we still think it justifiable to interpret factor 1 as political efficacy.

Factor 2 remains support for the vote, the earliest and most enduring of our cognitive structures. The highest loading variables are the following:

1. A country is not really free until every person can vote. (.796)
2. The government ought to make sure that all people can vote. (.761)
3. If people are not allowed to vote, they may use force to get their way. Therefore, we must make sure they can vote. (.575)

It is at this point that twelfth-graders begin to show interesting differences from ninth-graders, both in cognitive clarity and cognitive priorities. Twelfth-graders replace liberalism-conservatism, factor 3 for ninth-graders, with a rudimentary sense of the rules of the game. The three high loading variables on this new factor are as follows:

1. I don't mind how a politician does his job so long as he gets the right things done. (.648)

2. A book that has wrong political ideas should not be printed. (.600)

3. It is all right to get around the law if you don't actually break it. (.578)

Questions 1 and 3 clearly deal with the place of procedural norms in a democracy; item 2, which involves censorship, does not tap the ends-means problem directly. Nevertheless, the three items share a common concern with acceptable political practices. Their clustering suggests that twelfth-graders have acquired a sense for the more abstract of democracy's problems. Factor 3 therefore signifies a considerable leap in conceptual sophistication between the ninth and twelfth grades.

Factors 4 and 5 for twelfth-graders are unintelligible. We will, therefore, look at only one other dimension, factor 6. Skipping factors is not normally acceptable in factor analysis, but the exploratory, tentative character of our research, the weakness of the data in this section, and our desire to speculate as well as to report all seem to justify flexibility in this instance. Factor 6 turns out to be the liberal-conservative dimension, much less salient among twelfth-graders than it was among ninth-graders. Its high loading variables are the following:

1. Government ought to see to it that old and poor people get good medical care. (−.732)

2. The government should see to it that every American has enough money to live on. (−.723)

3. The government should see to it that schools in need get money. (−.470)

In general, the factor analysis reveals only minimal cognitive organization for any grade level. Item correlations are uniformly low. Moreover, although several intelligible factors emerge as children age, the proportion of the attitudinal variance explained by the factors actually remains virtually constant at all three grade levels. Our examination of the unrotated factor matrix, which orders the factors by the proportion of attitudinal variance they explain, indicates that the first six factors together account for only 30 percent of the sixth-grade variance, 28 percent of the ninth-grade variance, and 30 percent of the twelfth-grade variance. These findings suggest that, while twelfth-graders have a greater grasp of democratic concepts than do younger children, democratic attitudes are never cohesive. Put differently, age, instead of tightening political cognition, simply makes what cognitive organization there is more intelligible.

Not only is cognitive structure limited at all grade levels, but some components of democratic theory remain entirely unstructured. For example, we can discover no cognitive organization involving majority rule, civic obligation, or minority rights. Instead, cognitive structure is limited to the symbol of the vote, the closeness of the citizen to his government, policy differences, and, rudimentarily, some rules of the political game. It is clear that most adolescents enter adulthood with an incomplete understanding of democracy.

GROWTH IN SUPPORT FOR DEMOCRACY

The best attempts of the school fail to develop much understanding of democracy among students, but the school's lack of success in this task may not signify total ineptitude. After all, the school is a motivational as well as an educational tool. Perhaps it does succeed at inculcating support for democratic norms.

Do children, regardless of whether they structure their perceptions of democracy, approve more of democratic values as they proceed from the sixth through the twelfth grade? If our findings are affirmative, we can at least contend that the schools aid in the acceptance, if not in the understanding, of democratic values.

To explore this question, we treated each of our subsets of questions alike. That is, we used both those items that had crystallized into recognizable dimensions and those that had not. However, once a value dimension cohered, we measured attitude change by following the course of the crystallization through the grades. For example, we assessed political efficacy among ninth-graders by using the three questions that were the high correlates of that ninth-grade factor. But for sixth-graders, who have not yet structured political efficacy, we employed our original and slightly different set of three political-efficacy questions. Consequently, though they assess the same general norm, dimensions that crystallize sometimes include different items for different grade levels. Of course, in the case of values that never crystallize, such as majority rule, we needed to make no such adjustment, but simply employed the original items at each grade level.[30]

The developmental framework that forms the core of this chapter provides a rationale for expecting that, as children mature, they become more democratic. Much empirical work points to the same conclusion. Horton reports that "the higher the grade level in school, the greater the acceptance of the Bill of Rights. . . ."[31] Summing up their meticulous examination of political efficacy in the child, Easton and Dennis state that "a marked change occurs in these years in the degree of the child's sense of political efficacy. . . . The shift for those expressing opinions on these questions is distinctly in the direction of a development of a higher sense of political efficacy. . . ."[32] Other studies, such as that by Siegman, not only show that authoritarianism is labile, but also indicate that it decreases markedly with age.[33]

Of course, merely demonstrating that pro-democratic change occurs leaves open the place of various socialization agencies in the process. For that reason, we found it necessary to undertake a comparative study. Many of those who document a pro-democratic shift are quite skeptical about the school's contribution. For ex-

[30] We recognize the criticisms of those who feel that comparing scores on one scale with scores on another is an unacceptable procedure. However, we feel our practice defensible on two grounds. First, any other procedure would have misrepresented the actual course of development that students apparently go through. Second, in the case of the few values affected, we are not comparing scores on totally different values or items. In a sense, we are comparing one sort of apple with another rather than an apple with a pear. A political-efficacy dimension that has crystallized is quite similar in composition to one that has not. However, a crystallized political efficacy *is* different enough from an uncrystallized efficacy dimension to require measurement in its new form and comparison with its earlier form. Otherwise, we ignore the developmental process through which the child has passed.

[31] Roy E. Horton, Jr., "American Freedom and the Values of Youth," in H. H. Remmers (ed.), *Anti-Democratic Attitudes in American Schools* (Evanston, Ill.: Northwestern University Press, 1963), p. 53.

[32] Easton and Dennis, "The Child's Acquisition of Regime Norms," p. 33.

[33] Aaron W. Siegman, "Authoritarian Attitudes in Children: The Effects of Age, IQ, Anxiety and Parental Religious Attitudes," *Journal of Clinical Psychology*, 13, No. 4 (October 1956), pp. 338–340.

ample, Remmers writes, "Possibly because applications of the First Amendment of the United States Constitution are 'controversial,' they are not well taught by the agencies primarily responsible. . . ."[34] And James Garvey claims that deficiencies in the methods by which the schools have taught the Bill of Rights have robbed them of their effectiveness. According to Garvey, the study of the Bill of Rights, by relying excessively on textual description and chronology, has deprived students of any insight into the protections such rights afford to everyday conduct.[35] If the schools have failed to convey those political values that are an integral part of the curriculum, how much worse might they perform in transmitting norms that, while also aspects of democratic theory, are not central to the curriculum? We refer in this connection to such beliefs as political efficacy, civic obligation, and majority rule.

Table 3-1 summarizes the growth in student support for democracy, by value dimension. We may employ Table 3-1 for a number of purposes. We can first compare the rates of change in specific attitude clusters. Next, we can identify those dimensions that enjoy high support early in the educational process—in the sixth grade—and those that gain support only relatively late in the educational cycle, in the twelfth grade. Let us examine these two aspects of the table in some detail.

The rank order for the four-item dimensions in terms of their support by sixth-graders is the following: minority rights, civic obligation, importance of elections, and majority rule. There is no change in the relative support for these values over time. In other words, the identical order may be observed among twelfth-graders. Contrary to what Remmers has suggested, we find that young children are already favorably disposed toward the rights of minorities, at least when these rights are stated in the abstract. By contrast, there is never much support for majority norms. Indeed, majority rule provides one notable exception to the proposition that age increases acceptance of democracy. The schools would do well to teach majority rule more effectively.

Turning now to values indexed by three questions, we dis-

---

[34] H. H. Remmers and Richard D. Franklin, "Sweet Land of Liberty," in Remmers (ed.), p. 61.

[35] James F. Garvey, "Teaching Controversial Issues: The Bill of Rights," *California Journal for Instructional Improvement*, 9, No. 1 (March 1966), pp. 32–39.

TABLE 3-1. MEAN DEMOCRATIC SUPPORT BY GRADE LEVEL
AND DIMENSION

Dimension	Grade level 6th	Grade level 9th	Grade level 12th	Number of items in dimension	Percent growth from 6th to 12th[b] grade
Freedom of speech	1.82 (563)	2.23 (507)	2.40 (413)	3	61 to 77 (16)[c]
Majority rule	2.00 (562)	2.06 (509)	2.11 (413)	4	50 to 52 (2)[c]
Importance of elections	2.26 (563)	2.47 (510)	2.76 (409)	4	57 to 67 (10)[c]
Minority rights	2.75 (565)	3.09 (505)	3.13 (414)	4	69 to 79 (10)[c]
Sense of civic obligation	2.49 (563)	2.74 (503)	2.83 (414)	4	62 to 72 (10)[c]
Support for the vote	1.91 (560)	1.79[a] (499)	1.49[a] (408)	3	64 to 50 (−14)[c]
Political efficacy	1.59 (561)	1.54[a] (497)	1.66[a] (403)	3	53 to 55 (2)[c]
Rules of the game	2.95 (562)	3.33 (501)	2.02[a] (409)	5 for 6th & 9th, then 3	59 to 66 (7)[c]
Opportunity to participate	1.29 (562)	2.20 (504)	2.19 (408)	3 (6th & 12th) 4 (9th)	43 to 70 (27)[c]
Support for domestic liberalism	2.05 (564)	1.97[a] (509)	1.71[a] (411)	3	68 to 57 (−11)

[a] Crystallized dimensions.

[b] We calculated this figure by treating the items in each dimension as a continuum running from 0 to n items. A score of 0 equaled 0 percent and n items answered democratically equalled 100 percent. In short, we merely converted the means into percentile scores.

[c] Difference in percentage points from sixth to twelfth grades.

cover the following order of approval among sixth-grade pupils: support for the vote, freedom of speech, political efficacy, and opportunity to participate. Twelfth-graders exhibit a different ranking, however: freedom of speech, opportunity to participate, rules of the game, political efficacy, and support for the vote. Freedom of speech, as important a civil-libertarian value as minority rights, receives high levels of approval across the age spectrum. This finding takes on greater significance when we add the moderate and continuing support for the rules of the game. Let us also recall that twelfth-graders have acquired a reasonably clear conception of these rules. Taken together, the firm showing of the rules of the game, minority rights, and freedom of speech constitutes one of the major findings in this section of the study. Internalization of these three values provides a motivational base for libertarian democracy.[36]

Of all the values we examined, support for the vote behaves most distinctly. Although young children have a clear picture of the vote, their faith in voting actually falls precipitously as they proceed through school. Simultaneously, their appreciation of more sustained political participation (opportunity to participate) rises sharply. We can only speculate about this paradox. One possible explanation involves the increasing political militancy to which students at all levels of the educational structure are exposed, even in districts—such as Chalmers and Moss City—that have been relatively free of disruption. It may be that as today's children mature they come to see the vote more as a formal than as an effective method of exerting influence. If so, they may develop an inchoate, yet very real sympathy for less conventional forms of political expression and participation.

We were surprised to find that political efficacy does not gain much student support between the sixth and twelfth grades. This finding conflicts with those of Easton and Dennis, but there are not only methodological differences between our study and theirs but also differences in samples and time periods of study.[37]

---

[36] I do not wish to push this conclusion too far, however. The low cohesion in the rules of the game dimension and the absence of cohesion in the other two realms remain a source of concern.

[37] Easton and Dennis collected their data in the early 1960s. They based their findings on an eight-city sample of 12,000 children. In addition, they used a scoring method different from ours. Still, their mean political efficacy

Where do the greatest changes in support occur during the educational cycle, between the sixth and ninth grades, or between the ninth and twelfth? The answer to this question can only be ambiguous. Approximately equal numbers of values shift the most in both periods. The following norms change the most between sixth and ninth grades: (1) freedom of speech, (2) majority rule, (3) minority rights, (4) sense of civic obligation, and (5) rules of the game. The values that undergo the most change between the ninth and twelfth grades are (1) importance of elections, (2) political efficacy, (3) opportunity to participate, and (4) support for the vote. The deterioration of support for domestic liberalism also occurs most rapidly between ninth and twelfth grades. Thus, although they do not fit easily into any summary paradigm, these disparate rates do support Jennings and Niemi's contention that important political learning continues throughout the adolescent years.[38] In sum, our findings confirm our expectation that investigating the high-school period would be fruitful.

Any conclusions about the extent of a shift in pro-democratic attitudes between the sixth and twelfth grades should be considered with care, for the percentile figures, with but a few exceptions, do not indicate major pro-democratic changes during this period. Still, some important dimensions, such as freedom of speech and opportunity to participate, do make important strides. These data implicitly support the contentions of those who believe that much progress in a pro-democratic direction occurs before the sixth grade; they also suggest, however, that the adolescent is open to both pro- and anti-democratic movement. On balance, while the democratic terrain the student traverses between the sixth and twelfth grades varies in distance and evenness, in most cases it is limited.

Approval of domestic liberalism is the only value other than support for the vote that actually declines over time. As the child matures, he becomes increasingly pessimistic about the capacity

---

cores, though more variable than our own, moved only 3.6 on a scale of 6 from grades 3–8. Easton and Dennis, "The Child's Acquisition of Regime Norms," pp. 30–33. Finally, they did not investigate beyond grade 8. Discrepancies nonetheless remain substantial, particularly because we used three of their political-efficacy items.

[8] M. Kent Jennings and Richard G. Niemi, "Patterns of Political Learning," *Harvard Educational Review*, 38, No. 3 (Summer 1968), pp. 443–467.

of government to solve domestic problems. We cannot explain this finding with certainty, but it may reflect the child's growing suspicion of the benevolence and omnipotence of all authority.

GROWTH IN PARTICIPATION-RELATED ATTITUDES

Democratic attitudes cohere only moderately between sixth and twelth grades. In addition, the amount of pro-democratic attitude movement can only be characterized as restrained. But attitudes are not the sole support of a democratic system. What about the growth of sentiments and knowledge related to actual participation? We now examine three indices of such behavior—partisan identification, political information, and intended participation in politics.

It is difficult to imagine a democracy that lacks the contributions of an active, freely competitive party system.[39] The success with which the parties capture adherents among the young will not only affect the viability of those parties in later years, but will also, in turn, be reflected in the vitality of democracy. We know, for example, that party identifiers generally participate in all aspects of politics more than do those people who remain outside the party system.[40] Thus, the amount of partisanship in the public sets a limit on citizen participation in the democratic system.

There is ambiguity about the orientations and behavior of self-professed Independents,[41] but no ambiguity exists about those

[39] There are, of course, many statements about the importance of parties to a functioning democracy. See especially Frank J. Sorauf, *Political Parties in the American System* (Boston: Little, Brown and Company, 1966), chap. 1. For a highly sophisticated comparative discussion of parties in democracies, see Seymour M. Lipset and Stein Rokkan. "Cleavage Structures, Party Systems and Voter Alignments: An Introduction," in Lipset and Rokkan (eds.), *Party Systems and Voter Alignment* (New York: The Free Press, 1967), pp. 1–65. Jack Dennis has reported findings that suggest the ambivalence with which Americans view their parties; his findings, as we shall shortly see, parallel our own. See Jack Dennis, "Support for the Party System by the Mass Public," *American Political Science Review*, 60 No. 3 (September 1966), pp. 600–616.

[40] For a review of the evidence, see Lester W. Milbrath, *Political Participation* (Skokie, Ill.: Rand McNally and Company, 1965), p. 52.

[41] Alternative views of independents may be found in William H. Flanigan *Political Behavior of the Electorate* (Boston: Allyn and Bacon, Inc., 1969)

who cannot even place themselves within the Independent-party identification rubric. Such people contribute little to the democratic system. Hence, one sure measure of a student's commitment to democratic participation is the extent to which either his partisan identification or independence supplants total indecision about his position in the party system. Persistent inability to accept the partisan terms of the system is an indication of incomplete and potentially destabilizing socialization.

The literature on the subject suggests the following modal pattern. Most American children inherit a partisan identification early in their lives, but this youthful partisanship, although often lasting, is not all-encompassing. There are at least three major sources of adolescent independence. First, as Froman and Skipper point out, adolescence conveys the ability to evaluate both the parties and the party system in concrete terms.[42] Adolescents feel themselves prone to reassess their early partisan commitments in the light of their growing sensitivity to political issues. This retrenchment process may result in considerable instability and equivocation. Indeed, Jennings and Niemi believe that the twelfth grade concludes a full ten years of party reevaluation.[43] Hess and Torney postulate another source of adolescent political fluidity. They argue that the stress secondary-school teachers place upon open-mindedness and critical thinking encourages a sharp diminution of student partisanship. The effect of this training, they argue, culminates in an Independent rate of over 40 percent among tenth-graders.[44] Finally, Ball claims that the process of adolescent rebellion in the United States is accompanied by a withdrawal from politics and

---

p. 34; Robert E. Agger, "Independents and Party Identifiers in 1952," in Eugene Burdick and Arthur J. Brodbeck (eds.), *American Voting Behavior* (New York: The Free Press, 1959), pp. 308–330; Alan S. Meyer, "The Independent Voter," in William N. McPhee and William A. Glaser (eds.), *Public Opinion and Congressional Elections* (New York: The Free Press, 1962), pp. 65–78; Samuel Eldersveld, "The Independent Vote: Measurement, Characteristics, and Implications for Party Strategy," *American Political Science Review*, 46, No. 3 (September 1952), pp. 735–754; Campbell *et al., The American Voter*, pp. 143–145.

[42] Lewis A. Froman, Jr., and James K. Skipper, Jr., "An Approach to the Learning of Party Identification," *Public Opinion Quarterly*, 27, No. 3 (Fall 1963), pp. 473–480.

[43] Jennings and Niemi, "Patterns of Political Learning," p. 454.

[44] See chap. 3, fn. 16.

a deterioration of partisanship.[45] Again, however, let us distinguish carefully between the student's choice of independence, which has an assured history and referent within the current party system, and the student's reluctance to express any preference at all, which has no such referent.

Table 3-2 sheds some interesting new light on these questions.

TABLE 3-2. PARTY IDENTIFICATION AT THREE GRADE LEVELS
(IN PERCENT)

Party	6th		Grades 9th		12th		Totals	
Democrat	23	(129)	34	(166)	27	(111)	28	(406)
Republican	23	(131)	24	(118)	19	(76)	22	(325)
Independent	9	(49)	13	(65)	22	(89)	14	(203)
Don't know	43	(237)	26	(129)	27	(109)	33	(475)
Other	2	(6)	8	(14)	5	(21)	3	(41)
Totals	38% (552)		34% (492)		28% (406)		100% (1450)	

As Table 3-2 indicates, the party system succeeds only minimally in capturing the youthful electorate. Our findings are foreshadowed by Jennings and Niemi's recent discovery of the low correlations between parent and child partisan identifications.[46] Our figures are extreme, however, and therefore especially revealing. As few— 46 percent—of our twelfth-graders as of our sixth-graders classify themselves as Republicans or Democrats. Neither maturation nor schooling incorporates students into the major parties.

Age and education do reduce the proportion of students who remain totally outside the party system. This percentage, indexed by the don't-know statistic, falls 16 percent between sixth and twelfth grades. There is no change in the figure, however, between ninth and twelfth grades. The entire process of incorporation, such as it is, occurs *before* high-school social-studies courses treat the place of partisanship and independence in the political system. Either teaching in this subject area is poor, or else other pressures limit its effectiveness.

[45] Donald W. Ball, "Covert Political Rebellion as *Ressentiment*," *Social Forces*, 43, No. 1 (October 1964), pp. 93–101.
[46] Jennings and Niemi, "The Transmission of Political Values from Parent to Child," p. 173.

The proportion of Independents rises 13 percent between the sixth and twelfth grades. This increase, though marked, does not approach that reported in Hess and Torney's study. The main reason for the divergence in findings, one suspects, is the difference in the wording of questions. Let us recall that Hess and Torney, rather than employing the Survey Research Center self-identification question, chose to infer partisanship from the preferred voting strategies of their respondents. Our findings support the belief that the Hess and Torney procedure may have inflated the number of Independent responses.

In any case, the Independent figures are overshadowed by the fact that more than a quarter of our twelfth-graders are either so confused or so alienated by the American system that they cannot accept any of its partisan terms. The current wave of youthful protest, directed against established institutions such as the party system, is reflected in these data. Needless to say, our findings contrast sharply with others drawn from less turbulent times.[47]

A second participation-related measure is knowledge about the institutions and the leaders of the political system. Democratic government presupposes popular control of policy through citizen choice of leaders. Rational choice depends upon a secure base of information in the public. Although many studies contend that Americans know little about government and current events,[48] some observers have recently reacted against such pessimistic conclusions. The reaction takes two forms. First, there is evidence that

[47] This seems particularly true of those studies conducted in the late 1950s and early 1960s. However, let us enter a caveat. Many of the former studies were directed toward assessing basic system-support attitudes, such as orientations toward authority, which were associated with rather young children. Our own interest has been in more sophisticated attitudes that grow at later times. Thus, our findings do not directly contradict these earlier studies of the Chicago group and Greenstein. Put another way, it is perfectly possible that a young child can feel benevolent about and loyal to our system, support its authority structures, and yet, later develop an anti-democratic ideology. We know that though many Americans are not particularly democratic, they are strong nationalists and perhaps even hyperpatriotic. Indeed, as Edgar Litt points out in a private communication, much socialization literature ignores the distinction between support for the nationalistic aspects of a system and support for the system's principles.

[48] For an important formulation of the relationship between knowledge, partisanship, and voting, see Philip E. Converse, "Information Flow and the Stability of Partisan Attitudes," in Philip E. Converse *et al., Elections and the Political Order* (New York: John Wiley and Sons, Inc., 1965), chap. 8.

citizens perceive the connection between their party preference and their policy preference accurately. In other words, most Americans are apparently informed enough to use the parties as a rational channel for their own individual policy preferences.[49] Second, some normative theorists, of whom the most auspicious is Peter Bachrach, argue that believers in democracy are obligated to educate the electorate whatever its current state of knowledge. Bachrach also claims that, once aroused, the electorate possesses a greater capacity to absorb political information than is generally acknowledged.[50]

The educational system should excel in the conveyance of political information. The teacher need feel no trepidation in passing on neutral political facts and, as a consequence, should perform optimally. In addition, the transmission of information about governmental structures and political personalities is the core of the social-studies curriculum. Finally, the evaluational neutrality of political information may permit the teacher to circumvent any barriers that children erect against value-laden material. Thus, we have reason to expect marked increases over time in the level of student political information.

Table 3-3 reports the mean student information scores in two areas, political personalities and political institutions. Although Table 3-3 documents a substantial growth in the amount of political information that students possess, we would not be justified in attributing this growth entirely to the schools. After all, the mass media also foster the child's exposure to politics.[51] Our sixth-grade mean scores indicate that young children know more about political personalities than about political institutions; this finding not only confirms our earlier hypothesis, but also supports the child-development thesis that has provided the theoretical backbone of this

[49] V. O. Key, *The Responsible Electorate* (Cambridge, Mass.: Harvard University Press, 1966). See also Donald R. Matthews and James W. Prothro, "The Concept of Party Image and Its Importance for the Southern Electorate," in M. Kent Jennings and L. Harmon Zeigler (eds.), *The Electoral Process* (Englewood Cliffs, N.J.: Prentice-Hall, Inc., 1966), pp. 139–175.

[50] Peter Bachrach, *The Theory of Democratic Elitism* (Boston: Little, Brown and Company, 1967), pp. 99–103.

[51] For some excellent evidence on television's ability to stimulate the child and raise his interest in public affairs, see Hilde Himmelweit *et al.*, *Television and the Child* (New York: Oxford University Press, 1958), pp. 267–282.

chapter. However, Table 3-3 also shows that age does not reduce the child's interest in political personalities. Information about leaders keeps pace with student mastery of institutions. Perhaps

TABLE 3-3. MEAN STUDENT INFORMATION ON POLITICAL
PERSONALITIES AND POLITICAL INSTITUTIONS,
BY GRADE LEVEL[a]

Grade level	Personalities		Institutions		Percent change between 6th and 12th grades
6th	3.25	(556)	1.85	(563)	
9th	4.35	(504)	2.91	(502)	Personalities: 29%
12th	5.61	(406)	4.14	(401)	Institutions: 33%
Totals	4.28	(1466)	2.84	(1466)	

[a] Measurement of knowledge about personalities was based on eight questions; measurement of knowledge about institutions, on seven. Hence, the means are not directly comparable. The percentile-change column facilitates comparison, however.

the emphasis by the mass media on political personalities neutralizes the aspect of psychological development that normally shifts the child's attention to political institutions.

Let us pause briefly to examine a subsidiary question emerging from the literature on public opinion. We know that by their senior year, high-school students find national politics substantially more interesting and involving than state politics, and the latter similarly more attractive than local politics.[52] But how early do these different levels of involvement manifest themselves in the child? We can investigate this question with the aid of several of our information items. Table 3-4 reports the proportion of correct responses to three items, each of which measures knowledge of national, state, and local political institutions.

Although item 1 does not compare with the other two as neatly as we would ideally desire, we can still see that the expected

[52] M. Kent Jennings, "Pre-Adult Orientations to Multiple Levels of Government," *Midwest Journal of Political Science*, 11, No. 3 (August 1967), pp. 291–317.

TABLE 3-4. PERCENTAGE OF CORRECT RESPONSES TO THREE
QUESTIONS ABOUT LOCAL, STATE, AND NATIONAL
GOVERNMENT, BY GRADE LEVEL

| Question | Percent correct at grades | | | Totals |
	6	9	12	
1. What type of government does the city of Los Angeles have?	6 (32)[b]	10 (53)	17 (70)	10 (155)
2. The two branches of the California State Legislature are called:	9 (50)	20 (102)	47 (194)	23 (346)
3. The three branches of the United States Government[a] are:	23 (132)	30 (159)	62 (256)	37 (547)

[a] By accident, "United States Government" was substituted for "federal government." Despite the resulting awkwardness and inaccuracy in wording, we believe the findings remain indicative.
[b] Number of students at each grade level responding correctly.

order of salience becomes fixed in childhood and intensifies with age. A similar finding from the political-personalities data supports the same conclusion. Among sixth-graders, 94 percent recognized Ronald Reagan as the governor of California, but only 72 percent identified the vocal and colorful Sam Yorty as mayor of Los Angeles. In fact, fewer twelfth-graders named Yorty correctly than sixth-graders Reagan: 87 percent of the twelfth-graders knew of Yorty, 7 percent fewer than the sixth-graders who identified Reagan.

A third participation-related measure is the perceived attractiveness of holding political office. It seems obvious that people who find a political career inviting will participate more than those who do not. In addition, the democratic system demands that its citizens recruit themselves into politics; it therefore retards the formation of any self-perpetuating, hereditary elite that would take it upon itself to handle the reins of government. Democratic theory requires that the motivation to participate should be dispersed widely. Such a distribution would also prevent whole segments of the population from feeling themselves unrepresented in the policy-making process. But does the socialization process succeed in conveying the participation norm? Table 3-5 answers this question clearly. As the child becomes more familiar with politics, his desire to participate almost vanishes.

TABLE 3-5. RESPONSES BY GRADE LEVEL TO "WOULD YOU LIKE, SOMEDAY, TO RUN FOR POLITICAL OFFICE?"

Grade level	Percent "Yes"	Response Percent "No"	Totals	
6th	31 (171)	69 (376)	100%	(547)
9th	18 (92)	82 (407)	100%	(499)
12th	11 (43)	89 (363)	100%	(406)
Totals	21 (306)	79 (1146)	100%	(1452)

We can only speculate about the reasons for this precipitous decline. We have already reviewed those findings that indicate that the young child not only imbues the political system with drama and nobility, but also idealizes its leaders. This perceptual framework, whatever its other drawbacks, is conducive to a desire for political activity. But as the child matures, he learns about the moral, physical, and emotional demands of politics, and he also discovers frailties in formerly admired leaders. The high gloss in which politics was once enveloped understandably begins to dull. The school, along with other socialization agencies, apparently cannot prevent this process of deterioration; thus, the school does little to increase the pool of recruits to the American political process.

SUMMARY AND CONCLUSIONS

Let us summarize our findings in terms of the developmental framework we have employed as our guide:

1. Twelfth-graders exhibit sophisticated conceptualization of only three democratic values—the vote, political efficacy, and rules of the game. In addition, twelfth-graders have a good grasp of the liberal-conservative policy dimension. Political efficacy and the vote

are primarily symbolic values, but appreciation of policy issues and of the rules of the game are substantive. By this statement, we mean only that the vote and an individual's perceived closeness to the system are rather far removed from the actual operation of government.[53] The rules of the game, which specify operating procedures for the system, and policy issues, which delineate the conflicts around which the system revolves, are the heart of the governmental process. Understanding the rules of the game informs a person when leadership actions conform to democratic norms and when they do not; such knowledge enables the individual to make rational judgments about groups and individuals within the system. Likewise, the capacity to think along a left-to-right continuum conveys the information necessary for responsible choice among alternative programs. Emergence of the predominantly symbolic dimensions earlier than the predominantly abstract dimensions supports Piaget's model of maturation. We must remember, however, that the overall degree of cognitive structure is limited. Indeed, many democratic values possess little cohesion at all.

2. Pro-democratic progress from sixth through twelfth grades is modest. Age does elicit greater support for democratic norms, but the movement is neither as marked nor as uniform as developmental theory might have predicted. In fact, some values show either no movement or actual retrogression.

3. Students become much better informed as they mature. Political knowledge is clearly the most volatile factor we have investigated. Whether we conclude that the twelfth-grader has acquired enough information to make rational political choices depends, of course, on beliefs about the amount of knowledge required for responsible decisions in the American political system.

4. Age does not encourage support for the party system. Large numbers of twelfth-grade students find no place for themselves in the current structure of American partisanship.

5. The child's desire to participate in politics recedes sharply as maturation proceeds. In sum, then, because the gain in support for democratic values is only modest, because the party system exerts little attraction, and because participation motivation disinte-

---

[53] A much clearer formulation about the role of symbols in a democracy may be found in Murray Edelman, *The Symbolic Uses of Politics* (Urbana, Ill.: University of Illinois Press, 1964), chaps. 2 and 9.

grates, we feel justified in concluding that maturation produces less acceptance of than understanding of democracy.

It is conjectural, yet legitimate, to speculate upon the meaning of these findings. Our data appear to presage a darker future for the democratic system than do other findings from previous studies of socialization. We should not generalize these findings too widely, of course; after all, the two school districts from which they came are undoubtedly different in many ways from other districts around the country. Despite this methodological caveat, we remain impressed by the generally mixed results of socialization to democracy in these white, middle-class settings. How much bleaker might be findings from the ghetto?[54]

The maturational paradigm that we borrowed from Piaget has proved a useful, though not definitive guide. The general picture of development that it offered fits most of the data, but we find little support for Piaget's faith that maturity would encourage a belief in democracy. Political socialization is too complex a process to be encompassed by any single developmental model, even one as sophisticated and subtle as Piaget's. We have yet to fix the place of the schools in the socialization process. Does educational quality in Chalmers raise the level of support for democratic values among the students of that district? Let us now attempt to answer that question.

---

[54] For some hints, see David O. Sears, "Black Attitudes toward the Political System in the Aftermath of the Watts Insurrection," *Midwest Journal of Political Science*, 13, No. 4 (November 1969), pp. 515–545; see also Dwaine Marvick, "The Political Socialization of the American Negro," *The Annals of the American Academy of Political and Social Science*, 361 (1965), pp. 112–128.

Chapter 4

The Effect
of the School:
Direct Impacts

In Chapter 3 we described some major age differences in political conceptualization. Age is an individual property; that is, each person possesses an age that is uniquely his and that we can use to describe him. In Chapter 5 we will again investigate the political learning process, this time as it interacts with other individual properties, such as sex and scholarly attainment.

Assessing the effects of social class, which we shall also attempt in Chapter 5, presents complexities not found in the investigation of age, sex, and attainment. A person's class identification has a different theoretical standing than his sexual or intellectual status. Our society, because it lacks a rigid class structure, does not force people to conceive of themselves as members of a class, yet society continually thrusts a person's sex, age, and accomplishment into his consciousness, and these individual characteristics become signs of personal identity as well as role components. Thus, although we are free to describe an individual by reference to his social class, neither the terms we use nor the meanings we imply are as clear as we might desire.[1]

In addition, of course, class has a uniquely relational component not encountered in personal characteristics. Age and sex are part of the biological makeup of the individual, whereas scholarly attainment depends heavily on inherited intelligence. Class, however, gets its meaning solely from groups of men. A person's actions as a member of a social class must be explained primarily by reference to his identification with and ties to others in his class. For example, "misidentifiers" in a certain social class are less likely to vote with others in their income group than are those whose class perception is congruent with their income.[2] These differences are matters of degree, of course, and even biological characteristics leave room for social manipulation.

If assessing the effects on the individual of social class is problematic, it is even more difficult to explain a person's behavior by reference to his school district. Here we enter another realm entirely. The aggregate measures by which we have distinguished between our two school districts describe two political units, not any particular student. To say that one school district has a higher teacher-student ratio than another tells us nothing about the experience of particular students or teachers. Since the school district indices describe large masses of people, not individuals, we cannot legitimately explain the behavior of any single member of the aggregate by reference to the aggregate measures themselves.[3]

In this chapter we are engaged in inferring the effects of aggregate differences on the responses of individual students and teachers. Our independent variables in this chapter are school districts, but our dependent variables remain those discussed in Chapter 3, the attitudes of individuals. Therefore, we are moving

---

[1] For a good introduction to the problem, see Melvin Tumin, *Social Stratification: The Forms and Function of Inequality* (Englewood Cliffs, N.J.: Prentice-Hall, Inc., 1967).

[2] Bernard R. Berelson, Paul F. Lazarsfeld, and William N. McPhee, *Voting* (Chicago: University of Chicago Press, 1954), p. 56.

[3] W. S. Robinson, "Ecological Correlation and the Behavior of Individuals," *American Sociological Review*, 15, No. 3 (June 1950), pp. 351–357.

between social levels in our research, or, as Price would say, we are hypothesizing the effect of a macro factor on micro outcomes.[4]

By now, it should be easy to see why such a practice is even more difficult to defend than to explain. None of us would hesitate to say that certain of a person's characteristics cause certain of his actions, but to claim that a person's behavior depends upon factors that do not describe the individual himself seems, on its face, inadmissible.

This problem of matching individual behavior to aggregate characteristics is anything but new. The ancient aphorism, "The whole is more than the sum of its parts," sums up many of the attendant paradoxes. Still, despite the fact that logic cannot bridge the behavior of individuals and the actions of a group, we know that people often do things in concert or in the presence of others that, alone, they would never even contemplate. For instance, groups occasionally lynch, but the people composing such groups by and large deny any desire to lynch.[5]

The recent intellectual history of this problem has shaped our methodologies of political research. That history began with Robinson's analysis of the "ecological fallacy."[6] Before the appearance of Robinson's article, a generation of political scientists had relied upon the manipulation of aggregate data, such as census figures, to generate conclusions about the political behavior of individuals.[7] Once Robinson had pointed out the logical impossibility of this approach, political scientists resorted to two contradictory strategies.

The first of these strategies, according to Price, was reduction-

[4] Douglas Price, "Micro- and Macro-politics: Notes on Research Strategy," in Oliver Garceau (ed.), *Political Research and Political Theory* (Cambridge, Mass.: Harvard University Press), pp. 102–143.

[5] Thus, they must find rationalizations for their distasteful behavior. See Neil S. Smelser, *Theory of Collective Behavior* (New York: The Free Press, 1962), p. 108.

[6] Robinson, "Ecological Correlation and the Behavior of Individuals."

[7] This tradition persisted in Europe, where it brought some interesting research into electoral behavior. See, particularly, Herbert Tingsten, *Political Behavior: Studies in Electoral Statistics* (Totowa, N.J:. The Bedminster Press, 1963). See also François Goguel-Nyegaard, *Nouvelles Études de Sociologie Électorale* (Paris: Librairie Armand Colin, 1963).

ism.[8] Most behavioralists, because they accepted Robinson's injunction completely, attempted to scale down all their explanations to propositions about individuals. Their decision was sweetened by the fact that suddenly newfound survey techniques permitted the reliable interviewing of large samples of people. For a long time behavioralists were oblivious to all the implications of describing political behavior as a set of individual attitudes. Traditionalists, however, alerted them to the problem. One noted political theorist even charged that the behavioralists, by reducing political man to a bundle of psychological orientations, had robbed political science of the actual substance of governmental action.[9]

The reductionist solution may indeed have had the curious result of banishing "politics" from political science, but the traditionalists themselves could offer nothing better. Frustrated and outflanked, most anti-behavioralists contented themselves by pursuing the legal-historical method that had for so long been their staple approach to inquiry. The traditionalists' withdrawal assured that only the reductionist strategy would produce major advances in political knowledge and theory during the 1950s and early 1960s.

Today the problem has reemerged, again partly because of the effects of technology on political research. We have already observed that much of the original attraction of reductionism lay in the availability of the sample survey. Now, however, computers enable social scientists to analyze great masses of aggregate data. Consequently, political scientists have again become interested in the relationships among such aggregate data as governmental expenditures, voting rates, and party structures in states and localities.[10] They have been aided in this endeavor by David Easton's

[8] Price, "Micro- and Macro-politics," pp. 135–140. For an interesting inquiry into the methodological utility of reductionism, see Donald E. Stokes, "Analytic Reduction in the Study of Institutions," paper delivered at the annual meeting of the American Political Science Association, September 1966.

[9] Leo Strauss, "Epilogue," in Herbert Storing (ed.), *Essays in the Scientific Study of Politics* (New York: Holt, Rinehart and Winston, Inc., 1962), pp. 305–329.

[10] See particularly Thomas R. Dye, *Politics, Economics and the Public* (Skokie, Ill.: Rand McNally and Company, 1966). See also Ira Sharkansky, *Spending in the American States* (Skokie, Ill.: Rand McNally and Company, 1968).

systems theory, which emphasizes the links between inputs and outputs in political structures.[11] Already this new research direction has supplanted the reductionist strategy in some parts of the discipline.

The new concentration on macrostructure has only given our problem a more sophisticated, more compelling form. After all, few belittle the attitudinal studies that have increased our understanding of so large a unit as the electorate and so small a unit as the presidency.[12] In fact, it is precisely because we now possess reliable knowledge about both individuals and structures that our problem has become more urgent, yet less tractable.

Granted that this chapter encounters the macro-micro problem, of what further relevance is this discussion? Does it have general pertinence to education and political socialization? The answer becomes clearer in reconsidering some major studies of educational effects. Almost every important research project concerned with the impact of educational structure on student achievement, motivation, and life chances confronts this identical methodological and philosophical ambiguity. A few examples support our contention.

In *Equality of Educational Opportunity*, Coleman examines over one hundred correlates and possible determinants of educational achievement. His argument, like our own, moves back and forth between the macro and micro level; he ignores, however, the methodological paradoxes surrounding this portion of his research.[13] His lack of awareness is all the more puzzling because he has elsewhere written trenchantly about the macro-micro problem.[14] We do not mean to imply, however, that Coleman's failure to appreciate this problem vitiates his research. Otherwise, how would we justify our own inquiry? We introduce the example only to indicate the ubiquity and subtlety of the difficulty we face.

[11] David Easton, *A Systems Analysis of Political Life* (New York: John Wiley and Sons, Inc., 1965).

[12] Angus Campbell *et al., The American Voter* (New York: John Wiley and Sons, Inc., 1960); and Alexander L. and Juliette L. George, *Woodrow Wilson and Colonel House* (New York: Dover Publications, Inc., 1956).

[13] James Coleman, *Equality of Educational Opportunity* (Washington, D.C.: Government Printing Office, 1966).

[14] James Coleman, "Foundations for a Theory of Collective Decisions," *American Journal of Sociology*, 71, No. 6 (May 1966), pp. 615–628.

Equality of Educational Opportunity provides a useful example, not only because it has deservedly become a landmark, but also because its author is an accomplished social scientist unusually sensitive to methodological problems. Many other studies, such as those by Burkhead[15] and by Mollenkopf and Melville[16] on the relationship of educational inputs to student achievement, by Barker[17] on the impact of school size on student behavior, and by Edwards and Wilson[18] on the effects of educational environment on individual motivation, are plagued by the same problem of inference.

Rossi, after lamenting the inability of educational research to demonstrate that school differences contribute much to student achievement, remarks that, "to some unspecified degree, this failure may be due to the lack of ingenuity displayed by the researchers, who have measured only the grossest aspects of either schools or educational practices."[19] The observation gives us some leverage on our problem. It suggests, for example, that the effects of differences in such macro factors as student-teacher ratios depend upon the position of the teacher-student ratio within the entire structure of teacher-student relationships. Knowing the teacher-student ratio tells us only a little about this structure.

Although we can propose no solution to the problem that plagues us, we can at least explicate the theoretical premises that guide this chapter's attempt to infer the effects of school quality on political attitudes. These premises, and some of their limitations are as follows:

1. The gross measures that differentiate the two school dis-

---

[15] Jesse Burkhead *et al., Input and Output in Large-City High Schools* (Syracuse, N.Y.: Syracuse University Press, 1967).

[16] William G. Mollenkopf and S. Donald Melville, "A Study of Secondary School Characteristics as Related to Test Scores," (Princeton, N.J.: Educational Testing Service, 1956), unpublished.

[17] Roger Barker, *Big School—Small School: Studies of the Effects of High School Size upon Behavior and Experiences of Students* (Stanford, Calif.: Stanford University Press, 1962).

[18] T. Bentley Edwards and Alan B. Wilson, *A Study of Some Social and Psychological Factors Influencing Educational Achievement* (Berkeley, Calif.: University of California, Department of Education, June 1961).

[19] Peter Rossi, "Some Factors in Academic Achievement: A Brief Review," in A. H. Halsey *et al.* (eds.), *Education, Economy, and Society* (New York: The Free Press, 1961), p. 269.

tricts under study combine to portray divergent educational environments. The districts, in other words, offer distinct educational contexts to their teachers and students.

2. These educational contexts are composed of more or fewer opportunities and choices. Thus, the generally lower student-teacher ratio in Chalmers gives pupils in that district a relatively great opportunity to discuss academic and social problems with their teachers. It is this opportunity structure that forges the link between educational climates and individual responses.[20]

3. The structure of opportunities affects the motivation of individual students and the interaction of students with each other. In this way, the educational context contributes to particular attitudes and encourages specific actions among both teachers and students.

So much for our premises. Although we do not pretend that they unravel the macro-micro paradox, we do believe they constitute a reasonable approach to a difficult problem. Unfortunately, our research can only suggest the channels through which an educational climate produces a distinctive structure of opportunities that in turn shapes individual attitudes. We can, however, identify two prerequisites to the discovery of any such channels.

First, we should visualize social structure as a set of relationships, for it is only among these relationships that we will discover the linkage mechanisms between gross system characteristics and individual attitudes. The fundamental datum of such a study should not be the individual, but the bonds between individuals. Now, finally, political scientists have gained techniques that can describe a structure of social relationships precisely.[21]

But even an economical depiction of structures will not suffice unless we can agree upon a standardized unit of relationships. Through what device does an individual encounter organization?

---

[20] Cole takes a similar approach in his study of contextual effects on a teachers' strike. See Stephen Cole, "Teachers' Strike: A Study of the Conversion of Predisposition into Action," *American Journal of Sociology*, 74, No. 5 (March 1969), pp. 506–521.

[21] For suggestive approaches, see S. F. Nadel, *The Theory of Social Structure* (London: Cohen and West, 1957); and Steven Brams, "Measuring the Concentration of Power in Political Systems," *American Political Science Review*, 62, No. 2 (June 1968), pp. 461–476.

An answer to this question will provide us with the structural unit upon which we can build our description.

We believe that the most promising concept available for the analysis of social relationships is that of role. Properly employed, a theory of role can describe both the individual's orientation to his environment and the entire structure of an organization. At the micro level, role theory sees the individual constrained within a certain range of choice. This perspective encourages us to investigate the priorities of such role takers as teachers, students, and administrators. At the macro level, role theory focuses on the relationships among all role takers. The role approach culminates in the portrayal of a structure as an organization of role relationships. Thus, the concept of role may ultimately bring system and individual together.[22]

DISTRICT DIFFERENCES IN STUDENT SUPPORT FOR DEMOCRACY

In keeping with a developmental perspective, we assumed that a student's cognitive sophistication depends upon autogenetic factors, of which the most important is age. Consequently, we doubted that school-district quality would greatly affect the way in which a student conceptualized democracy. We agree with Freyberg that education may affect the rate, but not the shape, of cognitive maturation.[23] We therefore move directly to an examination of student support for democracy in the two districts. Table 4-1 compares the students' acceptance of democracy by value dimension, grade level, and district.

A definite pattern emerges from Table 4-1. In every case,

[22] For a good introduction to role theory, see Michael Banton, *Roles* (New York: Basic Books, Inc., 1965). An excellent study, in an educational context, of the relationship between structure and the individual is Neal Gross, Ward S. Mason, and Alexander W. McEachern, *Explorations in Role Analysis: Studies of the School Superintendency Role* (New York: John Wiley and Sons, Inc., 1958).

[23] P. S. Freyberg, "Concept Development in Piagetian Terms in Relation to School Attainment," *Journal of Educational Psychology*, 57 (June 1966), pp. 164–168.

Moss City sixth-graders are more democratic than their counter-parts in Chalmers, but by the twelfth grade, students in the two districts are virtually indistinguishable. In short, more pro-democratic change occurs in Chalmers than in Moss City.

Over time, change is ubiquitous in both districts, but major interdistrict differences usually disappear by the ninth grade. Al-

TABLE 4-1. MEAN SUPPORT FOR DEMOCRACY IN MOSS CITY AND CHALMERS, BY GRADE LEVEL AND VALUE DIMENSION

Dimension	Grade level	District Moss City	Chalmers	Totals
Freedom of	6th	1.89 (263)	1.76 (300)[c]	1.82 (563)
speech	9th	2.19 (283)	2.29 (224)	2.23 (507)
	12th	2.37 (246)	2.45 (167)	2.40 (413)
	Totals	2.15 (792)	2.10 (691)	2.12 (1483)
Majority	6th	2.17 (262)	1.86 (300)[c]	2.00 (562)
rule	9th	2.11 (282)	2.00 (222)	2.06 (504)
	12th	2.06 (247)	2.17 (166)	2.11 (413)
	Totals	2.12 (791)	1.98 (688)	2.05 (1479)
Importance	6th	2.43 (263)	2.12 (300)[c]	2.26 (563)
of elections	9th	2.43 (284)	2.52 (226)	2.47 (510)
	12th	2.75 (245)	2.76 (164)	2.76 (409)
	Totals	2.53 (792)	2.40 (690)	2.47 (1482)
Minority	6th	2.89 (264)	2.65 (301)[c]	2.76 (565)
rights	9th	3.18 (281)	2.99 (224)	3.09 (505)
	12th	3.18 (249)	3.05 (165)	3.13 (414)
	Totals	3.08 (794)	2.85 (690)	2.98 (1484)
Sense of	6th	2.65 (263)	2.35 (300)[c]	3.49 (563)
civic	9th	2.80 (280)	2.66 (223)	2.74 (503)
obligation	12th	2.88 (249)	2.76 (165)	2.83 (414)
	Totals	2.78 (792)	2.55 (688)	2.67 (1480)
Support	6th	2.06 (264)	1.81 (301)[c]	1.94 (560)
for the	9th	1.75 (280)	1.86 (225)	1.80 (505)
vote[a]	12th	1.45 (247)	1.57 (164)	1.50 (411)
	Totals	1.81 (791)	1.77 (690)	1.79 (481)
Political	6th	1.64 (264)	1.55 (299)	1.59 (563)
efficacy	9th[a]	1.56 (283)	1.52 (220)	1.54 (503)
	12th[a]	1.82 (245)	1.39 (161)[c]	1.65 (406)
	Totals	1.67 (792)	1.50 (680)	1.59 (1472)
Rules of	6th	2.99 (263)	2.91 (298)	2.02 (561)
the game[b]	9th	3.29 (284)	3.39 (223)	2.40 (507)
	12th[a]	2.07 (242)	1.91 (165)	2.00 (407)

TABLE 4.1 (*continued*)

| Dimension | Grade level | District | | Totals |
		Moss City	Chalmers	
Opportunity to participate[b]	6th	1.32 (264)	1.27 (298)	1.29 (562)
	9th	2.13 (286)	2.29 (224)	2.20 (510)
	12th	2.17 (246)	2.19 (165)	2.18 (411)
Support for domestic liberalism	6th	2.09 (263)	2.02 (301)	2.05 (564)
	9th	1.94 (284)	2.00 (225)	1.97 (509)
	12th	1.57 (246)	1.91 (165)[c]	1.71 (411)
	Totals	1.88 (793)	1.95 (692)	1.93 (1485)

[a] Crystallized dimension.

[b] Number of items for rules of the game: 5 for 6th and 9th grades, 3 for 12th. Number of items for opportunity to participate: 3 for 6th and 12th, 4 for 9th. For number of items in other dimensions, see Table 3-1. No means were calculated for rules of the game and opportunity to participate, since the number of items in these dimensions varied by grade level.

[c] District differences significant at .05 level using t test (two-tailed).

though it may be pure coincidence, the schools begin to expose their students to sophisticated training in social studies and history between sixth and ninth grades. Our ninth-grade scores may reflect the differential impact of such training.

Do these findings support our hypothesis that Chalmers' superior input to education produces effective democratic socialization? Yes and no. Had we discovered that Chalmers' students at all levels were more democratic than those in Moss City and also gained more between sixth and twelfth grades, we would have answered strongly in the affirmative. Had we found that students in Moss City were not only more democratic at all levels than those in Chalmers but also became proportionately more democratic as they proceeded through school, we would have had to reject our hypothesis completely. But we possess no such definitive findings.

Table 4-1 does lend some comfort to our hypothesis. After all, educational success can be measured in the amount of change that the school produces over time, and, in this regard, Chalmers excels.[24] But how are we to account for the sixth-grade findings?

[24] In general, the impact of a service is one of the least investigated aspects of public policy. The question "What difference does it make if a program

Yet, the logic of our research design should have predicted the sixth-grade differences. The social-class factors that favor Moss City exert their greatest influence in the early grades. The elementary school offers little social-studies training that might offset the effects of social-class differentials. Thus, the pro-democratic social-class bias in favor of Moss City operates unimpeded until the school overtly attempts to inculcate democratic attitudes. The school takes on its full responsibility only after the sixth grade. It is for these reasons that the rise of Chalmers during the high-school years encourages us to infer the importance of educational quality as an explanatory factor.

This interpretation suggests that we reconsider those aspects of public education that other researchers have discounted.[25] Particularly, it dictates a close examination of high-school teachers generally and social-studies teachers especially. Should we discover parallels between the attitudes of high-school students and their teachers, we could make a better case for the effects of school quality after sixth grade.

A second interpretation, which complements the first, focuses on the way in which educational quality is manifested in a school district. High input systems such as Chalmers' may have their greatest success at the secondary-school level. We can think of numerous reasons for such a pattern. For one thing, the elementary school is a less flexible educational instrument than the secondary school. Parents and elementary-school teachers apparently feel that the elementary school should be as concerned with discipline as with knowledge.[26] Furthermore, elementary-school teachers are trained less well and are more resistant to change than are high-school teachers. Fewer elementary-school than high-school teachers possess enough subject-matter competence to induce marked intel-

---

exists?" has rarely been asked. Instead, political scientists have concentrated on determining the major sources of program variation. For a study that highlights the subject of program impact, see Michael Lipsky, *Protest in City Politics* (Skokie, Ill.: Rand McNally and Company, 1970), chap. 5.
[25] We refer particularly to the work of Jennings and Langton on civics courses. See Kenneth P. Langton and M. Kent Jennings, "Political Socialization and the High School Civics Curriculum in the United States," *American Political Science Review*, 62, No. 3 (September 1968), pp. 852–868.
[26] In this connection, we recall that kindergarten teachers in Chalmers resisted the introduction of reading instruction for their pupils.

lectual change in their students.[27] Differences in the sex composition of teaching staffs may also be a factor. According to Zeigler, male teachers are the major agents of change in education,[28] and male teachers, of course, cluster in the secondary schools. Finally, curriculum experimentation may become more attractive and effective when teachers believe their students mature enough to profit from change. High-school teachers, because they are abler to take the maturity of their students for granted than are elementary-school teachers, are relatively free to concentrate on subject matter and on innovation. Admittedly, these observations are speculative, but in Chapter 6 we will support them with data from the teacher sample.

Table 4-1 reveals substantial interdistrict attitudinal homogeneity among twelfth-graders. High-school seniors in Moss City and Chalmers apparently end their public-school careers on the same plateau of democratic support. What explains the existence of this plateau and what implications does it have for the role of the schools in political socialization?

Interdistrict uniformity of support for democracy among twelfth-graders may be the result of two factors. First, student age may set cognitive limits on the capacity of the schools to inculcate democratic values. Perhaps laboratory schools, such as those found at many universities, can expand these limits, but most public schools lack the theoretical and practical tools for such a job. A good public-school system may have to content itself either with positioning its students favorably within their cognitive limits or with moving them to their limits rapidly.

Second, most public schools operate with relatively standardized packages of curricula. Rarely can even the most innovative district restructure its entire scholastic program. This incrementalism of experimentation persists for several reasons, the most obvi-

---

[27] See the contrasts between elementary-school and secondary-school teachers reported by Gordon C. Lee, "The Changing Role of the Teacher," in John I. Goodlad (ed.), *The Changing American School*, 65th Yearbook of the National Society for the Study of Education, pt. II (Chicago: University of Chicago Press, 1966), pp. 9–32.

[28] Thus, male teachers see their representative organizations as political lobbying agencies, while women do not. Harmon Zeigler, *The Political Life of American Teachers* (Englewood Cliffs, N.J.: Prentice-Hall, Inc., 1967), pp. 65–66.

ous of which is the financial constraints placed upon innovation. Experimentation is expensive. It requires the hiring and training of specialized personnel, the reorganization of classes, and the close monitoring of student progress. Therefore, few school systems can afford to try out more than a small number of innovations at any one time. Nor should we ignore the psychological costs of experimentation. Many administrators and teachers, because they have become used to a particular style of education with a small number of goals, cannot adjust to change. Willing innovators may finally conclude that mobilizing and supporting an experimental cadre within the instructional staff may cause unacceptable disruption to the process of education.

Other factors that produce curricula standardization lie wholly beyond the control of the school. Universities, preoccupied with selecting a freshman class, demand comparative data on student performance. Only school systems that teach similar subjects in similar ways can provide such data. Universities must also depend upon the high schools to prepare students in comparable fields; otherwise, it becomes difficult to plan a university curriculum. Likewise, businesses require some information about the comparative aptitudes and achievements of job seekers, and such data would be extremely difficult to evaluate were it not for the standardized curriculum in the public schools. Even teachers, whose rhetoric emphasizes the importance of educational innovation, have a stake in standardized curricula, for curriculum overlap permits many teachers to avoid adjustment problems when transferring between schools. Finally, state politicians, who dispense tax money to school districts, desire some information about the impact of their allocations. Were every district able to employ state money as it saw fit, politicians would be unable to obtain such information and would therefore have trouble legitimizing their decisions. State politicians also standardize curricula by mandating certain courses to be taught at the high-school level.[29]

For all these reasons, course curricula differ little between districts.[30] Schools of varying quality teach much the same material.

[29] Until 1968, for example, the state mandated a host of courses for California schools. These courses ranged from physical education and driver training to state history. The legislature in 1968 finally loosened these requirements.

[30] There are, of course, some differences, most of which involve extra, en-

A good district simply imparts the curriculum effectively, with the occasional result that, as in Chalmers, children from relatively disadvantaged backgrounds are elevated to the democratic support levels of more fortunate children. But standardized curricula and student limitations combine to prevent good schools from doing more.

Let us now order our value dimensions in terms of their sensitivity to district differences. Does any recognizable pattern emerge from this ranking as shown in Table 4-2? We will examine four

TABLE 4-2. SCHOOL-DISTRICT DIFFERENCES IN THE DEGREE OF STUDENT PRO-DEMOCRATIC GAIN, BY VALUE DIMENSION

Dimension	Differences in gain between districts[a]	Better performing district
Domestic liberalism	.63	. . [b]
Majority rule	.42	Chalmers
Support for the vote	.38	Chalmers
Political efficacy	.34	Moss City
Importance of elections	.32	Chalmers
Freedom of speech	.21	Chalmers
Sense of civic obligation	.18	Chalmers
Minority rights	.12	Chalmers
Rules of the game	.07	Moss City
Opportunity to participate	.07	Chalmers

[a] We computed this figure by subtracting the sixth-grade from the twelfth-grade score in each district, then subtracting the smaller of the two remainders from the larger.
[b] Not a measure of support for democracy.

aspects of this table. First, notice that it is policy attitudes that are most closely associated with district differences. The explanation

---

riching courses that wealthy school districts and large schools are able to afford. For a discussion of this problem and an estimate of the resulting inequalities, see James B. Conant, *The American High School Today* (New York: McGraw-Hill, Inc., 1959).

Nonetheless, the standard curriculum is offered by most schools. For a description of the most common social-studies offerings, see Edwin R. Carr, *The Social Studies* (New York: The Center for Applied Research in Education, 1965), p. 7.

for this is not immediately apparent, nor are we certain that the datum itself can be traced to the schools. Even if teachers in Chalmers were more liberal than those in Moss City (and we have no evidence that they are), we doubt that they discuss their policy preferences any more than do Moss City teachers. We suspect that our finding only reflects the process by which maturing children in the two districts assume the modal policy preferences of their communities. We have already noted that Chalmers is the more consistently Democratic of the two districts. The people in Chalmers may, therefore, be comparatively supportive of domestic liberalism.

Second, majority rule, which we believe is underemphasized in the high-school curriculum, emerges as the most sensitive of the democratic values. This finding is consistent with our expectation that school differences would become most apparent on subjects not constrained by a standardized textbook treatment. It is in the teaching of such norms as majority rule, whose imprecision in social-studies texts gives teachers broad latitude, that instructional quality may reveal itself most completely.

The three values below majority rule are primarily symbolic. Two of them, support for the vote and political efficacy, crystallize early in the learning process. Differences in school-district quality apparently influence the extent to which early support for key democratic symbols survives the onset of adolescent cynicism. We recognize that this conclusion seems at first inconsistent with the developmental approach that has guided us, for according to developmental theory, political maturation involves a transition from symbolic to abstract and logical thought. But here we find that schooling does little to assist that transition. Moreover, educational quality in Chalmers actually places extra inhibitions on the child's withdrawal from symbolic thought, at least as evidenced by the behavior of Chalmers students on the two electoral dimensions. In some sense, therefore, good schools may work against rather than capitalize on the course of development.

Finally, we note that variations in educational inputs have little effect on those democratic values that demand the most rigorous thought. Freedom of speech, minority rights, and rules of the game are all insensitive to district differences. That the districts have virtually identical impacts upon sophisticated dimensions provides just another indication of the restricted influence the school exerts.

DISTRICT EFFECTS
ON PARTICIPATION-RELATED ATTITUDES

Schick and Somit, after studying innovative political-science courses, conclude that while such educational experiments cannot transmit an appreciation for political activity to students, they can produce substantial leaps in political knowledge.[31] Our findings parallel these conclusions. The evidence comes from student responses to our three participation indices—desire to run for political office, party identification, and level of political information.

As Table 4-3 indicates, Chalmers can no more prevent the erosion of student interest in political office seeking than can Moss City.

TABLE 4-3. PERCENTAGE OF STUDENTS WHO DESIRE TO RUN FOR
POLITICAL OFFICE IN TWO SCHOOL DISTRICTS,
BY GRADE LEVEL (IN PERCENT)

| Grade level | District | | Totals |
	Moss City	Chalmers	
6th	33 (98)[a]	27 (82)	32 (180)
9th	17 (48)	19 (43)	18 (91)
12th	11 (28)	9 (15)	11 (43)
Totals	21 (174)	20 (140)	21 (314)

[a] Number wishing to run for office at each grade level in each district.

Some might explain these findings by arguing that, in their discussion of government, teachers unconsciously transmit a distrust of politicians. In Chapter 6, however, we will present evidence that makes this possibility unlikely. The real explanation probably resides in the nature of the developmental process and in the character of American attitudes about politics. One recurrent aspect of maturation is sloughing off childhood fantasies about recognition and power. The progressive disparagement of political ambitions may simply be a political expression of this general process; faced with so fundamental a phase of development, the schools

[31] Marvin Schick and Albert Somit, "The Failure to Teach Political Activity," *American Behavioral Scientist*, 6, No. 5 (January 1963), pp. 5–7.

may be helpless. In addition, American ambivalence toward politicians may be so deeply rooted in culture and society as to engulf counterpressures from the schools.[32] Thus, it appears that individual growth and cultural sanctions combine to defeat the schools.

Table 4-4 demonstrates that Chalmers can hold only a few more of its students within the confines of the American party system than can Moss City. In Chalmers, 5 percent fewer twelfthgraders than in Moss City give themselves no partisan label. These differences are so small, however, as to be trivial.

TABLE 4-4. PARTISAN IDENTIFICATION IN MOSS CITY AND CHALMERS, BY GRADE LEVEL (IN PERCENT)

Grade level	Party	District					
		Moss City		Chalmers		Totals	
6th	Democrat	21	(54)	25	(75)	23	(124)
	Republican	26	(69)	21	(62)	23	(131)
	Independent	8	(21)	9	(28)	9	(49)
	No answer and other	45	(110)	45	(137)	45	(247)
	Totals	100	(254)	100	(302)	100	(556)
9th	Democrat	31	(89)	34	(77)	32	(166)
	Republican	25	(71)	21	(47)	22	(118)
	Independent	12	(36)	13	(29)	12	(65)
	No answer and other	32	(93)	32	(85)	34	(178)
	Totals	100	(289)	100	(238)	100	(527)
12th	Democrat	27	(68)	26	(44)	26	(112)
	Republican	19	(48)	17	(28)	18	(76)
	Independent	18	(46)	26	(43)	21	(88)
	No answer and other	36	(88)	31	(53)	35	(141)
	Totals	100	(250)	100	(168)	100	(418)

Chalmers demonstrates a statistically significant superiority over Moss City only in the conveyance of political information. Table 4-5 presents these data. The pattern in Table 4-5 is, of course, the one first encountered in Table 4-1. Again Moss City's

[32] For some illuminating early polling data on American attitudes toward politicians, see Hadley Cantril and Mildred Strunk (eds.), *Public Opinion 1935–1946* (Princeton, N.J.: Princeton University Press, 1951), p. 534.

TABLE 4-5. MEAN POLITICAL INFORMATION SCORES IN MOSS CITY
AND CHALMERS, BY GRADE LEVEL

Grade level	District		Totals
	Moss City	Chalmers	
6th	5.21 (262)	4.99 (292)	5.09 (554)
9th	7.16 (275)	7.33 (222)	7.23 (497)
12th	9.33 (240)	10.25 (156)[a]	9.70 (396)
Totals	7.17 (777)	6.99 (670)	7.09 (1447)

[a] Twelfth-grade difference significant $< .01$ using t test.

sixth-graders perform better than their Chalmers' counterparts;
however, Chalmers makes up these differences by twelfth grade.
There is one feature that Table 4-5 introduces. Chalmers never
managed to push its students significantly beyond those in Moss
City on value dimensions, but Chalmers is significantly more successful than Moss City in conveying political information.

Our earlier discussion led us to expect that educational
quality would bear its closest relation to the transmission of political knowledge. It is reasonable to expect that teachers who need
worry neither about the possible repercussions of their instruction
nor the sensitivities of their students will perform at their best.
Conveyance of neutral political facts meets these conditions. It
may also be that teachers are hired and retained more for their
ability to impart information than to explain complex values. After
all, the success of teachers in their own college careers determines
their chances of employment by school districts; all too often, this
success depends more upon the ability to retain information than
to think well. Thus, administrators who select new teachers on
the basis of college performance may well be recruiting people who
are themselves unable to deal with political complexities, much
less to train others to analyze such complexities. Finally, administrators search for criteria to guide their tenure decisions.[33] Standardized student information tests permit the administrator to

[33] For a review of the most commonly used methods, see Hazel Davis,
"Evolution of Current Practices in Evaluating Teacher Competence," in
Bruce J. Biddle and William S. Ellena (eds.), *Contemporary Research on
Teacher Effectiveness* (New York: Holt, Rinehart and Winston, Inc., 1963),
pp. 41–67.

compare the performance of teachers. In this way, the capacity to convey information becomes a convenient yardstick for the measurement of teacher competence. Teachers undoubtedly realize the importance of this criterion and therefore probably stress it in their instruction.

To summarize, the effects of educational quality are limited but varied. Educational quality increases the absorption of political information and raises student support for those democratic values that are submerged in the standard cirriculum. Educational quality also appears to retard the child's alienation from such key symbols of democracy as elections and the vote. However, educational climates exert little influence on the partisan motivations of students or on student support for complex democratic values. Educational quality is also unrelated to political motivation among students. Let us turn to the theoretical implications of these findings.

THE RESULTS OF QUALITY: COMPENSATION AND CONSERVATION

We have seen that quality education sustains support for the most visible democratic symbols, thereby extending public approval for the existing structures of democracy. This accomplishment should not be dismissed lightly. After all, most people, because they never gain the capacity to visualize politics in a sophisticated way, must rely on symbolic identifications to tie them to the democratic system.[34] Most people are, in other words, symbolic democrats.

But there is a darker side to this picture. Adherence to symbols, as Edelman has pointed out, is primarily a conservative force.[35] Symbols focus the individual's attention on the hallowed traditions, but not on the contemporary problems of democracy. In addition, symbolic democrats lack an appreciation of the more

[34] The symbolic components of political thought in mass societies are highlighted in Philip E. Converse, "The Nature of Belief Systems in Mass Public," in David E. Apter (ed.), *Ideology and Discontent* (New York: The Free Press), pp. 206–262.

[35] Murray Edelman, *The Symbolic Use of Politics* (Urbana, Ill: University of Illinois Press, 1964), chap. 1. See also Thomas J. Anton, "Roles and Symbols in the Determination of State Expenditures," *Midwest Journal of Political Science,* 11, No. 1 (February 1967), pp. 27–44.

subtle and complex of democratic principles, such as minority rights and free speech.

Thus, although quality education can create symbolic democrats, it seems unable to convey much tolerance for or comprehension of those minorities who would criticize the democratic system. Educational quality, as it presently operates, therefore supports the status quo rather than those who would change the status quo.

Of the abstract democratic values, only those that are unclear and have little prominence in curricula, such as majority rule, react to differences in educational quality. If it seems paradoxical that quality education has its major impact in the lacunae of the educational program, it is at least as paradoxical for the schools to pour large amounts of money into an unreconstructed social-studies curriculum that homogenizes the abilities and presentations of teachers. This latter practice hamstrings teachers and students alike, virtually assuring uniformity in the treatment of democratic values.

Its success in transmitting mainly the symbols of democracy reduces the importance of Chalmers' superiority in conveying political information. Political knowledge becomes most useful to people who are motivated politically, who understand the complex principles of democracy, and who support those principles. But it is precisely these kinds of people that even good schools cannot produce. We agree with Zeigler that educational quality ought to do more than reinforce the status quo,[36] create lukewarm support for poorly understand democratic values, or transmit political information. The public schools of a democracy have as great a responsibility to turn out a participating and critical citizen as an informed and loyal subject, for loyalty is no more a democratic virtue than is political understanding or participation. It is as important for a child to respect the subtle procedures and protections of democracy as it is for him to cleave to the visible trappings of a particular democratic regime. Thus, the American educational system, even when it receives unusually great support, does not meet its responsibility.

On the other hand, we realize that educators and teachers are

---

[36] Harmon Zeigler, "Education and the Status Quo," paper delivered at the annual meeting of the Western Political Science Association, Honolulu, Hawaii, May 1969.

too busy to be aware of all the consequences of their efforts. Most of them also lack the information necessary to plan the implementation of important goals; indeed, one outcome of this study might be the provision of such information. Nor do educators agree on the aims of political socialization. Yet, it is also true that the predispositions of many educators are all too well-served by their limited success. According to Jennings and Zeigler, the public-school establishment prefers to buttress rather than to assess the status quo.[37] Educational quality, when it is found, seems to pass on this uncritical mentality to students.

These observations provide a framework within which we can consider perhaps the most important and certainly the most visible effect of quality education on political socialization. Chalmers ultimately succeeds in boosting its students to a level of democratic support and knowledge equal to that of students in Moss City, who begin school at a higher support level. Chalmers thus engages in what might be called "compensatory political socialization." Let us briefly examine the relationship of compensatory political socialization to political theory and American politics.

It is a truism to state that equality is one of the most cherished of American values. As early as the 1830s, De Tocqueville recognized the centrality of equality in the American value system,[38] but it does De Tocqueville no disservice to admit that Americans themselves have never agreed upon a precise meaning of equality. At least three separate and occasionally inconsistent usages of the term may be found in American public rhetoric.

The first of these is "equality of opportunity," the belief that all people should have roughly the same life chances at birth. Those who believe in equality of opportunity would ensure that a person's ultimate position in society is the product only of his intelligence and energy. Perhaps the earliest legislative embodiments of this concept are the progressive income tax and the inheritance tax.

The second meaning of equality may be called "equality of circumstances." Those who advocate equality of circumstances would decree that, whatever the accidents of birth, during their lifetime people should not be allowed to develop such widely dif-

[37] M. Kent Jennings and Harmon Zeigler, "The Politics of Teacher-Administrator Relations," unpublished, 1966.

[38] Alexis de Tocqueville, *Democracy in America*, vol. 1 (New York: Vintage, 1960), chap. 3.

fering life styles as to be unable to compete with each other. Such New Deal measures as Social Security embody this concept.

James Coleman believes that a third usage of equality has recently entered American thought. Although differing only in emphasis from equality of circumstances, this concept, "equality of accomplishment," deserves recognition in its own right. When it is applied to the schools, equality of accomplishment states that all students, regardless of their origins, should achieve at the same levels; furthermore, it implies an obligation on the part of the schools to equalize student achievement.[39]

Those who believe in equality of opportunity would make it possible for individual differences to express themselves. Those who believe in equality of circumstances would mitigate the unequal effects of individual differences. Those who believe in equality of accomplishment would deny the legitimacy of individual differences. This brief description makes it clear that the three conceptions of equality do not rest easily together.

Studies other than ours have demonstrated that quality education can compensate for individual inequalities and produce equal academic accomplishments. Coleman discovered that although above-average educational inputs had little effect on affluent, middle-class white children, disadvantaged Negro children profited significantly.[40] Quality education apparently overcame some of the racial barriers to equal academic accomplishment. Our findings directly parallel Coleman's. Quality education can produce not only compensatory intellectual training, but also compensatory political socialization.

This conclusion is not as surprising as it first appears. Were not the public schools performing compensatory functions for the children of immigrants eighty years ago? The substitution effects of quality education have been present in America for a long time.

[39] James S. Coleman, "The Concept of Equality of Educational Opportunity," in *Harvard Educational Review, Equal Educational Opportunity* (Cambridge, Mass.: Harvard University Press, 1969), pp. 9–25.
[40] Coleman, *Equality of Educational Opportunity*, p. 21. Edwards and Wilson discovered, however, that motivational levels of students tended to conform to the motivational norms of whichever social class was dominant in the school. Edwards and Wilson, *A Study of Some Social and Psychological Factors*, pp. 5–6. But for evidence paralleling Coleman's, see Neil V. Sullivan, "Compensation and Integration: The Berkeley Experience," in *Harvard Educational Review, Equal Educational Opportunity*, pp. 220–228.

Until recently, compensatory socialization occurred informally and unofficially. Some educators may have been aware of the compensatory effects of their efforts, but the schools themselves never chose compensatory education as a goal. Most teachers busied themselves with their best students, although, ironically, their major contributions were actually being made among less promising pupils.

Equality of accomplishment is no longer the stepchild of the schools. Such programs as Operation Headstart have elevated the concept to the status of a distinct educational goal. The total legitimation of this goal, should it occur, will bring unforeseeable changes to public education. Schools that are judged by their ability to provide a common level of accomplishment for all their students will undoubtedly redirect their educational resources. Such a massive reorientation of efforts deserves careful preliminary scrutiny, especially because the doctrine of equal accomplishment has much about it to which one might take exception.

Believers in equal accomplishment lay much of the responsibility for social inequality at the schoolhouse door. But the factors that produce social inequality are not in the first instance traceable to the structure of the school.[41] Emphasis upon equality of educational accomplishment, no matter how laudable in producing needed school reform, diverts attention from the root causes of inequality—poverty, discrimination, unemployment, and family disintegration.

Equality of accomplishment also endorses intellectual homogeneity among students. Few would deny the desirability of homogeneity in certain areas of education. For example, we would like all our children to be able to read well, but whether we want students to manifest equal amounts of support for the same political values is more problematic. Attitudinal homogeneity is not necessarily in the long-range interest of democracy. Worse yet, as our findings show, there is no guarantee that the uniformity of opinions will be strongly pro-democratic.

[41] Coleman, *Equality of Educational Opportunity*, p. 22.

For an interesting study of the linguistic sources of inequality in early childhood, see Robert D. Hess and Virginia C. Shipman, "Early Experience and the Socialization of Cognitive Modes in Children," in Robert J. Havighurst, Bernice L. Neugarten, and Jacqueline M. Falk (eds.), *Society and Education* (Boston: Allyn and Bacon, Inc., 1967), pp. 74–86.

We should also recognize that homogeneous support for political values may encourage uniform and automatic responses to value-laden political events. Value heterogeneity, on the other hand, not only produces creative challenges to the political system, but also assures fruitful discussion of those challenges. Value homogeneity can ensure no such debate. Thus it is that mildly allegiant value homogeneity among students can be as conservative a force as the persistence of student support for the symbols of democracy.

Of course, as Chapter 5 points out, twelfth-grade students differ among themselves in their support for democratic values. But these divisions have their sources outside the school—in factors related to sex, class, intelligence. The school itself does little to promote value diversity.[42] Thus, the consequences of compensatory socialization are not all salutary.

Our criticisms have not been intended to discount Chalmers' accomplishments, but only to put them in reasoned perspective. More important than the potential changes of compensatory education, however, is the inability of the school to convey to students a clear understanding of democratic values. Let us, therefore, reconsider this problem in conclusion.

Is it really necessary that the mass of citizens understand the operating principles of the democratic system? Many political scientists apparently believe that ignorance and its correlate, apathy, are conducive to the smooth functioning of a democracy. Too much ideological dispute, they fear, will destabilize and ultimately destroy democratic government.[43]

We would agree that in normal times the widespread ignorance of democratic values constitutes more of a moral than a practical problem. But these are not normal times. Many alienated

---

[42] Coleman discovered the same thing when he focused on the social structure of the high school and the dominant values transmitted therein. See James S. Coleman, *The Adolescent Society* (New York: The Free Press, 1961), especially chap. 10.

[43] The earliest statement of the thesis may be found in Frances G. Wilson, "The Inactive Electorate and Social Revolution," *Southwestern Social Science Quarterly*, 16, No. 1 (1936), pp. 73–84. For an influential elaboration, see Berelson, Lazarsfeld, and McPhee, *Voting*, chap. 14. For a far-ranging critique of this view, see Jack L. Walker, "A Critique of the Elitist Theory of Democracy," *American Political Science Review*, 60, No. 2 (June 1966), pp. 285–295.

young people are putting democracy to a severe test. Their failure to appreciate or, in some cases, even to understand democratic practices is now evident. The price of their ignorance may be paid by all. We would agree with Hess that in times of youthful protest and fundamental social change it is vital that the young understand the fundamental principles upon which democracy works, so that they can restructure the regime intelligently.[44]

Our educational system, which generates only moderate comprehension of democracy, presents society with a dual risk. On the one hand, those who support democracy without understanding it may respond undemocratically to criticism of the system. Uncomprehending support may degenerate into destructive, chauvinistic reaction. On the other hand, the absence of either support for or comprehension of democracy encourages the blind rejection of the system and can lead only to the excesses of the New Left. It follows, therefore, that a sophisticated public can reduce democracy's vulnerability to extremist politics. It is important that the schools convey an understanding of democracy.

The critic, of course, enjoys the enviable hypocrisy of not having to remedy the deficiencies he observes. How, in fact, does one go about teaching democratic principles? We will set forth some recommendations in Chapter 8, but, more important than any of our conclusions, is the fact that at last educators, for a variety of reasons, have become interested in the problem.[45]

The success of innovative science curricula first put educators on the alert.[46] New science curricula stress the logic of a discipline rather than its factual minutiae; drill and memorization are replaced by conceptualization. Emboldened by the apparent success of these new approaches to the sciences, social-studies educators have begun to search for analogous approaches.

[44] Robert D. Hess, "Discussion: Political Socialization in the Schools," *Harvard Educational Review*, 38, No. 3 (1968), pp. 528–536.

[45] For evidence of the ferment, the reader need only peruse the essays in Benjamin C. Cox and Byron G. Massialas (eds.), *Social Studies in the United States: A Critical Appraisal* (New York: Harcourt Brace Jovanovich, Inc., 1967).

[46] Much of the interest in designing such curricula stems from Jerome S. Bruner, *The Process of Education* (Cambridge, Mass.: Harvard University Press, 1960). The emphasis upon process learning and conceptualization in the early years is now being reassessed. See John I. Goodlad, "The Curriculum," in Goodlad (ed.), *The Changing American School*, pp. 32–59.

More recently, the Black Revolution and the New Left have contributed to the recognition of the problem. Educators are now fully aware that young people from different backgrounds come to school with different perceptions about the processes of democracy. Without their experience of political militance among the young, the nation's educators would not have realized the depth of the school's failure to teach democratic principles.

Finally, research in political socialization has at last trickled down to a few educators. At least some have absorbed the now reliable findings that document the lack of political motivation, comprehension, and information among parents and students. These educators have spurred the attempt to develop new methods of teaching democratic principles.

It is too early to evaluate the new approaches to the social studies. Implementation of techniques such as the inquiry method are still scattered and uneven.[47] Indeed, effects will never be known unless proper evaluation methods are rapidly devised. Nonetheless, we can still raise a general question about the reforms. Not only is it difficult to train teachers in the new methods, but it is also questionable whether the assumptions of the inquiry approach are compatible with what we know about the young child's learning capacity. If the inquiry technique makes excessive demands on the child's cognitive skills, it may do more harm than good. On balance, however, it is encouraging that educators are now confronting the failure of quality public education to have more than a slight impact on the student's acquisition and understanding of democratic values.

[47] At least one study, cited by Getzels, indicates that the inquiry method succeeds in the teaching of physics. J. W. Getzels, "Creative Thinking, Problem-Solving, and Instruction," in Ernest R. Hilgard (ed.), *Theories of Learning and Instruction*, 63d Yearbook of the National Society for the Study of Education, pt. 1 (Chicago: University of Chicago Press, 1964), pp. 240–268.

Chapter 5
The Effect
of the School:
Conditioning Agents

Standing between the environment that the school creates for the student and the impact of that environment on the student is a series of barriers. These barriers consist of the capacities and orientations that the child brings with him to school. The child's ethnic background, his sexual identity, his intelligence, his desire to perform well in school, his parents' social class and political orientation—all may condition the degree to which the school can influence him. It is to the role of these intervening variables that we now turn our attention.

Let us consider first the most autogenetic of the conditioning agents, the child's sex. Why should we expect to find sex differences in political socialization? The answer is that sexual identity, besides being clearly visible, influences a host of behaviors. But can we expect to find evidence for sex differences in political behavior among children and adolescents? Yes. As the Dubins point out, the child adopts a sexual identification very early.[1] Therefore, should sex roles embody differing perceptions of political involvement or democratic values, we would expect such differences to reveal themselves in our study.

There are two theories about the effects of sex differentiation on political socialization. The first focuses upon the discrimination females experience when they attempt to enter the more competitive areas of life. The political side of this argument asserts that girls, seeing little opportunity to participate in politics, withdraw gracefully. Some studies support this theory of female disengagement. For example, Stephenson found that 20 percent of his female sample in an Appalachian community refused even to listen to the questions he wanted to ask.[2] The theory of female disengagement therefore leads us to expect girls to know less about politics and to manifest much less political motivation than boys.

The second sex-role theory derives from the childrearing function of women. Some observers believe that preoccupation with childrearing attunes women to questions of morality, corruption, and personality in politics.[3] Others claim that the woman's responsibility in childrearing leads to female support for sacred values over secular ones and for political traditionalism over political modernity. These considerations suggest that women are less tolerant of democracy than men. Again there is evidence to support the theory. One set of researchers has succeeded in showing that girls score higher on a fascism scale than boys.[4] But as yet there is no conclusive proof of the theory. In sum, all we have is reason

[1] Robert Dubin and Elizabeth Ruth Dubin, "Children's Social Perceptions: A Review of Research," *Child Development*, 36, No. 3 (September 1965), pp. 809–838.

[2] John B. Stephenson, "Is Everyone Going Modern? A Critique and a Suggestion for Measuring Modernism," *American Journal of Sociology*, 74, No. 3 (November 1968), pp. 265–276.

[3] For similar theoretical considerations, see David Easton and Jack Dennis, *Children in the Political System* (New York: McGraw-Hill, Inc., 1969), pp. 342, 335. See also Robert E. Lane, *Political Life* (New York: The Free Press, 1959), pp. 341–342.

[4] Roy E. Horton, "American Freedom and the Values of Youth," in H. H. Remmers (ed.), *Anti-Democratic Attitudes in American Schools* (Evanston, Ill.: Northwestern University Press, 1963), pp. 18–61.

to believe that sex differences affect political cognition, motivation, and values, and that such differences predispose men to favor democracy.[5]

From a genetic characteristic, sex role, let us turn our attention to an acquired characteristic, scholastic achievement. Many studies indicate that children of varying intelligence and academic accomplishment view politics in different ways. Hess and Torney show that children with high IQs not only manifest higher levels of political efficacy than their duller classmates, but also become comparatively more efficacious with age.[6] White's examination of the effect of IQ on political efficacy replicates the Hess and Torney findings.[7] In addition, Selvin and Hagstrom have discovered that academic achievement is loosely linked to attitudes toward civil liberties among college students. Those students who did well in school were consistently more libertarian than those who were struggling.[8] Lane reports that high grades among college students are usually associated both with support for welfare liberalism and with diminished ethnocentrism.[9] There is also evidence that children with high IQs quickly develop into political independents, while their slower schoolmates remain mired in traditional party identifications.[10] Finally, and not surprisingly, there appear to be high levels of political participation and information among good students.[11]

We can think of at least three different explanations for these findings. First, it is possible that good grades enhance the self-esteem and confidence of good students, thereby producing an

[5] For theorizing relevant to these considerations and for pertinent findings, see Elizabeth Douvan and Joseph Adelson, *The Adolescent Experience* (New York: John Wiley and Sons, Inc., 1966), chap. 7.

[6] Robert D. Hess and Judith Torney, *The Development of Political Attitudes in Childhood* (London: Aldine Publishing Co., 1967), p. 267.

[7] Elliot S. White, "Intelligence and Sense of Political Efficacy in Children," *Journal of Politics*, 30, No. 3 (August 1968), pp. 710–732.

[8] Hannan C. Selvin and Warren O. Hagstrom, "Determinants of Support for Civil Liberties," *British Journal of Sociology*, 11, No. 1 (1960), pp. 51–73.

[9] Robert E. Lane, "Political Education in the Midst of Life's Struggles," *Harvard Educational Review*, 38, No. 3 (Summer 1968), pp. 468–494.

[10] Hess and Torney, *The Development of Political Attitudes in Childhood*, p. 291.

[11] Lester W. Milbrath, *Political Participation* (Skokie, Ill.: Rand McNally and Company, 1965), p. 68.

elevated sense of efficacy, higher motivation, and increased tolerance of others. Buoyed confidence may also encourage good
students to participate in school organizations. In turn, such participation may convince the good student of his power to influence
events.

But might there be some inherent connection between intelligence and support for democracy? Perhaps democratic values are
so complex that only the brightest students can appreciate them
fully. Bright students may also be able to identify areas of the
political system that are open to influence, while dull students may
be unable to locate opportunities for themselves. If so, we could
hardly expect intelligent students to have a low sense of political
efficacy.

Finally, there is always the possibility that students succeed
in school partly because they agree to parrot the norms of the
educational system, some of which encourage support for democracy.[12] The existence of any such process would force us to characterize the successful student's belief in democracy as essentially
superficial and instrumental. By this statement we simply mean
that a new set of educational norms might radically alter the
student's view of democracy. Lest these remarks sound unduly
cynical, let us remember that the school, like any large organization, survives only by the provision of incentives that ensure conformity to administrative directives.[13] There is no intrinsic reason,
as Friedenburg demonstrates, why the meshing of organizational
rewards and student motivation cannot tie scholarly success to
superficial support for democratic norms.[14]

Our study does not provide the evidence necessary to choose
between these alternative theories, and we must be content mainly

[12] That there may, in fact, be an incompatibility between truly creative thinking and scholastic success becomes clear in J. W. Getzels, "Creative Thinking, Problem-solving, and Instruction," in Ernest R. Hilgard (ed.), *Theories
of Learning and Instruction*, 63d Yearbook of the National Society for the
Study of Education, pt. I (Chicago: University of Chicago Press, 1964),
pp. 240–268.

[13] For an interesting analysis of the sociology of education using this approach, see Burton R. Clark, "Sociology of Education," in R. E. L. Faris
(ed.), *Handbook of Modern Sociology* (Skokie, Ill.: Rand McNally and
Company, 1964), chap. 19.

[14] Edgar Z. Friedenburg, *Coming of Age in America: Growth and Acquiescence* (New York: Vintage, 1967).

with estimating the gap between brighter and duller children. By replicating existing findings and charting the magnitude of differences, we will at least be able to gauge the importance of intelligence and achievement not only to political socialization as a whole, but also to the impact of the school on the acquisition of democratic values.

We move next to a variable wholly outside the genetic process, social class. Despite the host of problems associated with understanding social class in the American context, the importance of class in socialization is well established.

According to the literature, working-class people not only view politics nonideologically, but also show little sympathy for either minority groups or civil liberties. Lipset gave this combination of findings the now famous label "working-class authoritarianism."[15] But again there are minor crosscurrents in the data. Hagstrom and Selvin have noted that, of all college students, it was the children of blue-collar parents who supported civil liberties most staunchly.[16] Whether these successful offspring of blue-collar families are representative of the rest of working-class children is conjectural, however.

There is also little disagreement about the state of political motivation and knowledge in the working class. A wealth of evidence indicates that lower-status children manifest diminished political efficacy, little political information, and little desire to enter politics.[17] Hess and Torney report class differences in political efficacy even among third-graders.[18] These authors also claim that working-class children are slower to move away from partisanship into informed, participant independence than are middle-class children.[19] Finally, there is ample indication of low political involve-

---

[15] Seymour Martin Lipset, *Political Man* (New York: Doubleday and Company, Inc., Anchor Books, 1960), chap. 4. There are, of course, exceptions to this general pattern. When specific problems become visibly urgent to the poor, they may develop sophisticated political conceptions. The most dramatic recent illustration of this principle is the rise of black militancy.

[16] Selvin and Hagstrom, "Determinants of Support for Civil Liberties," p. 59.

[17] Milbrath, *Political Participation*, pp. 57, 68, 116.

[18] Hess and Torney, *The Development of Political Attitudes in Childhood*, p. 267. For parallel findings, see David Easton and Jack Dennis, "The Child's Acquisition of Regime Norms: Political Efficacy," *American Political Science Review*, 61, No. 1 (March 1967), pp. 25–39.

[19] Hess and Torney, *The Development of Political Attitudes in Childhood*, p. 291.

ment among working-class adults; the poor vote less than the rich in virtually every kind of election.[20]

Again, it is easier to recapitulate the literature than to interpret it; once more alternative explanations compete for our attention. For example, some observers believe that the conditions of lower-class existence account for these findings. It has been argued that lower-class people are so busy fighting for day-to-day survival that they have no time to survey calmly the complex, long-range affairs of the larger society. Supporters of this theory can cite evidence that lower-class people possess relatively short-time perspectives and manifest little desire or ability to defer gratification.[21] The prevalence of such cognitive orientations undoubtedly weakens working-class comprehension of and support for the slow, painful, complicated processes of democracy. In addition, as Hoggart emphasizes, working-class life is cut off from and therefore resistant to the outside world.[22] Hoggart claims that the life of the working class revolves around home, family, and work; there is neither time nor interest left for political concerns.

A second explanation focuses on the relationship between the lower-status person and the political system. Poor people have little control over the circumstances of their own lives, much less over the political affairs of the larger society. They enjoy little access to those who wield power, they are inexperienced in the skills of collective action, and they lack the necessary information or contacts to exert influence. In short, those of lower status possess a quite realistic basis for their political alienation. The system does not reward the poor, and therefore, the poor are not interested in joining the system.[23]

There are some flaws in this explanation. The argument

---

[20] Milbrath, *Political Participation*, pp. 97–98.

[21] Thus, they evidence less willingness to extend their formal education or to strive for higher-paying occupations. See Herbert Hyman "The Value Systems of Different Classes," in Reinhard Bendix and Seymour Martin Lipset (eds.), *Class, Status and Power* (New York: The Free Press, 1953), pp. 426–442. For an interesting attempt to link shortened time perspectives to reduced political participation, see John H. Kessel, "Cognitive Dimensions of Political Activity," *Public Opinion Quarterly*, 29, No. 3 (Fall 1965), pp. 377–390.

[22] Richard Hoggart, *The Uses of Literacy* (Boston: The Beacon Press, 1961), chaps. 3–5.

[23] E. E. Schattschneider, *The Semisovereign People* (New York: Holt, Rinehart and Winston, Inc., 1960), chaps. 3–4.

assumes an interrelationship between belief in the values of the system, knowledge about the structure of the system, and loyalty to the system. However, belief in democratic values and knowledge about democratic structures are not always necessary conditions for loyalty to democratic symbols, and there is evidence to support this contention. Both Greenstein and Hess and Torney report that lower-status children loosen their hold on national symbols such as the President more slowly than do higher-status children. In addition, the children of the poor retain a belief in the benevolence of leaders longer than do the children of the rich.[24] Jaros even found that ghetto children had as intense an attachment to the President as did white children.[25]

We will not be able to disentangle these arguments. Instead, we will concentrate on describing class differences in socialization, focusing especially on the interaction of educational quality and social class as they influence attitudes toward democracy. We will try, however, to shed some light on one portion of the argument we have just reviewed. If lower-class alienation stems from a lack of opportunity to exercise power, it should follow that any chance to exert influence should reduce disaffection. It is only reasonable to expect people who occupy positions of power to feel a close attachment to the political system that has rewarded them. Such people should also experience increases both in political motivation and knowledge. There are already many studies that support these observations.[26]

Children and adolescents, of course, hold no political positions in our society, but the schools are providing students with increasing opportunities to influence educational policy. Do students who participate in school organizations manifest higher levels of democratic support than those who do not?

This question has important theoretical implications beyond those related to social class. Almond and Verba hypothesize that

[24] Fred I. Greenstein, *Children and Politics* (New Haven, Conn.: Yale University Press, 1965), pp. 101–102; Hess and Torney, *The Development of Political Attitudes in Childhood*, p. 137.

[25] Dean Jaros, "Children's Orientations towards the President: Some Additional Theoretical Considerations," *Journal of Politics*, 29, No. 2 (May 1967), pp. 368–387.

[26] Samuel Stouffer, *Communism, Conformity and Civil Liberties* (Gloucester, Mass.: Peter Smith, 1963), chap. 2. See also Milbrath, *Political Participation*, chap. 3.

the egalitarian character and openness of American schools encourage support for democracy among all students.[27] If Almond and Verba are correct, students who take advantage of this openness by participating in school organizations should be highly democratic. However, should we find no relationship between school participation and support for democracy, we would have reason to question the notion that by giving people a greater share of political influence we will automatically forge in them an attachment to the democratic system.

We will examine one other variable that intervenes between the school and the child, political partisanship. Until this point, we have treated partisanship as an outcome of the developmental process and of educational quality. But student partisans may also differ among themselves in the way they confront politics. For example, we already know that by ninth grade students have a well-developed sense of domestic policy. Do student Democrats and Republicans have different policy preferences and, if so, at what point do these differences manifest themselves? Surely party identification, if it is more than simple force of habit, must be linked to policy preferences. Should we find student Republicans more conservative than student Democrats, we can at least claim that early in the socialization cycle partisanship and policy preference combine to allow the student some understanding of party and policy in the political system.

But partisanship may be related to more than policy orientation. Does partisan identification among students affect political motivation, information, and support for democratic norms? Already there is evidence that Democrats participate less in politics than Republicans.[28] How early do these differences develop and how widespread are they?

We are interested not only in assessing the influence of these intervening variables, but also in relating their effects to those of our two major independent variables, age and school district. Hence, we will examine the interaction of age and school district with sex, grade average, class, partisanship, and school participa-

---

[27] Gabriel Almond and Sidney Verba, *The Civic Culture* (Boston: Little, Brown and Company, 1965), pp. 276–277. For parallel contentions, see Harry Eckstein, *A Theory of Stable Democracy* (Princeton, N.J.: Center of International Studies, 1961).

[28] Lane, "Political Education in the Midst of Life's Struggles," p. 144.

tion. We hypothesize that the older the child and the better the education he gets, the less influence intervening variables will have on socialization to democracy. Good schools and maturity should minimize the exogenous impact of sex, class, intelligence, partisanship, and participation. Whatever our findings, we will speculate about possible consequences for adult behavior in the American system.

SEX DIFFERENCES

Table 5-1 summarizes the attitude and information scores of males and females in our sample, according to grade.

As Table 5-1 indicates, not only are the differences between the sexes generally small, but most of them favor the girls by twelfth grade. In those dimensions where twelfth-grade girls are furthest ahead of boys—political efficacy, rules of the game, and opportunity to participate—major gains are made between ninth

TABLE 5-1. SUPPORT FOR DEMOCRACY, LIBERALISM-CONSERVA-
TISM, AND LEVELS OF POLITICAL INFORMATION,
BY SEX AND GRADE (MEAN SCORES)[a]

Dimension	Grade level	Sex Male	Female	Totals
Freedom of speech	6th	1.83 (300)	1.80 (261)	1.82 (561)
	9th	2.20 (249)	2.26 (252)	2.23 (501)
	12th	2.40 (194)	2.41 (216)	2.41 (410)
	Totals	2.10 (743)	2.15 (729)	2.13 (1472)
Majority rule	6th	2.16 (298)	1.90 (262)	2.00 (560)
	9th	2.10 (247)	2.01 (251)	2.06 (498)
	12th	2.21 (194)	2.01 (216)	2.11 (410)
	Totals	2.13 (739)	1.97 (729)	2.05 (1468)
Importance of elections	6th	2.28 (300)	2.25 (260)	2.27 (560)
	9th	2.53 (249)	2.41 (255)	2.47 (504)
	12th	2.77 (189)	2.74 (217)	2.76 (406)
	Totals	2.49 (738)	2.46 (732)	2.47 (1470)
Minority rights	6th	2.77 (300)	2.73 (262)	2.76 (562)
	9th	3.11 (249)	3.07 (250)	3.09 (499)
	12th	3.09 (194)	3.17 (217)	3.13 (411)
	Totals	2.97 (743)	2.98 (729)	2.98 (1472)

TABLE 5-1 (*continued*)

Dimension	Grade level	Sex Male	Female	Totals
Sense of	6th	2.45 (299)	2.55 (261)	2.50 (560)
civic	9th	2.67 (247)	2.78 (250)	2.73 (497)
obligation	12th	2.77 (195)	2.90 (216)	2.84 (411)
	Totals	2.61 (741)	2.74 (727)	2.67 (1468)
Liberalism	6th	2.07 (298)	2.03 (262)	2.06 (560)
	9th	1.88 (248)	2.03 (255)	1.96 (503)
	12th	1.62 (193)	1.79 (215)	1.71 (408)
	Totals	1.89 (739)	1.97 (732)	1.93 (1471)
Knowledge of	6th	3.44 (294)	3.06 (257)	3.25 (553)
political	9th	4.64 (248)	4.05 (251)	4.34 (499)
personalities	12th	6.02 (192)	5.23 (212)	5.61 (404)
	Totals	5.68 (734)	4.03 (722)	4.28 (1456)
Knowledge of	6th	1.73 (299)	1.38 (261)	1.57 (560)
political	9th	2.35 (250)	1.98 (251)	2.17 (501)
institutions	12th	3.59 (188)	3.08 (209)	3.32 (397)
	Totals	2.42 (737)	2.08 (721)	2.25 (1458)
Aggregate	6th	4.58 (297)	3.91 (258)	4.27 (551)
knowledge	9th	6.18 (243)	5.26 (246)	5.72 (493)
	12th	8.68 (186)	7.44 (208)	8.03 (394)
	Totals	6.17 (726)	5.41 (712)	5.80 (1438)

Dimensions that change between grades

Dimension	Grade level	Sex Male	Female	Totals
Support	6th	1.90 (300)	1.93 (262)	1.91 (562)
for the	9th	1.78 (249)	1.81 (250)	1.80 (499)
vote	12th	1.50 (193)	1.49 (215)	1.50 (408)
Political	6th	1.59 (298)	1.62 (261)	1.60 (599)
efficacy	9th	1.51 (245)	1.58 (252)	1.54 (497)
	12th	1.53 (192)	1.78 (211)	1.66 (403)
Rules of	6th	2.95 (299)	2.96 (259)	2.95 (558)
the game	9th	3.31 (248)	3.34 (253)	3.33 (501)
	12th	1.92 (190)	2.11 (214)	2.02 (404)
Opportunity to	6th	1.25 (299)	1.33 (260)	1.29 (558)
participate	9th	2.10 (246)	2.29 (258)	2.20 (504)
	12th	2.01 (191)	2.35 (217)	2.19 (408)

[a] Number of items for rules of the game: 5 for 6th and 9th grades, 3 for 12th. Number of items for opportunity to participate: 3 for 6th and 12th, 4 for 9th. For number of items in other dimensions, see Table 3-1.

and twelfth grades. This finding might signify the particular importance of high-school social studies to girls. It is at least intuitively reasonable to believe that boys come to their social-studies courses with an already settled view of democracy, while girls are less completely socialized.[29] The substantial movement between ninth and twelfth grades suggests that, for girls, the high school may play a compensatory role in political socialization.

Our interpretation, however, is not consistent with the fact that neither the sense of civic obligation nor majority rule shift as much between ninth and twelfth as between sixth and ninth grades among girls. In fact, girls score higher than boys on the sense of civic obligation all through the educational cycle.

One thing is clear. Sex-role typing in American society extends primarily to political participation, not to democratic values. This conclusion first becomes evident through our examination of the information scores in Table 5-1. Significant sex differences in political knowledge have already emerged by the sixth grade and accelerate rapidly thereafter. More persuasive are the total disintegration of female interest in political office seeking after the sixth grade and the slowness of girls to enter the party system. Tables 5-2 and 5-3 document these findings.

TABLE 5-2. SEX DIFFERENCES IN DESIRE TO RUN FOR POLITICAL OFFICE, BY GRADE LEVEL

Grade level	Sex	Percent desiring to run for office
6th	Male	31 (90)
	Female	31 (80)
9th	Male	26 (64)
	Female	10 (26)
12th	Male	18 (36)
	Female	3 (6)

Table 5-2 portrays the impact of sex-role socialization in bold relief. To our surprise, sixth-grade girls show as much interest in pursuing a political career as sixth-grade boys. But by twelfth

[29] Douvan and Adelson suggest that girls rarely internalize values fully. See Douvan and Adelson, *The Adolescent Experience*, chap. 7.

TABLE 5-3. SEX DIFFERENCES IN PARTY IDENTIFICATION,
BY GRADE LEVEL (IN PERCENT)

Grade	Sex	Party				Totals	
		Democrat	Republican	Independent	None		
6th	Male	28 (81)	24 (70)	9 (27)	39 (112)	100	(290)
	Female	19 (48)	24 (60)	8 (20)	49 (125)	100	(253)
9th	Male	38 (90)	25 (59)	14 (32)	23 (53)	100	(234)
	Female	31 (74)	24 (58)	13 (31)	32 (76)	100	(239)
12th	Male	24 (43)	24 (42)	28 (51)	24 (45)	100	(181)
	Female	33 (65)	17 (33)	19 (38)	31 (63)	100	(199)
Totals		29 (401)	24 (322)	14 (199)	33 (474)	100 (1396)	

grade, female adolescence, the awakening of interest in boys, and the acceptance of a nonoccupational role in society have all taken their toll. Twelfth-grade girls are six times less likely than twelfth-grade boys to be interested in a political career. Moreover, as Table 5-3 makes clear, sixth-grade girls already trail sixth-grade boys in socialization to partisanship. Even in the twelfth grade, almost one-third of the girls can find no place for themselves within the partisan-Independent configurations of our political system. Thus, Hess and Torney may be correct when they claim that "that school socializes both boys and girls to equal levels of attitudes,"[30] but they err if they believe that this equality implies comparable commitment to political involvement.

Why should girls have performed so unexpectedly well on democratic values, yet so poorly on participation-related measures? There are two possible reasons. For one thing, we may have been misled by the inadequacy of the existing literature. Findings about sex differences in politics have always been weak and mixed. One is almost tempted to believe that America's unfavorable image of women in the democratic system has been as much the product of folklore as of hard evidence. But there is another, more interesting possibility. Our data may reflect the changing status of women in American life. It is proverbial that the present generation of girls does not feel itself as constrained by sex-role barriers as did its predecessors. The cloistered family life that supposedly made

[30] Hess and Torney, *The Development of Political Attitudes in Childhood*, p. 308.

women anti-democratic in the past does not appeal to today's girls. Perhaps the conditions that once may have produced anti-democratic attitudes among girls are now disintegrating. Unfortunately, this interpretation is inconsistent with the marked sex differences on participation-related variables. We cannot explain away this inconsistency, but it is at least possible that a change of values must precede a change in participation. If so, our findings have merely photographed the middle of a long-term shift in female orientations toward politics.[31]

DIFFERENCES AMONG STUDENTS
OF VARYING ACHIEVEMENT LEVELS

Table 5-4 is analogous to Table 5-1. Like the latter, it too reports democratic support and knowledge scores of students, this time by reference to student scholastic averages and grade level.

Table 5-4 supports the hypothesis that scholastic achievement is directly related to acceptance of democratic values. The "A" students score highest among the three achievement groups on almost all value dimensions, regardless of grade level. Comparable, but even sharper differences appear when we consider levels of political information. The latter finding, while of little theoretical importance, does legitimize our risky procedure of allowing the students to place themselves in their own scholastic average bracket. Had we discovered no positive correlation between grade average and political information, we would have had severe doubts about the reliability of our student-achievement measure.

Substantial differences between students of varying achievement levels have already emerged by sixth grade. What is the fate of these differences as the child matures? Are twelfth-grade "A" students more like twelfth-grade "C" students than sixth-grade "A" students are like sixth-grade "C" students? If the gap between bright and dull students widens as children proceed through school, we can conclude that education stratifies intellectual acceptance of democracy. However, if students of different abilities grow together in their appreciation of democracy, we can conclude again that the school fulfills a compensatory, egalitarian function.

[31] For additional considerations, see Kenneth P. Langton, *Political Socialization* (New York: Oxford University Press, 1969), chap. 3.

TABLE 5-4. SUPPORT FOR DEMOCRACY AND LEVELS OF POLITICAL INFORMATION, BY SCHOLASTIC AVERAGE AND GRADE LEVEL[a]

Dimension	Grade level	"A"	"B"	"C"	Totals
Freedom	6th	1.99 (105)	1.88 (270)	1.65 (168)	1.83 (543)
of	9th	2.65 (41)	2.28 (242)	2.15 (201)	2.25 (484)
speech	12th	2.60 (33)	2.50 (207)	2.26 (165)	2.42 (404)
	Totals	2.26 (179)	2.20 (719)	2.02 (533)	2.13 (1431)
Majority	6th	2.09 (105)	1.95 (271)	2.00 (166)	1.99 (542)
rule	9th	2.14 (42)	2.04 (238)	2.07 (201)	2.07 (481)
	12th	2.15 (33)	2.12 (206)	2.11 (165)	2.11 (404)
	Totals	2.12 (180)	2.04 (715)	2.06 (532)	2.05 (1427)
Importance	6th	2.43 (105)	2.28 (271)	2.11 (167)	2.25 (543)
of elec-	9th	2.78 (42)	2.52 (241)	2.83 (204)	2.67 (487)
tions	12th	2.11 (32)	2.34 (204)	2.68 (164)	2.46 (400)
	Totals	2.57 (179)	2.52 (716)	2.38 (535)	2.45 (1430)
Minority	6th	2.93 (105)	2.83 (272)	2.47 (168)	2.73 (545)
rights	9th	3.12 (41)	3.14 (239)	3.01 (202)	3.08 (482)
	12th	3.15 (33)	3.20 (207)	3.03 (165)	3.12 (405)
	Totals	3.02 (179)	3.05 (718)	2.87 (535)	2.95 (1432)
Sense of	6th	2.74 (105)	2.58 (270)	2.26 (168)	2.51 (543)
civic	9th	2.87 (41)	2.79 (241)	2.63 (201)	2.73 (483)
obliga-	12th	2.67 (33)	2.86 (206)	2.82 (166)	2.82 (405)
tion	Totals	2.77 (179)	2.73 (717)	2.58 (535)	2.67 (1431)

Dimensions that change between grades

Support	6th	2.29 (105)	2.02 (272)	1.53 (168)	1.95 (545)
for the	9th	2.22 (41)	1.83 (241)	1.68 (201)	1.80 (483)
vote	12th	1.42 (33)	1.50 (204)	1.49 (165)	1.48 (402)
	Totals	2.11 (179)	1.81 (717)	1.57 (534)	1.76 (1430)
Political	6th	1.65 (104)	1.60 (270)	1.58 (168)	1.60 (542)
efficacy	9th	1.76 (42)	1.68 (239)	1.36 (199)	1.55 (480)
	12th	1.88 (33)	1.65 (200)	1.65 (164)	1.66 (397)
	Totals	1.72 (179)	1.65 (709)	1.52 (531)	1.60 (1419)
Rules of	6th	3.19 (105)	3.08 (269)	2.61 (168)	2.96 (542)
the	9th	3.02 (42)	2.50 (242)	2.18 (200)	2.41 (484)
game	12th	2.34 (32)	2.18 (203)	1.77 (163)	2.02 (398)
Opportu-	6th	1.42 (104)	1.32 (271)	1.21 (168)	1.30 (543)
nity to	9th	2.65 (43)	2.36 (243)	1.91 (201)	2.19 (487)
par-	12th	2.15 (33)	2.27 (206)	2.10 (163)	2.19 (402)
ticipate					

(TABLE 5-4 *continued*)

Dimension	Grade level	"A"	Scholastic average "B"	"C"	Totals
Knowledge of politi- cal per- son- alities	6th	3.81 (102)	3.30 (271)	2.86 (165)	3.27 (538)
	9th	5.62 (43)	4.55 (271)	3.85 (199)	4.35 (483)
	12th	6.46 (32)	5.98 (202)	5.05 (169)	5.62 (403)
	Totals	4.73 (177)	4.49 (712)	3.92 (528)	4.30 (1424)
Knowledge of politi- cal in- stitu- tions	6th	1.76 (105)	1.66 (271)	1.32 (168)	1.57 (544)
	9th	2.88 (43)	2.29 (242)	1.91 (199)	2.18 (484)
	12th	3.71 (31)	3.62 (198)	2.90 (163)	3.32 (392)
	Totals	2.37 (179)	2.42 (711)	2.02 (530)	2.26 (1420)
Aggregate knowl- edge	6th	4.98 (102)	4.36 (268)	3.72 (165)	4.28 (535)
	9th	7.56 (43)	6.01 (238)	5.08 (196)	5.72 (477)
	12th	9.13 (31)	8.71 (195)	7.08 (163)	8.35 (389)
	Totals	6.34 (176)	6.13 (701)	5.27 (524)	5.92 (1401)
Liberal- ism	6th	2.04 (105)	2.03 (271)	2.10 (167)	2.05 (543)
	9th	1.71 (42)	1.95 (241)	2.04 (202)	1.96 (485)
	12th	1.34 (33)	1.68 (205)	1.80 (164)	1.70 (402)
	Totals	1.83 (180)	1.90 (717)	1.99 (533)	1.92 (1430)

[a] Number of items for rules of the game: 5 for 6th and 9th grades, 3 for 12th. Number of items for opportunity to participate: 3 for 6th and 12th, 4 for 9th. For number of items in other dimensions, see Table 3-1.

Unfortunately, our findings are inconclusive. Of the nine dimensions of democracy, sixth-grade "A" and "C" students differ more than twelfth-grade "A" and "C" students on four dimensions, while the reverse holds for another four. In the case of freedom of speech, we find identical differences at the two grade levels. Education apparently has equal socialization effects on bright and dull students.

It is not surprising that the sharpest divergence between bright and dull students should involve political information. Moreover, such differences accelerate over time. We see a familiar pattern emerging. The school is weakest when it confronts the impact of exogenous variables on participation-related dimensions.

A closer examination of Table 5-4 reveals a peculiar finding.

Twelfth-grade "A" students seem to behave strangely. They usually experience little pro-democratic movement between ninth and twelfth grades; indeed, in some cases, they actually score lower than their ninth-grade counterparts. Twelfth-grade "B" and "C" students, on the other hand, have continued a regular, gradual, pro-democratic shift. Something must alter the development of bright students between ninth and twelfth grades. We shall speculate further on this paradox shortly.

The liberalism findings are also worthy of comment. Table 5-4 describes a definite and growing inverse relationship between academic success and support for domestic liberalism.[32] Strangely, however, as Table 5-6 shows, bright students tend disproportionately to be Democrats, and, as Table 5-10 will demonstrate, Democrats as a whole become more liberal over time. Putting these pieces together, we come to the paradoxical conclusion that many of the brightest students espouse a partisan identification not at all in accord with their policy views. It is among the duller student Democrats that party identification and policy view are most closely joined. It is bemusing to discover a more rational basis for future

---

[32] Lest it be thought that this finding is an outgrowth of social-class differences in scholastic attainment, we discover that the finding survives controls for social class. It is true that more "A" students are children of white-collar families than is true for the sample as a whole. It is also true that the children of blue-collar families make up a disproportionate number of the "C" category in scholastic achievement. Nonetheless, grade-average differences survive class controls, as the following table of domestic liberalism, by grade average and social class, indicates:

Class	Grade average	Liberalism score
White-collar	"A"	1.83 (121)
	"B"	1.85 (450)
	"C"	1.97 (310)
Blue-collar	"A"	1.82 (55)
	"B"	2.00 (248)
	"C"	2.01 (201)

When this relationship is reexamined with the addition of grade level, it still survives, though more weakly. The relationship is reversed at the sixth-grade level, with "A" students the most liberal and "C" students the least, within social class. The relationship reasserts itself, however, at the ninth-grade and twelfth-grade levels.

voting choice among the ordinary than among the bright Demo-crats.[33]

Earlier we suggested that scholastic attainment, like sex role, apparently has a major impact upon participation-related variables.

TABLE 5-5. PERCENT OF STUDENTS WITH VARYING SCHOLASTIC
AVERAGES WHO DESIRE TO RUN FOR POLITICAL
OFFICE, BY GRADE LEVEL

Grade level	"A"	Scholastic average "B"	"C"
6th	36 (37)	30 (30)	31 (51)
9th	24 (10)	19 (43)	18 (36)
12th	24 (8)	11 (21)	8 (14)

TABLE 5-6. PARTY IDENTIFICATION, BY GRADE LEVEL AND
SCHOLASTIC AVERAGE (IN PERCENT)

Grade level	Scho-lastic average	Demo-crat	Repub-lican	Inde-pendent	None	Totals
			Party			
6th	"A"	36 (36)	21 (22)	10 (10)	33 (33)	100 (101)
	"B"	25 (66)	25 (66)	8 (21)	42 (111)	100 (264)
	"C"	14 (23)	24 (40)	9 (14)	53 (86)	100 (163)
9th	"A"	52 (21)	18 (7)	10 (4)	20 (8)	100 (40)
	"B"	33 (76)	21 (58)	15 (35)	31 (59)	100 (228)
	"C"	33 (62)	26 (49)	12 (23)	29 (54)	100 (188)
12th	"A"	40 (12)	17 (5)	13 (4)	30 (9)	100 (30)
	"B"	24 (46)	24 (46)	26 (51)	26 (51)	100 (194)
	"C"	31 (47)	16 (25)	21 (33)	32 (48)	100 (153)
Totals		29 (389)	23 (318)	14 (195)	34 (459)	100 (1361)

We based this assertion on the different amounts of political knowl-edge that bright and dull students possessed. Does the assertion hold when we examine the relation of scholastic achievement to

[33] Of course, we have not examined ninth- and twelfth-grade "A" Democrats in contrast to other students, as we would have to in order to establish this relationship uncontestably. However, the great majority of ninth- and twelfth-grade "A" students are Democrats; thus, we can infer that the ninth- and twelfth-grade "A" scores are primarily the scores of Democrats as well.

partisan identification and desire to run for political office? Tables 5-5 and 5-6 provide the relevant data.

Our conclusions about scholastic average are not quite as clear-cut as those that involved sex differences. Table 5-5 reveals the expected results: an accelerating divergence between bright and dull students in their desire to enter politics. No doubt this pattern may be explained by the self-confidence that their academic success brings to the brighter students. However, Table 5-6 portrays ambiguities among "A" students similar to those noted above. Although sixth- and ninth-grade "A" students find it considerably easier than "B" or "C" students to absorb the partisan terms of our political system, these differences vanish among twelfth-graders.[34] Fully 30 percent of the twelfth-grade "A" students can choose no party-related label for themselves.

The reluctance of twelfth-grade "A" students to embrace democracy, their high degree of alienation from partisan choice, and the divergence of policy position from partisanship among their Democratic contingent, combine to form a picture of political confusion. It is possible to interpret these findings as evidence of a movement toward political reorientation among bright high-school seniors. Certainly the tie between academic achievement and student radicalism in college supports this view.[35] Unfortunately, because our twelfth-grade "A" sample is so small, we cannot support our interpretation as strongly as we would like. The distinctiveness of the twelfth-grade "A" students nonetheless stands out from all the data in this section.

---

[34] Notice that Table 5-6 does not reveal the rapid development of Independence among the bright students reported by Hess and Torney. Indeed, the proportion of our "A" students who are Independents rises only 3 percent from sixth through twelfth grade. The greatest Independence gains are in fact made among "B" students, where the rise is a continuous one of 18 percent. For the Hess and Torney formulation, see Hess and Torney, "The Development of Basic Attitudes and Values toward Government and Citizenship during the Elementary Years," Cooperative Research Project No. 1078, U.S. Office of Education (Chicago: The University of Chicago, 1965), p. 172. In addition, see Hess and Torney, *The Development of Political Attitudes in Childhood*, p. 278.

[35] For a suggestive essay bearing on this finding, see Seymour Martin Lipset and Philip O. Altbach, "Student Politics and Higher Education in the United States," in Seymour Martin Lipset (ed.), *Student Politics* (New York: Basic Books, Inc., 1967), pp. 199–253.

SOCIAL CLASS

We have already seen that, according to most observers, working-class children fall significantly below middle-class children in their devotion to democratic values and in their levels of political participation. But does public education moderate or exacerbate these value differences? There are two views on the matter. Wiggin speaks for many educators when she claims that the school helps create a homogeneous middle-class culture.[36] Edgar Litt disagrees strongly, arguing that the school's curriculum actually reinforces class differences in politics.[37] Litt's position is echoed by militant blacks, who point to incriminating inconsistencies between the political history dispensed in primarily black schools and that purveyed in middle-class white schools. It therefore becomes important for us not only to examine class differences in student political orientations, but also to assess the degree to which these differences grow or vanish as the child proceeds through school.

Let us say a word about our measure of class. We have already alluded to the complex dispute surrounding the comparative merits of various class indices. Any researcher interested in class effects on political socialization who does not want to become caught in this debate faces a difficult choice. It seems to us that the optimum strategy for such an investigator is to seek out an index of class that, while sophisticated enough to relate to socialization convincingly, is also straightforward enough to permit easy interpretation and analysis.

He may choose from at least three alternatives. First, he can use parental education to measure the child's class. The major appeal of this alternative lies in the fact that education has become an increasingly powerful determinant of both occupation and life style.[38] A formidable drawback to this measure, however, is that many young children know little about their parents' education. The investigator may then consider a second alternative, construct-

---

[36] Gladys Wiggin, *Education and Nationalism* (New York: McGraw-Hill, Inc., 1962), p. 39.

[37] Edgar Litt, "Civic Education, Community Norms, and Political Indoctrination," *American Sociological Review*, 28, No. 1 (February 1963), pp. 69–75.

[38] Gerhard E. Lenski, *Power and Privilege* (New York: McGraw-Hill, Inc. 1966), pp. 364–365.

ing a multifactor measure of class. This procedure, because it combines several class indices to utilize a maximum amount of information, at first appears an attractive option. However, the use of such a measure implies that the investigator has some theory about the ways in which class elements combine. Not only do we possess no such knowledge, but any pretense to knowledge on our part would thrust us into the very debate we are trying to circumvent.

Consequently, we have chosen as our measure of class a simple dichotomy between blue-collar and white-collar work. Our reasons for this decision are fourfold. First, because blue- and white-collar workers apparently possess very different value systems,[39] our index captures much beyond the purely occupational aspect of class. Second, according to Blau and Duncan, educational differences are heavily dependent upon and correlated with the white-collar—blue-collar dichotomy.[40] Thus, occupation is an adequate surrogate for an educational measure. Third, and most important, social mobility in the United States occurs primarily within, rather than between, white- and blue-collar occupations.[41] This pattern of restricted mobility provides inferential evidence for the existence of distinct social classes based on occupational differences. Finally, more youngsters are familiar with their parents' work than with their parents' educational background.

Table 5-7 reports class differences in democratic values and in levels of political information.

Our findings, although in the expected direction, are somewhat weak, especially when compared with those involving scholastic achievement. Class differences in support for democracy are consistent, but small. As Tables 5-8 and 5-9 make clear, the effects of class on participation-related measures are also less marked than were the effects not only of scholastic achievement, but also of sex.

Although social class apparently has only a muted effect on

[39] Hyman, "The Value Systems of Different Classes"; Joseph Kahl, "Educational and Occupational Aspirations of 'Common Man' Boys," *Harvard Educational Review*, 23, No. 2 (Summer 1953), pp. 186–203; Leonard I. Pearlin and Melvin L. Kohn, "Social Class, Occupation, and Parental Values," *American Sociological Review*, 31, No. 4 (August 1966), pp. 466–480.
[40] Peter Blau and Otis Dudley Duncan, *The American Occupational Structure* (New York: John Wiley and Sons, Inc., 1968), pp. 124–126.
[41] Blau and Duncan, *The American Occupational Structure*, pp. 77–79.

TABLE 5-7. SOCIAL-CLASS DIFFERENCES IN DEMOCRATIC VALUES AND LEVELS OF POLITICAL INFORMATION, BY GRADE LEVEL[a]

| Dimension | Grade level | Social class | | Totals |
		White-collar	Blue-collar	
Freedom of	6th	1.96 (301)	1.70 (196)	1.85 (497)
speech	9th	2.30 (258)	2.22 (145)	2.27 (403)
	12th	2.52 (201)	2.31 (140)	2.43 (341)
	Totals	2.22 (750)	2.04 (481)	2.13 (1241)
Majority	6th	2.06 (301)	1.90 (194)	1.89 (495)
rule	9th	2.08 (257)	2.08 (141)	2.08 (358)
	12th	2.07 (200)	2.18 (141)	2.11 (341)
	Totals	2.07 (760)	2.04 (475)	2.07 (1234)
Importance	6th	2.30 (301)	2.22 (195)	2.26 (496)
of elections	9th	2.48 (260)	2.39 (147)	2.44 (407)
	12th	2.79 (200)	2.74 (138)	2.76 (338)
	Totals	2.50 (761)	2.42 (480)	2.46 (1241)
Minority	6th	2.82 (301)	2.70 (196)	2.77 (497)
rights	9th	3.13 (257)	3.05 (145)	3.10 (402)
	12th	3.18 (202)	3.10 (139)	3.14 (341)
	Totals	3.03 (760)	2.92 (480)	2.99 (1240)
Sense of	6th	2.63 (301)	2.38 (194)	2.53 (495)
civic	9th	2.78 (256)	2.72 (145)	2.75 (401)
obligation	12th	2.88 (202)	2.79 (139)	2.84 (341)
	Totals	2.71 (759)	2.60 (478)	2.67 (1237)
Support	6th	2.18 (289)	1.70 (193)	1.98 (482)
for the	9th	1.79 (258)	1.83 (144)	1.80 (402)
vote	12th	1.54 (200)	1.50 (140)	1.53 (340)
	Totals	1.87 (747)	1.68 (477)	1.80 (1224)
Political	6th	1.59 (289)	1.62 (190)	1.60 (479)
efficacy	9th	1.61 (259)	1.44 (142)	1.54 (401)
	12th	1.66 (195)	1.62 (138)	1.65 (333)
	Totals	1.62 (743)	1.57 (470)	1.60 (1213)
Rules of	6th	3.13 (300)	2.77 (195)	2.99 (495)
the game	9th	3.43 (260)	3.14 (144)	3.36 (404)
	12th	2.14 (198)	1.96 (137)	2.06 (335)
Opportunity	6th	1.34 (298)	1.21 (196)	1.28 (494)
to participate	9th	2.27 (263)	2.21 (144)	2.25 (467)
	12th	2.16 (199)	2.31 (140)	2.23 (339)
Knowledge	6th	3.44 (299)	3.07 (191)	3.29 (490)
of political	9th	4.52 (256)	4.13 (145)	4.37 (401)
personalities	12th	5.90 (194)	5.40 (139)	5.69 (333)
	Totals	4.46 (749)	4.08 (475)	4.31 (1224)

TABLE 5-7 (*continued*)

Dimension	Grade level	Social class White-collar	Blue-collar	Totals
Knowledge	6th	1.76 (299)	1.37 (192)	1.55 (491)
of political	9th	2.22 (256)	2.07 (150)	2.16 (406)
institutions	12th	3.33 (194)	2.28 (139)	2.90 (333)
	Totals	2.36 (749)	2.12 (475)	1.92 (1230)
Aggregate	6th	4.57 (299)	3.98 (192)	4.33 (491)
information	9th	5.86 (256)	5.41 (150)	5.69 (406)
	12th	8.15 (194)	7.82 (139)	8.02 (333)
	Totals	6.04 (749)	5.52 (475)	5.82 (1230)
Liberalism	6th	2.01 (300)	2.14 (195)	2.06 (495)
	9th	1.90 (260)	2.02 (146)	1.94 (406)
	12th	1.67 (199)	1.77 (140)	1.81 (339)
	Totals	1.89 (759)	1.99 (481)	1.92 (1240)

[a] Number of items for rules of the game: 5 for 6th and 9th grades, 3 for 12th. Number of items for opportunity to participate: 3 for 6th and 12th, 4 for 9th. For number of items in other dimensions, see Table 3-1.

TABLE 5-8. PERCENT OF STUDENTS DESIRING TO RUN FOR POLITICAL OFFICE, BY GRADE LEVEL AND SOCIAL CLASS

Grade level	Social class Percent white-collar	Percent blue-collar
6th	31 (94)	33 (70)
9th	19 (62)	18 (28)
12th	12 (29)	9 (13)

the acquisition of democratic attitudes, some aspects of our findings do bear extended comment. We had expected working-class children to view government much more benevolently than white-collar children. Instead, we find that class differences in liberalism, though in the hypothesized direction, are relatively small. Working-class children are only slightly more likely than white-collar children to approve government's paternalistic responsibility in social affairs. This finding should be juxtaposed against the puzzling fact that greater numbers of working-class than of middle-class children are Democrats, and, as we shall see, Democrats are considerably more

TABLE 5-9. PARTISAN IDENTIFICATION OF STUDENTS BY GRADE LEVEL AND SOCIAL CLASS (IN PERCENT)

Grade level	Social class	Party Demo-crat	Party Repub-lican	Party Inde-pendent	None	Totals
6th	White-collar	24 (75)	24 (76)	10 (32)	42 (124)	100 (307)
	Blue-collar	23 (49)	24 (50)	8 (17)	45 (93)	100 (209)
9th	White-collar	36 (116)	26 (82)	12 (38)	26 (82)	100 (318)
	Blue-collar	30 (45)	20 (29)	17 (25)	33 (45)	100 (144)
12th	White-collar	27 (66)	21 (51)	24 (57)	28 (67)	100 (241)
	Blue-collar	31 (43)	17 (23)	23 (31)	29 (40)	100 (137)
Totals		30 (394)	23 (311)	15 (200)	32 (451)	100 (1356)

liberal than Republicans. Apparently the policy views of student Republicans and Democrats cannot be explained primarily by reference to the class composition of the parties.[42]

[42] Another hypothesis suggests itself to explain these findings. If there are only small differences in liberalism between the classes, but large differences between partisans, then the bulk of the difference between partisans may be traced to the class misidentifiers. In other words, these findings suggest that white-collar Democrats or blue-collar Republicans provide the ideological distinctiveness of the parties. The relevant literature linking sociological marginality and ideological overcompensation involves the concept of status inconsistency. See Gerhard E. Lenski, "Status Crystallization: A Non-Vertical Dimension of Social Status," *American Sociological Review*, 19, No. 2 (August 1954); Gerard Brandmeyer, "Status Consistency and Political Behavior: A Replication and Extension of Research," *Sociological Quarterly*, 6, No. 3 (Summer 1965), pp. 241–257; and Joseph R. Gusfield, *Symbolic Crusade* (Urbana, Ill.: University of Illinois Press, 1963).

However, although the aggregate differences between the classes are low, those members of each class who select themselves into different parties may represent very distinct views on liberalism. We do not have the data to compare white- and blue-collar Democrats in their liberalism scores, nor do we have the data for Republicans. Nonetheless, we can make some extremely tentative inferences. We have already seen that there is an inverse relation between grade average and liberalism. Thus, 69 percent of the "A"

As Table 5-7 indicates, class differences among sixth-graders exceed those among twelfth-graders on all but two value dimensions: political efficacy and opportunity to participate. In short, the school minimizes the effects of class over time much more successfully than it reduces the impact of intelligence. The school also neutralizes the effect of class on policy attitudes; by twelfth grade, the children of blue-collar parents have become almost as disillusioned with liberalism as have the children of white-collar parents. Only class differences in political knowledge actually widen with age. We can conclude, therefore, that with regard to social class, the school again plays a compensatory role.

To summarize, there are consistent value, information, and participation-related differences between bright and dull, and rich and poor pupils. By and large, with the exception of twelfth-grade "A" students, the findings fit our expectations. Surprisingly, differences between the sexes are confined primarily to participation-related measures. Particularly in the case of social class, we observe the schools generating a relatively homogeneous attitudinal climate by twelfth grade.

PARTISANS AND PARTICIPANTS

We suggested earlier that the relationship between partisan identification and policy preference is central to any theory of democratic politics. If the public is to control its leaders, the voter must link his party choice to his policy preferences. In his last work, Key demonstrated the widespread existence, but not the origin, of such a link.[43] Our intent, therefore, is not only to show that youthful

---

students, 65 percent of the "B" students, and 60 percent of the "C" students are from white-collar families. We know that there is a strong relationship between liberalism score and partisan identification. Now 73 percent of the Democrats (257) are from white-collar families, with only 27 percent from blue-collar families. It seems clear that the distinctive liberalism score for Democrats must be, in large measure, due to the 73 percent of white-collar adherents. Yet, since the differences between the classes as a whole are smaller than between partisans, it seems clear that these 257 Democrats from the white-collar community must not only be more liberal than other white-collar students, but also more liberal than the remaining 27 percent of their fellow Democrats.

[43] V. O. Key, *The Responsible Electorate* (Cambridge, Mass.: Harvard University Press, 1966).

Republicans and Democrats differ significantly on policy matters, but also to sketch the development of their views. Do student Democrats oppose the policy orientations of youthful Republicans and, if so, at what rate and at what age does such opposition emerge?

We have already demonstrated that a consistent left-right orientation cannot be discerned until ninth grade. For this reason, we would be surprised to discover major ideological differences between sixth-grade partisans. However, we would expect to find progressively sharper differences thereafter. Table 5-10 supplies the necessary data.

TABLE 5-10. SUPPORT FOR DOMESTIC LIBERALISM AMONG REPUBLICANS AND DEMOCRATS, BY GRADE LEVEL

Grade level	Party Republican	Democrat	Totals
6th	2.09 (130)	2.06 (129)	2.08 (259)
9th	1.70 (116)	2.14 (164)	1.95 (280)
12th	1.30 (72)	1.92 (110)	1.68 (182)
Totals	1.77 (318)	2.06 (403)	1.93 (721)

As we suspected, Republicans and Democrats have similar policy views until they become capable of structuring the policy dimension. Many sixth-graders may identify themselves with the two parties, but by and large, such identification is innocent of ideological rationality. Cognitive development forges the link between policy preference and partisan identification. It therefore follows that cognitive development underlies purposive, policy-oriented, rational voting.[44]

Even among Democrats, liberalism deteriorates as maturation proceeds. It is difficult to know whether these data signify a generic developmental process or a difference in political generations. Perhaps our sixth-graders are more liberal than were our twelfth-

[44] For a fuller investigation of the relationship between cognitive development and the development of political ideology, see Richard M. Merelman, "The Development of Political Ideology: A Framework for the Analysis of Political Socialization," *American Political Science Review*, 64, No. 3 (September 1969), pp. 750–767.

graders six years earlier. After all, there is a general consensus that the political spectrum among the young has moved to the left in recent years. The problem, however, is that child-development theory also predicts our findings. Theoretically, whatever his generation, the young child's belief in the omnipotence of government and in the paternalistic benevolence of political leaders should convince him that government ought to assume major social responsibilities. Aging should destroy the child's automatic psychological support for liberalism.[45] Once again, therefore, we can offer no clear explanation for our findings.

There are no other relationships between partisanship and socialization to democratic values, nor are there interesting differences between students who report working for school political candidates and those who do not. Our negative finding in the latter area has both theoretical and educational import. Not only does it contradict Almond and Verba's contention that participation in nongovernmental politics builds support for the political community,[46] but it also disputes those educators who claim that school elections and student councils convey democratic norms. By itself, participation in school affairs can do little to instill respect for democratic values.

There is a good reason for this null relationship. More often than not, student government is a social rather than a political process. Because most student organizations have limited power, the few students truly interested in exerting political influence need feel no loss should they focus their attention beyond the school.

THE SCHOOLS AND THE BARRIERS

Sex, social class, and scholarship not only have their own impact on political socialization, but also condition the ability of the

[45] For a study that describes the young child's high support of the current scope of government, see Easton and Dennis, "The Child's Acquisition of Regime Norms: Political Efficacy," p. 130. They characterize the child as a "conservative collectivist," willing to tolerate the current level of government intrusion, but not much willing to extend it.

[46] For a finding similar to our own, see David Ziblatt, "High School Extracurricular activities and Political Socialization," *Annals*, 361 (September 1965), pp. 20–31.

schools to inculcate democratic attitudes. How do these variables affect the two school districts? To answer this question, we re-analyzed the student populations by grade level, school district, and, in order, sex, social class, and scholarship.

Instead of reproducing the massive tables reporting these data, however, we will present two summary formulations. Table 5-11 indicates that the two districts have generally similar effects

TABLE 5-11. RANK ORDER OF SCHOLARSHIP TYPES IN PROGRESS TO DEMOCRATIC ATTITUDES, BY DIMENSION AND SCHOOL DISTRICT

Dimension	School district	Scholarship type		
		"A"	"B"	"C"
Freedom of speech	Chalmers	3	2	1
	Moss City	1	2	3
Majority rule	Chalmers	3	2	1
	Moss City	1	2	3
Importance of elections	Chalmers	3	1	2
	Moss City	3	2	1
Minority rights	Chalmers	3	2	1
	Moss City	2	1	1 (tie)
Sense of civic obligation	Chalmers	3	2	1
	Moss City	3	2	1
Importance of the vote	Chalmers	3	2	1
	Moss City	3	2	1
Political efficacy	Chalmers	2	1	1 (tie)
	Moss City	1	3	2
Rules of the game	Chalmers	3	2	1
	Moss City	1	3	2
Opportunity to participate	Chalmers	2	3	1
	Moss City	3	2	1
Knowledge of political personalities	Chalmers	3	1	2
	Moss City	1	2	3
Knowledge of political institutions	Chalmers	2	1	3
	Moss City	1	2	3
Aggregate information	Chalmers	3	1	2
	Moss City	3	1	2
Partisanship (including Independence)	Chalmers	2	1	3
	Moss City	3	2	1
Desire to run for office	Chalmers	2	1	3
	Moss City	1	3	2

on students of different ability; however, as Table 5-12 demonstrates, the districts diverge markedly in their effects on the sexes. We have no table for social class because the districts affect the classes randomly. First, let us examine the interaction of the stu-

TABLE 5-12. SEX DIFFERENCES IN PROGRESS TO DEMOCRATIC ATTITUDES, BY DIMENSION AND SCHOOL DISTRICT

Dimension	*School district*	*Sex*[a] *Male*	*Female*
Freedom of speech	Chalmers	x	
	Moss City		x
Majority rule	Chalmers	x	
	Moss City		x
Importance of elections	Chalmers	x	
	Moss City		x
Minority rights	Chalmers		x
	Moss City		x
Sense of civic obligation	Chalmers	x	
	Moss City		x
Importance of the vote	Chalmers	x	
	Moss City		x
Political efficacy	Chalmers	x	
	Moss City		x
Rules of the game	Chalmers	x	
	Moss City		x
Opportunity to participate	Chalmers		x
	Moss City		x
Knowledge of political personalities	Chalmers	x	
	Moss City	x	
Knowledge of political institutions	Chalmers		x
	Moss City	x	
Aggregate political information	Chalmers	x	
	Moss City	x	
Partisanship (including Independence)	Chalmers		x
	Moss City		x
Desire to run for office	Chalmers	x	
	Moss City	x	

[a] *x* designates the sex that became most democratic on the dimension between the sixth and twelfth grades.

dent's scholastic average with his school district, grade level, and support for democratic values.

Table 5-11 orders by rank the scholarship types in the two districts on the basis of their progress to democratic attitudes over the sixth- to twelfth-grade time span. The table should be read in the following way: on freedom of speech in Moss City, "A" students showed the greatest democratic change over the grade span, "B" students ranked second, and "C" students brought up the rear. The order in Chalmers, however, was reversed.

Table 5-11 shows that both school districts succeed best in moving their dullest students to support democratic values. Of the twenty-eight comparisons within districts, "C" students travel furthest in a pro-democratic direction fourteen times, with "A" and "B" students splitting the remaining fourteen cases.

Here we observe the school's compensatory effect once more. If we are correct in assuming that Chalmers is the better of the two districts, we should expect to find compensation especially marked in that district. And so it is. Of the fourteen cases in which "C" students proceed fastest, eight occur in Chalmers; more important, not once do Chalmers "A" students move most rapidly. This is compensatory education with a vengeance.

But compensatory education also has a dark side. It is apparently impossible to produce comparable democratic gains in dull and bright students simultaneously. Perhaps bright students disdain as dull, repetitive, and simplistic the training that motivates their duller classmates. Indeed, in two cases, Chalmers "A" and "C" students actually move in opposite directions. On these dimensions, the sixth-grade "C" students are markedly less democratic than the sixth-grade "A" students; by twelfth grade, however, "A" students have actually regressed, while "C" students have forged far ahead of them.

More support for these observations comes from the Moss City findings. Superficially, Moss City appears to affect its students more uniformly than Chalmers. In eight cases, Moss City "A" students move furthest while in another six, "C" students lead the way. But closer examination yields another important finding. On five of the eight values that Moss City "A" students internalize most rapidly, "C" students proceed the least. Only one time of the six during which "C" students move furthest in Moss City, do "A" students not progress least. The identical finding holds for

Chalmers. Only one of the eight cases where Chalmers "C" students progress furthest does not involve "A" students moving least.[47]

Is training that falls so unevenly on bright and dull students desirable? Is it avoidable? Our questions are not meant to imply that the schools alone are responsible for the pattern we have observed. Bright students, no matter what their educational environment, may become especially sensitive to and cynical about various aspects of our political system. All that is clear is that the schools do not have equal impact on bright and dull students.

Table 5-12 indicates that the districts have markedly different effects on the sexes. On ten of the fourteen dimensions, boys progress faster than girls in Chalmers, while the opposite applies for ten cases in Moss City. In short, the schools influence boys more than girls in Chalmers, and girls more than boys in Moss City.

That Chalmers has its greatest success in reaching males carries interesting implications. Males control politics. Therefore, the political effect of Chalmers' concentration on boys far exceeds that of Moss City's success with girls. Put differently, Chalmers capitalizes on the culturally sanctioned and developmentally based interests of boys to make its own impact on political socialization greater.

THE SCHOOLS AMID THE BARRIERS

Let us now summarize briefly our major conclusions about the impact of educational quality on the political values of students. Good schools are only one factor amidst the many that structure political socialization. Indeed, for purely suggestive purposes, we can order the effects of our variables into two socialization hierarchies. The first hierarchy ranks the variables in terms of their con-

[47] These findings qualify those of Langton and Jennings, who report few significant effects of civics courses on students. As Langton and Jennings themselves admit in reference to Negro students, such courses can have important effects on students who do not find them redundant. Our conclusions are similar. See Kenneth P. Langton and M. Kent Jennings, "Political Socialization and the High School Civics Curriculum in the United States," *American Political Science Review*, 63, No. 3 (September 1968), pp. 852–868.

FIGURE 5-1. THE HIERARCHY OF SOCIALIZATION
TO DEMOCRATIC VALUES[1]

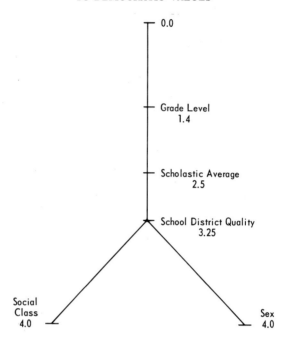

[1] For a description of the construction of this figure, see footnote 48.

tribution to the conveyance of democratic values. The second is identical, except for its concentration on the participation-related variable of political information.[48]

[48] Figures 5-1 and 5-2 are based not only on the findings reported, but also on a multiple-regression analysis of our data. Early in the data analysis and for suggestive purposes only, we attempted to use our five major independent variables—grade level, sex, scholastic average, school district, and social class—to account for variance in our attitudinal and information measures. We recognized at the time that the statistical requirements for the use of multiple regression, notably the requirement of interval scales, did not fit our data. Therefore, we determined not to report the multiple-regression scores in the text, but to use them only as a guide. Another reason for not making more of the regression analysis is that, after it was completed, we rearranged some of the data into the form in which we now find it. Consequently, our regression findings are only suggestive.

Our five variables, with the addition of two other variables, years in

The contributions of school quality to democratic values override the effects of class and sex. But educational quality can do little to alter the influence of exogenous factors on political information. The effects of school quality are limited and, as we have seen, mainly compensatory. Quality schools encourage standardized political values and knowledge.

The homogenizing impact of quality education moderates value differences among students. Unabated, such differences might harden in adulthood, thereby dividing the public so thoroughly as to defeat any hope for democracy. Thus, good schools help create a rudimentary democratic consensus. However, this consensus *is* rudimentary, neither as democratic as earlier socialization studies have portrayed it, nor well-structured cognitively. It is not even an

---

district and political party, explained 18 percent of the total attitudinal variance, $r = .419$. Not surprisingly, predictive value was much higher with the information items. The independent variables explained 47 percent of the information variance, $r = .683$.

These figures for the democratic-value scores are misleading, however, for they are inflated by the moderate $(.15–.35)$ correlations between dimensions. Thus, for individual dimensions, the total variance explained never rose over 14 percent and, in the egregious case of majority rule, equaled a whopping 2 percent. We ranked each of our five independent variables in relation to their explanatory power on the information and attitude dimensions. That is, each variable was ranked for its capacity to explain a dimension, and the sum of its rank scores, divided by the total dimensions, produced a summary ranking of each independent variable's explanatory power. The ranks, for democratic dimensions and political information, respectively, are as follows:

Grade level	1.4	Grade level	1.0
Scholastic average	2.5	Scholastic average	2.0
School district	3.25	Sex	3.0
Social class	4.0	Social class	4.0
Sex	4.0	District	5.0

District brings up the rear on political information, yet places moderately high on attitudes. This finding seems paradoxical, particularly since we have already seen that Chalmers was able to produce significant differences from Moss City at the twelfth-grade level only with regard to information. The paradox can be resolved by the fact that there was a great deal more actual movement on the information than the attitudinal findings; thus, comparatively, the school-district findings were overwhelmed by the other variables. In Figures 5-1 and 5-2 the distance between the variables corresponds to the rankings reported.

informed consensus; worse, it seems to penalize the most alert students. But if good schools can do no more for democracy than provide compensatory democratic socialization, perhaps, given the localized, undirected, and fragmented government of education, democracy has no right to demand more from them.

FIGURE 5-2. THE HIERARCHY OF SOCIALIZATION
TO POLITICAL KNOWLEDGE[1]

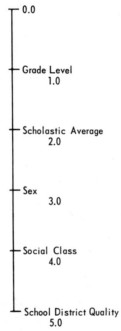

[1] For a description of the construction of this figure, see footnote 48.

Chapter 6

The Environments
of Teaching

A reading of the press almost any morning reveals that many teachers are dissatisfied with the schools. Teachers are, of course, concerned about the rewards and perquisites of their own craft; but their unhappiness extends beyond occupational goals to the larger aims of education. Unrest in teaching has been symbolized most recently by rapid growth in the American Federation of Teachers, a union sufficiently dedicated to the protection of teachers as to resort to a prolonged and illegal strike in the nation's largest city.[1]

But the press is not an accurate guide to the current state of the teaching profession. The majority of American school districts

[1] For a discussion of the New York teachers' strike, see Marilyn Gittell, "Community Control of Education," in Marilyn Gittell and Alan G. Hevesi (eds.), *The Politics of Urban Education* (New York: Frederick A. Praeger, Inc., 1969), pp. 363–377; and Martin Mayer, *Teachers Strike* (New York: Harper & Row, Publishers, 1968).

has remained relatively untouched by AFT militance. These are districts—and Chalmers and Moss City are good examples—that rarely make the headlines. For example, though teachers in both Chalmers and Moss City have pressed for better working conditions, AFT membership is small in each district. Neither in Chalmers nor Moss City has the AFT chapter even gained formal entrance into salary negotiations. The teachers in the two districts probably typify the majority of their fellows around the country. Not only are they untrained to militance and generally unfamiliar with the politics of education in their districts, but they are also surprisingly agreed on the worthiness of their status, their students, and themselves. Thus, the most striking characteristics of these teachers are their moderation and their homogeneity; we were rarely able to distinguish many differences among them, and even when such differences appeared, they were, at best, trends. If our sample is indicative, the teaching profession exerts socialization pressures far beyond that of most other occupations.[2]

A PROFILE OF TEACHERS—THE COMMITTED CLASS

There is evidence throughout our data that teachers are generally satisfied with their choice of occupation. Let us illustrate this by

TABLE 6-1. LIKELIHOOD THAT TEACHERS IN TWO DISTRICTS WOULD REENTER TEACHING, IF GIVEN THE OPPORTUNITY

Likelihood	Percent
Quite likely	81 (170)
Somewhat likely	12 (25)
Not very likely	7 (13)
Totals	100 (208)

reporting our respondents' assessments of the likelihood that they would reenter teaching if "they had it to do over again." Our findings appear in Table 6-1.

[2] For a related set of conclusions, see M. Kent Jennings and Harmon Zeigler, "Political Expressivism among High School Teachers; The Intersection of Community and Occupational Values," unpublished, 1967.

There is no way of knowing whether other professions generate as high a sense of commitment as does teaching. Surely a combination of self-selection, retrospection, and rationalization can buttress support for any occupation. Nevertheless, it is striking that teachers, so burdened and so ill-paid, are so agreed upon the worth of their craft.

One reason for the high level of teacher satisfaction may be the predominantly feminine composition of the profession. Thus, Zeigler presents evidence that men are the least content of teachers.[3] Male teachers not only resent taking orders from female supervisors, but also object to salaries that are barely sufficient to meet family obligations. We too can document some male dissatisfaction, but their unhappiness does not prevent men from committing themselves as strongly to teaching as do women. (See Table 6-2.)

TABLE 6-2. SEX DIFFERENCES IN LIKELIHOOD THAT TEACHERS WOULD REENTER TEACHING, IF GIVEN THE OPPORTUNITY

Likelihood	Percent men	Percent women	Totals
Quite likely	79 (65)	83 (101)	80 (166)
Somewhat likely	12 (10)	12 (14)	12 (24)
Not very likely	9 (7)	5 (6)	8 (13)
Totals	100 (82)	100 (121)	100 (203)

Widespread support for the teaching profession becomes evident in other ways throughout our data. For instance, 74 percent of our sample planned to teach for six years or more, while 36 percent specifically contemplated teaching until retirement. This retirement percentage is clearly understated. A number of teachers who had only a few years to go before retirement chose the years rather than the retirement option on our question. The actual retirement statistics may run as high as 50 percent.

It might be expected that, if men are unhappier than women in teaching, more of the former than the latter would be planning to leave the profession. However, as Table 6-3 indicates, this expectation is inaccurate.

[3] Harmon Zeigler, *The Political Life of American Teachers* (Englewood Cliffs, N.J.: Prentice-Hall, Inc., 1967), chap. 1.

The findings reported in Table 6-3 become less paradoxical on reflection. We suspect that many of the women who plan to leave teaching are not dissatisfied with their choice of profession. They simply want time off to begin to raise their families. Indeed, one of the chief attractions that teaching has for women is the possibility of leaving when family demands require and reentering when family opportunities permit. But the situation is different for men. Many male teachers may be unhappy, but few can foresee a bright future for themselves outside of teaching. There are many

TABLE 6-3. PROPORTIONS OF TEACHERS PLANNING TO TEACH FOR VARIOUS PERIODS, BY SEX (IN PERCENT)

Period	Percent men	Percent women	Totals
Less than six years	17 (10)	30 (41)	25 (51)
Six to ten years	9 (5)	11 (15)	10 (20)
Eleven or more	10 (6)	22 (30)	18 (36)
To retirement	60 (39)	34 (46)	43 (85)
No answer	4 (4)	3 (4)	4 (8)
Totals	100 (64)	100 (136)	100 (200)

reasons for this pessimism. Some male teachers are too old to shift careers easily; others hope to advance into the increasingly male administration, where they can enjoy bigger salaries and more prestige. Still others believe, quite correctly, that they do not have enough intellectual acumen to make leaving profitable. As early as high school, those boys who aspire to teach do less well in school than other boys.[4] We are therefore not surprised that only 14 percent of the male teachers as opposed to 23 percent of the women reported undergraduate grade-point averages of 3.3 or more. By contrast, 43 percent of the men confessed to grade averages in the low 2.0 to 2.9 range, whereas only 32 percent of the women scored as low. Their limited capacities prevent many men from leaving teaching.

Most of the teachers are committed not only to their profes-

[4] Ronald M. Pavalko, "Aspirants to Teaching: Some Differences between High School Senior Boys and Girls Planning on a Career in Teaching," *Sociology and Social Research*, 50, No. 1 (October 1965), pp. 47–62.

sion, but to their district. Seventy percent (146) intended to remain in the district where they were and only 10 percent (20) admitted any plans to leave. The remaining 20 percent (41) declined to answer our question. Even if we make the most damaging assumption, that every nonrespondent intended to leave, but was afraid to say so for fear of retribution from administrators, the depth of commitment to these districts remains impressive. After all, the ease of transportation in Los Angeles, coupled with the size of the region, opens many districts to teachers. But neither of these factors influences the teachers significantly. Therefore, the question arises: What do these teachers find so compelling about their districts?

We investigated this question by inquiring of the teachers what things in their districts they most enjoyed. We reasoned that if the answers revolved around intangible items, such as atmosphere, teachers would be unlikely to move, for it is difficult to assess the intangibles of another district before actually moving. Therefore, teachers who value intangible aspects of their current districts have little motivation to move. However, if what teachers prefer is tangible and easily compared with other districts—such as salary—moving becomes more likely; all that is required is the readily available evidence that teaching in another district pays more than teaching in one's current district.

What do the data say? As we suspected, it is the atmosphere of their district that attracts most teachers. But we can be more specific. More than anything else the teachers crave professional autonomy. Thus, 44 percent (91) mention freedom as the thing they like most about their district; only 3 percent (5) name salary as their district's most attractive feature. Because Chalmers and Moss City succeed in giving their teachers a sense of professionalism, they enhance their capacity to prevent turnover.[5]

Of course, other factors also contribute to the teachers' commitment to their districts. Perhaps the most significant is the fact that in both Moss City and Chalmers teachers enjoy generally good relations with their key reference groups—students, other teachers,

[5] Salary is much less important to occupational motivation than one might have expected. One of the first things sociologists interested in the nature of occupational commitment found was that, even in relatively menial positions, occupants are as much concerned with intangibles as with salaries. For elucidation, see Morris Rosenberg, *Occupations and Values* (New York: The Free Press, 1957), pp. 17–19.

and administrators. The amity of these relationships increases the districts' holding power.

Solid majorities of teachers claim that their students are quite responsive and cooperative. Sixty-five percent of the respondents (136) believe their students to be quite responsive, while only 3 percent (6) accuse their students of being unresponsive. The remainder, 32 percent (67), view students as only moderately responsive. Similarly, 70 percent (147) of the teachers say that their students are quite cooperative; barely 2 percent (4) feel that their students are not very cooperative. The balance, 28 percent (58), describe their students as moderately cooperative. There are no "blackboard-jungle" schools and relatively few difficult students in Moss City or Chalmers.

The respondents are much less sanguine about their students' diligence. Only 29 percent (61) believe that their pupils try very hard in school, while 8 percent (16) admit that their students do not work very hard at all. The majority of the teachers, 63 percent (131), describes the students as working only moderately hard. The portrait that emerges from these data depicts two middle-class school districts, both of which are populated by respectful, friendly, but somewhat detached students. We cannot help but be struck by the resemblance between the respondents' characterizations of their pupils and Friedenburg's description of high-schoolers.[6]

A comparable profile of satisfaction emerges when we examine the ties between teachers. We had expected few of our respondents to feel close to each other. After all, many live outside their district, and many others have been teaching in their district for only a short time. But we were wrong. In fact, these teaching communities seem surprisingly well integrated. We investigated the nature of teacher relationships by questioning the respondents about their friendship with colleagues, the commitment their colleagues felt to teaching, the extent to which they themselves found other teachers interesting people, and the degree to which teachers cared about each other as people rather than simply as fellow employees.

The great majority of teachers, 65 percent (134), reports having more than six friends in the district. Another 20 percent even claim over twenty friends among their colleagues. Most of the

[6] Edgar Z. Friedenburg, *Coming of Age in America: Growth and Acquiescence* (New York: Vintage, 1967), chap. 3.

teachers, 68 percent (142), rate their friends as only moderately close, but many more state that their friends are very close than admit that their friends are not very close. The respective proportions are 23 percent (47) and 6 percent (12). No doubt this high degree of friendly interaction takes place among the vast majority of teachers who think each other to be interesting and attractive people. Only 11 percent (22) demur from this judgment.

Perhaps one explanation for the high degree of teacher interaction in the two districts is that most teachers prefer the social to the intellectual characteristics of their colleagues. More are attracted by the "niceness," "helpfulness," and integrity of their fellows than by any intellectual excitement they might generate. Most teachers apparently rank qualities that can make their professional experience humane over qualities that can make it stimulating.

As Table 6-4 indicates, our generalization does not apply to

TABLE 6-4. PROPORTION OF TEACHERS WITH VARYING UNDER-
GRADUATE GRADE AVERAGE WHO CHOOSE SOCIAL AS OPPOSED
TO INTELLECTUAL REASONS FOR FINDING THEIR
COLLEAGUES INTERESTING (BY PERCENT)

Grade-point average	Reasons for interest		Totals	
	Social	Intellectual		
"A"	44 (11)	56 (14)	100 (25)
"B"	59 (49)	41 (34)	100 (83)
"C"	68 (45)	32 (21)	100 (66)
Totals	60 (105)	40 (69)	100 (174)

all teachers. Those with undergraduate grade-point averages in the "A" range were more likely than other teachers to portray their colleagues as being interesting intellectually. More generally, there is a pronounced inverse relationship between the academic success of the teacher and the tendency to see other teachers as being attractive for social reasons.

These responses indicate some selectivity of perception and association in teaching ranks.[7] Not only may the more intelligent

[7] This distinction between teachers of different achievement levels is about the only one that divides these groups from each other. In other words, teacher differences are generally unrelated to academic achievement. This

teachers seek each other out for friendship, but some may also project onto the entire group of teachers the same characteristics they value in each other. Likewise, teachers who did not do well in college probably associate mainly with others who, like themselves, can bring only social gifts to interaction. At any rate, there is certainly intellectual segregation in teaching.

More convincing evidence of teacher solidarity in the two districts comes from responses to our question whether teachers cared about each other as people and not only as fellow professionals. A majority of the respondents, 53 percent (111), claimed only that their colleagues cared about them as people "somewhat." More significant, however, is the fact that over a third, 35 percent (73), believes that colleagues care about them as people "very much," while only a handful, 9 percent (19), feels that colleagues care "very little" about them.

Our teachers also profess generally good relationships with administrators. Unfortunately, but perhaps understandably, we could not probe this sensitive subject as completely as we would have liked.[8] Thus, our conclusions are commensurately tentative. We are forced to rely principally on responses to only two items, both of which are indirect. Nonetheless, it is noteworthy that during an era of teacher militance generally, and at a time when teachers in Moss City were demonstrating because of low salaries, most of the respondents in both districts reported acceptable arrangements with their superiors. A clear majority of teachers, 79 percent (164), stated that their experience with administrators was "quite satisfactory." Most of the remainder, 20 percent (42), claimed that their dealings with administrators still were "moderately satisfactory," and only a minuscule 1 percent (2) admitted to having "unsatisfactory" relations with administrators.

---

negative finding is interesting because we know that academic and educational background is a major source of status differences in the larger society. Again, we can infer the great power of the teacher socialization experience.

[8] We were discouraged from becoming too explicit about teacher-administrator relations in the sample districts early in our discussions with administrators. It became clear that questions that specifically probed such relationships would be prohibited and, if insisted upon, might vitiate the entire project. Consequently, we had to resort to the circumventions reported in the text. For an investigation of the determinants of teacher-administrator relations, see M. Kent Jennings and Harmon Zeigler, "The Politics of Teacher-Administrator Relations," unpublished, 1967.

There are several plausible interpretations of these findings. One is the lack of overt dissatisfaction in the districts. After all, neither in Moss City nor Chalmers is there much teacher militance. The Moss City demonstrations against low salaries were token; never did the teachers seriously consider striking. The AFT chapters in both districts are too small to divide teachers from administrators. Perhaps the findings accurately reflect the actual state of affairs.

We have also seen that the teachers genuinely appreciate their classroom autonomy; possibly, they attribute their freedom to the efforts of superiors. It does appear that teachers in both districts believe themselves to be exceptionally well-protected.

However, a less charitable interpretation might be that the teachers, fearing the retaliation of administrators, refrained from admitting their real hostility. We inquired, indirectly, into this possibility. We asked the respondents to choose between the two following statements about administrators:

a. Administrators are skilled and experienced former teachers who play an integral role in the instruction of the young.

b. Administrators are ex-teachers who have sought their present positions primarily because of salary considerations.

We assume that teachers who chose alternative *a* view administrators more favorably than those who chose *b*. We believe that because the question does not refer to any particular group of administrators, it need not provoke fear in the teachers. On the other hand, it seems likely that most teachers will base their judgments of administrators primarily on personal experience in their own districts. Consequently, we feel justified in applying responses to Moss City and Chalmers. Table 6-5 shows that the teachers

TABLE 6-5. PROPORTION OF TEACHERS EXPRESSING POSITIVE AND NEGATIVE VIEWS OF ADMINISTRATORS, BY DISTRICT

District	Percent choosing a	Percent choosing b	Total
Chalmers	51 (47)	49 (45)	100 (92)
Moss City	64 (74)	36 (41)	100 (114)
Totals	58 (120)	42 (86)	100 (206)

are divided in their views, with some interdistrict differences emerging.

The teachers are somewhat less happy wtih administrators than they at first appear. Still, a majority maintains a favorable view of administrative contributions to education.[9] The relative dissatisfaction of the Chalmers respondents at first comes as a surprise, but as we shall see shortly, it fits into an enlightening pattern of findings; consequently, we leave it for the moment.

Perhaps the most convincing indication of teacher contentment involves the reactions of the teachers to their districts. In response to our invitation, a full 78 percent of the sample (161) described their tenure either in Chalmers or Moss City as "quite satisfying." Twenty-one percent (44) found their experience "moderately satisfactory," and only 1 percent (2) saw their experience as "not very satisfactory." A more overwhelming vote of confidence in our districts would be difficult to imagine.[10]

POLITICAL ATTITUDES: THE EXPRESSIVE INGENUES

How does the teacher view politics as it impinges on her professional role? Does she feel free to undertake political discussion in the classroom? What does she think about the propriety of certain topics? How much support for democratic values does she evince? Does she possess much information about the political structure of her district? Does she, as Hess and Torney argue, convey a norm of political independence to her students? Our data give some unexpected answers to these questions. For example, we were surprised to discover teachers more strongly committed to the classroom discussion of controversial issues than previous

[9] Unhappiness with administrators, as we shall see in Chapter 7, centers in the high school, particularly in Chalmers. If we were to remove the Chalmers high-school group from our sample, we would find that substantial majorities were satisfied with their relationships with administrators.

[10] It is possible that teachers were afraid to express dissatisfaction with their districts for fear of administrator retribution. Nonetheless, we doubt that this was a common reaction, both because an expression of dissatisfaction would be sufficiently general as not to antagonize any particular parties in the district and because the teachers were assured both by ourselves and by the superintendents in their districts that their responses would be entirely confidential and that identities would not be revealed in our study.

studies had led us to foresee. Nor is political debate confined to special niches in the school; instead, it permeates the teaching culture.

Other investigators have concluded that the teacher feels so constrained by pressures both external and internal to her situation that she avoids controversial political subjects. Reporting on a national sample of high-school teachers, M. Kent Jennings states that there is only "a cautious acceptance" of political controversy.[11] Elsewhere, Jennings and Zeigler complain that even social-studies teachers, who are closest to the relevant subject matter, eschew classroom discussion of controversial political topics. For example, only 57 percent of their national sample of social-studies teachers felt free to advocate socialism.[12]

Our findings are different. A first indication of the teachers' openness to political discussion came from their responses to the question "Are there any political or social issues that you think should not be discussed in the classroom?" Roughly four-fifths, 81 percent (170), of the sample responded that, in principle, anything should be open to discussion. Only 16 percent (33) demurred.

But do teachers actually discuss controversial topics? After all, it is easy enough to voice general agreement with a proposition, but it may be more difficult to act on that belief in concrete cases. Therefore, we asked the teachers if they had dealt in class with several delicate political and social issues during the past year. Table 6-6 reports the proportions of respondents who claim to have discussed these subjects.

There are two especially notable aspects of Table 6-6. The first is that discussion takes place at all grade levels and in most courses. Let us remember that the sample includes teachers of every grade and subject. It therefore seems clear that classroom consideration of political problems is no longer (if it ever was) confined to high school or to the social studies. Second, the discussion of controversial issues depends at least as much on the interests of the students as on the desires of the teacher. The table offers no direct evidence for our statement, but it does provide

[11] M. Kent Jennings, "Observations on the Study of Political Values among Pre-Adults," unpublished, Survey Research Center, University of Michigan, Ann Arbor, Mich., October 1966, p. 19.

[12] Jennings and Zeigler, "Political Expressivism among High School Teachers," p. 6.

TABLE 6-6. PERCENT OF RESPONDENTS REPORTING CLASS
DISCUSSION OF SEVERAL CONTROVERSIAL ISSUES
IN THE PRECEDING YEAR

Topic	Percent discussing
The hippie phenomenon	73 ($n = 152$)[a]
The war in Vietnam	70 ($n = 146$)
Narcotics and LSD	67 ($n = 140$)
Rioting in American cities	65 ($n = 135$)
Communism	55 ($n = 114$)
Tuition at the University of California	26 ($n = 54$)

[a] n refers to the number of teachers discussing the topics.

inferential support. Notice that communism, a staple of social-studies courses, ranks second-lowest among the issues discussed. However, such topics as Vietnam, narcotics, and the hippie phenomenon—all of which strike closer to the California teen-ager—are heavily discussed. Students no doubt spill the consideration of these latter problems over the confines of social-studies classes. We not only doubt whether most teachers take the initiative on these subjects, but we would not be surprised to discover that some try to discourage their discussion. Still, for whatever reason, most teachers find themselves involved.

Why do our findings differ from those reported by other investigators? One reason might be the fact that Jennings and Zeigler inquired into the willingness of social-studies teachers to take value positions on political issues. They found many teachers unwilling to do so. By contrast, we asked teachers only if they had discussed certain delicate subjects in the classroom. The teachers had the maximum latitude to give an affirmative answer because, unlike Jennings and Zeigler, we specified no particular mode of discussion. Which is the more significant finding? We cannot say, but we suspect that college professors are almost as reluctant as high-school teachers to use the classroom in order to proselytize. Few would contend, however, that the college classroom is not a forum for vigorous political debate and learning. Nor should we immediately conclude that a teacher's refusal to advocate political values is a sign of fear. Instructors who refrain from value pronouncement may simply want to keep their teaching as objective as possible. In addition, it is certainly possible to use the discussion of controversial issues for teaching purposes without introducing one's own prejudices. We therefore feel that our findings convey as true a picture of the contribution that political discussion brings to teaching as do Jennings' and Zeigler's.

Equal proportions of elementary-school and secondary-school teachers reported engaging in political controversy during class periods. Today's youngsters are apparently unwilling to wait until they are "old enough" before they confront sensitive problems. One can only speculate about the relationship between the structured discussion of these controversial issues in high-school social-studies classes and the earlier informal discussion to which the child has been exposed in elementary school. At the very least, the average student does not come to the high school's treatment of political problems bearing a tabula rasa upon which the social-studies teacher has only to leave her mark.[13]

What political values do teachers bring to their interchange with students? Specifically, how democratic are teachers and how do their political values compare with those of their pupils? Much controversy swirls about this subject. Zeigler, for example, discovered that his teachers manifested a conservative and, in some cases, antidemocratic set of attitudes.[14] Weizer and Hayes found that only minorities of Michigan teachers favored a free press and free speech. Michigan teachers, according to Weizer and Hayes, are barely more democratic than their students.[15] Rabkin, however, reports that teachers in Washington state score lower on the Rokeach Dogmatism scale than any of Rokeach's original test groups.[16] Rabkin's finding has political significance because, as a number of studies have shown, open-mindedness is positively related to support for democratic norms.[17]

---

[13] Indeed, as Easton and Dennis demonstrate, by the sixth grade, children have developed a large repertory of system-relevant sentiments. See David Easton and Jack Dennis, *Children in the Political System* (New York: McGraw-Hill, Inc., 1969), pt. 3.

[14] Zeigler, *The Political Life of American Teachers*, pp. 21–25.

[15] John C. Weizer and James E. Hayes, "Democratic Attitudes of Teachers and Prospective Teachers," *Phi Delta Kappan*, 47, No. 9 (May 1966), pp. 476–481.

[16] Leslie Y. Rabkin, "Dogmatism of Teachers," *Journal of Teacher Education*, 17, No. 3 (Spring 1966), pp. 47–49.

[17] See, for example, Else Frenkel-Brunswik, "Further Explorations by a Contributor to 'The Authoritarian Personality,'" in Richard Christie and Marie Jahoda (eds.), *Studies in the Scope and Method of "The Authoritarian Personality"* (New York: The Free Press, 1954), pp. 226–276.

Our interest in the political attitudes of teachers may be traced directly to Hess and Torney's contention that the school is the American society's major conveyor of democratic values.[18] We have already presented evidence that, while disputing this position, still affirms a positive role for educational quality. We now return to the question in a new context. We assume that a sizable gap between the political attitudes of twelfth-graders and their teachers would weaken the Hess and Torney hypothesis even further. If the school is effective, students should finish their education with values closely parallel to those of their teachers. Thus, should we discover a close correspondence between twelfth-graders and teachers, Hess and Torney's contention would gain support.

TABLE 6-7. MEAN MAJORITY RULE AND POLITICAL EFFICACY
SCORES OF TEACHERS AND TWELFTH-GRADERS
IN TWO SCHOOL DISTRICTS

Dimension	Group	Mean
Majority rule	Twelfth-graders	2.11 (413)[a]
	Teachers	2.72 (209)
Political efficacy	Twelfth-graders	1.40 (403)[a]
	Teachers	1.68 (208)

[a] Majority rule was measured by four items, political efficacy by two.

We were unfortunately unable to compare teachers and twelfth-graders on each of our value dimensions. We were forced to restrict ourselves to two values and also to the investigation of party identification. The two dimensions we selected are majority rule and political efficacy.[19] As Table 6-7 reveals, there is a sizable

[18] Robert D. Hess and Judith Torney, *The Development of Political Attitudes* (London: Aldine Publishing Co., 1967), p. 101.
[19] Because we performed our factor analysis of student attitudes only after planning and administering the teacher questionnaire, we could not include one of the twelfth-grade political-efficacy items in our analysis of teachers. This item was "The poor person should be helped to take part in politics because he doesn't have as good a chance as the rich man." Hence, the political-efficacy score here involves a comparison of teacher and student responses to the remaining two twelfth-grade political-efficacy components: (1) people in the government care what people like my parents think and (2) the whole

gap between teachers and twelfth-graders on both of these dimensions. Teachers are markedly more democratic than their twelfth-grade students in each case.

The teachers have not elevated their students to the high level of democratic support that they themselves occupy. Do we find the same discrepancy when we examine party identification? Specifically, are Hess and Torney correct in their belief that teachers transmit the norm of independence from partisanship to their students?[20] As we mentioned earlier, Hess and Torney utilize voting intention to measure partisan identification. We anticipated findings substantially different from theirs if we employed the standard Survey Research Center self-identification question. Our expectations are confirmed, as Table 6-8 demonstrates.

TABLE 6-8. PARTY IDENTIFICATION OF TEACHERS AND STUDENTS IN TWO SCHOOL DISTRICTS (IN PERCENT)

Group	Party			
	Republican	Democrat	Independent	Don't know
6th-graders	23 ($n = 131$)	23 ($n = 129$)	9 ($n = 49$)	42 ($n = 237$)
9th-graders	23 ($n = 118$)	32 ($n = 166$)	12 ($n = 65$)	25 ($n = 129$)
12th-graders	18 ($n = 76$)	27 ($n = 112$)	21 ($n = 89$)	26 ($n = 109$)
Teachers	33 ($n = 69$)	45 ($n = 94$)	19 ($n = 39$)	1 ($n = 5$)

Table 6-8 illustrates two things. The first is the critical importance of the wording of questions in social research. Hess and Torney, using their unusual index of partisanship, report that 26 percent of their sixth-graders and 55 percent of their teachers were Independents.[21] We find, however, that teachers do not even

---

government is run by a few big, powerful men, and they don't care about us ordinary people. Of course, in the teacher protocols the wording of item 1 was altered to read, "People in the government care what people like me think."

[20] Hess and Torney, *The Development of Political Attitudes*, p. 90.

[21] Hess and Torney, *The Development of Political Attitudes*, p. 90.

possess a norm of independence. In fact, teachers are no more independent than any other population subgroup with comparable education.[22] Students do become more independent as they progress through school, but their shift is not nearly so drastic as Hess and Torney believe it to be.

This methodological point is less important than our substantive conclusion that teachers fail to socialize their students to partisanship. The substantial "don't-know" rate among twelfth-graders, when compared to the absence of partisan confusion among teachers, documents the inability of teachers to attract students into the party system that they themselves inhabit so easily.

Let us now return our attention exclusively to teachers. Why have we characterized them as political ingenues? There are two major reasons. The first is that teachers possess only a fragmented picture of the communities in which they teach. The second is that teachers maintain little contact with other groups in the community. Thus, the respondents function in a political vacuum, having neither the knowledge nor the connections necessary to understand decision making in their districts. Indeed, our guess is that teachers in ghetto schools are more sensitive to the politics of education within their communities than are teachers in districts like Chalmers and Moss City.

That our teachers are profoundly ignorant about the local politics of education became obvious early in the analysis. A third of the sample, 33 percent (68), could not identify a single community group that affected the schools in their districts. Of those who could name any groups, almost half specified only one. Most of the respondents did not even mention the local Parent-Teacher Association, a group constantly and visibly in touch with the doings of education. The only organizations that teachers believe have a continuous and widespread effect on the schools consist of businessmen; here the Chamber of Commerce appears prominently. In answer to another question, one-fifth of the respondents could not name any local group that consistently supported education. In this case, however, 36 percent (76) mentioned the PTA. The only other pro-education groups teachers specified were again composed mainly of businessmen.

---

[22] For indications of party identification among comparably educated white-collar groups, see Angus Campbell *et al., The American Voter* (New York: John Wiley and Sons, Inc., 1960), p. 479.

Despite their efforts, such lay supporters of education as the Chalmers Tax-Override Committee and the Chalmers School-Community Coordinating Council have not had much impact on teachers. The failure of most lay groups is even more surprising when we realize that, at least in Chalmers, their political activities have attracted much newspaper coverage. By contrast, the groups that teachers mention most frequently, the PTA and businessmen, exert little overt political influence on education. The Parent-Teacher Associations are generally impotent at the state level and, in local affairs, usually function as spokesmen for the superintendent.[23] Despite their desire that the schools produce competent employees, businessmen usually become most politically involved as opponents of rising school costs. Therefore, it is hard to view them as consistent friends of education.

However ill-perceived are the supporters of education, almost invisible are the opponents of the schools. Three-fourths of our teachers, 72 percent (151), could not name a single community group that was critical of the educational system. The only organization a reasonable number, 11 percent (22), mentioned was the John Birch Society, which, so far as one could tell, had little influence on educational policy in the two districts.[24]

We can offer two interpretations of these findings. The first is that the teachers perceive their communities accurately. Perhaps in middle-class communities the schools inhabit a kind of political vacuum.[25] Certainly, the low voter interest in school elections lends

[23] For indications of the comparative unimportance of PTA's in state politics, see Nicholas Masters, Robert H. Salisbury, and Thomas H. Eliot, *State Politics and the Public Schools* (New York: Alfred A. Knopf, 1964), pp. 176 ff. On the supportive role of PTA's in local politics, see Neal Gross, *Who Runs Our Schools?* (New York: John Wiley and Sons, Inc., 1958), pp. 36–37.

[24] Observation suggests that local opposition to the schools, though widespread, is disorganized. This pattern clearly seems to hold in the case of the recent Chalmers referendum loss, where the newspaper continued to point out that there was no organized opposition. It appears that the supporters of education, though better organized than their opponents, are unable to make their organization pay off. For further discussion of the role of citizen organizations in local school politics and in related local political matters, see James S. Coleman, *Community Conflict* (New York: The Free Press, 1957).

[25] For an empirical investigation supporting this interpretation, see David W. Minar, "The Community Basis of Conflict in School Politics," *American Sociological Review*, 31, No. 4 (December 1966), pp. 822–835.

credibility to this contention; maybe there is no structure to school politics in districts like Moss City and Chalmers.

However, a comparison of our findings with those reported by Gross in his study of superintendents leaves us much less impressed with this interpretation. Many more of Gross's respondents than of our teachers reported organized opposition to the public schools. For example, while 38 percent of his superintendents named public officials as opponents of public education,[26] not one of our teachers even mentioned government figures. Teachers are somehow less aware than superintendents of what local politics of education does exist.

We believe that teacher ignorance about the local politics of education may be explained partly by the relative isolation of the teaching profession. Our interpretation parallels that of Jennings, who writes, "Teachers . . . were seldom consciously aware that other people were trying to influence their handling of sensitive course content. . . ."[27] The isolation of teaching from the com-

TABLE 6-9. PROPORTION OF TEACHERS REPORTING SUGGESTIONS ABOUT THEIR INSTRUCTION FROM VARIOUS SOURCES

Source group	Percent of teachers reporting suggestions
Superiors	62 (132)
Other teachers	51 (108)
Parents	26 (56)
Community groups	2 (5)

munity first manifested itself when we examined the extent to which our respondents had received "suggestions" to "improve or change" their instruction from parents, other teachers, community groups, or superiors. That we were not permitted to ask a more direct question about outside interference in teaching becomes fortunate in retrospect, for the diffuseness of our items gave our respondents maximum leeway for an affirmative answer. Despite this fact, teachers rarely perceived themselves as subject to outside pressure. (See Table 6-9.)

[26] Gross, *Who Runs Our Schools?*, p. 20.
[27] Jennings, "Observations on the Study of Political Values among Pre-Adults," p. 20.

The major influences on the teacher came from within the school. Even the few teachers who reported parental pressure carefully noted that most parents were concerned primarily about discipline and teaching techniques. Only 2 percent (5) of the entire sample reported having parents question course content. In addition, as Table 6-9 also indicates, community groups almost never interfere in any way with teaching.

Explaining these findings again poses a challenge. Perhaps the teachers simply underestimated the total amount of interference to which they were subjected. This is clearly the interpretation that Jennings prefers, for he writes that his findings are "conservative."[28] It is also possible that, had we been able to ask a more direct set of questions, we might have obtained different results. We doubt, however, that another item would have altered the relative standing of the four groups. We also suspect that a teacher's unpleasant experiences with outsiders are vivid enough to trigger responses to the question we did ask.

It may also be true that teachers utilize the process of anticipated reactions to shape their material so that it will not offend others. But surely the respondents' widespread classroom treatment of controversial issues often finds them saying potentially dangerous things.

We are therefore led to a third, more attractive alternative. We believe that little of what occurs in the classroom travels from child to parent or from parent to community. Teaching is so wholly taken for granted that few parents check closely into the content of instruction. The few who do and become alarmed take their complaints to administrators, to the superintendent, or to the school board, but not to individual teachers. Consequently, the respondents operate in a strange sort of autonomy, cut off from most of the community. If their gain is control over their teaching, their loss is information about their clientele. Hence, a close relationship exists between the lack of community interest in the teacher and the absence of teacher knowledge about the community. Teachers thus become, within their limited sphere, expressive ingenues.

---

[28] Jennings, "Observations on the Study of Political Values among Pre-Adults," p. 20.

INTERDISTRICT COMPARISONS

Does Chalmers' extra educational effort produce a discernible impact on the characerictics and attitudes of its teachers? More broadly, do the beliefs and behaviors of teachers truly forge a link between educational policy making on the one hand and political socialization on the other? Our answers to these questions are consistent with those we ventured earlier about political socialization in the two districts. Teachers in Chalmers do differ in the expected directions from those in Moss City, but the trend is weak and incommensurate with the markedly different educational commitments of the two districts.

We questioned the teachers about five components of their professional environment. We predicted that teachers in Chalmers would excel in each area. In fact, Chalmers proved superior in but three—and in these, marginally. Only a few individual items distinguished strongly between teachers in the districts. We will judge the superiority of one district's teaching environment over the other's, first by surveying the sheer number of a component's items in which teachers in one district surpass teachers in the other, and then by paying special attention to the few items in each component that reach levels of statistical significance.

We first investigated teacher qualifications. We expected that Chalmers' high salaries, small classes, and innovative programs would attract teachers with superior credentials. The following items allowed us to compare teacher qualifications in the districts:

1. Cosmopolitanism of undergraduate colleges
2. Proportion of teachers holding advanced degrees
3. Proportion of teachers having academic rather than education degrees
4. Quality of undergraduate colleges from which teachers graduated
5. Undergraduate grade averages of teachers
6. Proportion of teachers currently taking courses to supplement teaching
7. Proportion of teachers possessing tenure

Taken together, these seven bits of information form a comprehensive quality index of the teachers' educational backgrounds.

The more cosmopolitan the collegiate training of a district's teachers, the more advanced degrees held, and the more work done in academic courses, the deeper and more diverse is education in the district likely to be.[29] In addition, the higher the quality of the undergraduate college from which a teacher received her degree, the richer should be her teaching performance.[30] The same consideration applies to the teacher's scholastic success, as measured by her grade-point average. Current course work usually grows out of the teacher's area of instruction and should, therefore, raise her effectiveness. Finally, we already have evidence of a positive relationship between the experience of a teaching staff and its capacity to raise student achievement.[31] The proportion of teachers posses-

TABLE 6-10. TEACHER QUALIFICATIONS IN MOSS CITY
AND CHALMERS[a]

| Item | District | |
	Moss City	Chalmers
Cosmopolitanism of universities	x	
Advanced degrees		x
Academic versus education preparation	(tie)[b]	
Quality of colleges		x
Undergraduate grade averages		x
Current course work		x
Possession of tenure		x

[a] x denotes the superior district.
[b] When no more than 5 percent separated the districts, we saw no reason to consider the difference worth reporting.

sing tenure is, of course, a rough measure of teacher experience. Table 6-10 summarizes the qualifications of teachers in the two districts.

[29] Coleman uses each of these indices to measure teacher quality. James S. Coleman *et al., Equality of Educational Opportunity* (Washington, D.C.: Government Printing Office, 1966), pp. 122, 135–140.
[30] The quality of a teacher's undergraduate college was judged by reference to the criteria offered in Alexander W. Astin, *Who Goes Where to College* (Chicago: Science Research Associates, Inc., 1965).
[31] William G. Mollenkopf and S. Donald Melville, "A Study of Secondary School Characteristics as Related to Test Scores," (Princeton, N.J.: Educational Testing Service, 1956), p. 21.

Teachers in Chalmers are superior on five of the seven items. Still, on only two, did we discover strong differences between the districts. Tables 6-11 and 6-12 report these two items in detail.

TABLE 6-11. QUALITY OF UNIVERSITIES FROM WHICH TEACHERS IN MOSS CITY AND CHALMERS GRADUATED (IN PERCENT)[a]

Quality	District	
	Moss City	Chalmers
Distinguished	00.0	2.3 (2)
Strong	15.7 (19)	31.4 (27)
Adequate plus	67.8 (82)	54.7 (47)
Adequate	9.1 (11)	10.5 (9)
Indeterminate	7.4 (9)	1.2 (1)
Totals	100 (121)	100 (86)

[a] $x^2 = 13.97$ with 4 degrees of freedom; significant at .007 level.

TABLE 6-12. PROPORTION OF TEACHERS IN MOSS CITY AND CHALMERS POSSESSING TENURE (IN PERCENT)[a]

Tenure	District	
	Moss City	Chalmers
Have tenure	53.3 (65)	70.9 (61)
Do not have tenure	46.7 (57)	29.1 (25)
Totals	100 (122)	100 (86)

[a] $x^2 = 5.86$ with 1 degree of freedom; significant at .01 level.

The Chalmers teaching staff is much more experienced and much better trained than the Moss City staff. For this reason, and also because scores on five of the seven items favored Chalmers, it seems fair to conclude that Chalmers teachers are more qualified than Moss City teachers.

Both our measurements of and judgments about teacher qualifications were comparatively straightforward. We find it considerably more difficult, however, to assess morale among teachers, for several reasons. One problem is that most behavioral indices—

such as the employee turnover rate or the amount of absenteeism in an industry—constitute ambiguous measures of morale.[32] For example, turnover is often related more closely to the peculiar economic conditions of an industry than to employee attitudes. There is no easy way out of this dilemma. Consequently, we have defined morale broadly as a patterned set of reactions to teaching. We view morale as a compendium of teacher attitudes about students, fellow teachers, self, and district. Thus, teachers who respect and like their colleagues, who have good friends in the district, who enjoy their students, who have a favorable view of their own efforts, and who feel the district to be a good environment in which to work manifest high levels of morale. Certainly such teachers are emotionally integrated into their districts. Accordingly, we have investigated the following teacher attitudes:

1. Teacher views of the salary schedule in the district
2. Teacher views of instructional conditions in the district
3. Teacher ratings of own performance
4. Teacher perception of own effort
5. Teacher perception of student responsiveness
6. Teacher perception of own acceptance by students
7. Teacher perception of cooperativeness of students
8. Teacher perception of students' willingness to work
9. Number of teacher's friends in the district
10. Closeness of teacher's friends in the district
11. Teacher perception of extent to which colleagues care about her teaching ability
12. Teacher perception of extent to which colleagues care about her as a person

A glance at Table 6-13 indicates how little there is to choose between teacher morale in the two districts. By and large, the Chalmers respondents do not believe that the instructional environment created for them by innovation and tax dollars has brought with it superior teaching conditions. Although Chalmers teachers have a high opinion of themselves, their views of students are no more generous than are the judgments of their Moss City counter-

---

[32] See Philip B. Appelwhite, *Organizational Behavior* (Englewood Cliffs, N.J.: Prentice-Hall, Inc., 1965), pp. 28 ff.

TABLE 6-13. TEACHER MORALE IN CHALMERS AND MOSS CITY

| Measure | District[a] | |
	Moss City	Chalmers
Views of the salary schedule		X
Views of teaching conditions	X	
Ratings of own performance		X
Perception of own effort as a teacher		X
Perception of student responsiveness	X	
Perception of own acceptance by students		X
Perception of cooperativeness of students	X	
Perception of students' willingness to work		X
Number of friends in the district	X	
Closeness of friends in the district		X
Perception of extent to which colleagues care about own teaching ability	X	
Perception of extent to which colleagues care about teacher as a person	(tie)	

[a] x denotes the district with the highest morale.

parts. In addition, neither the smallness of Chalmers nor the innovative character of its education produces a particularly warm or stimulating teaching environment.

The inconclusiveness of our findings is further highlighted by the fact that only one of our thirteen items reached statistical significance. Not surprisingly, this is the item that solicited opinions about the salary schedule, but even this finding is trivial. Had teachers in Chalmers not been aware of their favored salary position, we would have been forced to question all the assumptions that underlie the teacher portion of our study; the data reported in Table 6-14 saves us from such a painful task.

Our attempt to assess morale may have yielded ambiguous results, but there is no uncertainty about interdistrict differences in the perception of teaching burdens. As Table 6-15 indicates, Moss City teachers feel themselves much less pressured than Chalmers teachers. Perhaps in its anxiety to attain educational superiority, Chalmers finds it necessary to place a heavy work load on its teachers. On the other hand, the organization of the Chalmers

TABLE 6-14. VIEWS OF THEIR SALARY SCHEDULE BY MOSS CITY
AND CHALMERS TEACHERS (IN PERCENT)[a]

| | District | |
Response	Moss City	Chalmers
Unsatisfactory	33.9 (41)	14.0 (12)
Satisfactory	65.3 (79)	62.8 (54)
Superior	0.8 (1)	23.3 (20)
Totals	100 (121)	100 (86)

[a] $x^2 = 32.77$ with 2 degrees of freedom; significant at .0001 level.

schools may be less efficient in some ways than the organization of the Moss City schools.[33]

Not only is the pattern of teaching burdens unmistakable, but there are also more items that reach statistical significance on this dimension than on any other. The burdens index therefore distinguishes most clearly between the districts. Tables 6-16 through 6-19 report the strongest findings in this dimension.

Only with regard to the retention of credentials do Chalmers teachers feel comparatively little pressure. This finding, because it directly reflects the experience structure of the districts, has little importance. More teachers in Chalmers than in Moss City possess

TABLE 6-15. TEACHING BURDENS IN MOSS CITY AND CHALMERS

| | District[a] | |
Measure	Moss City	Chalmers
Burden of classroom instruction	x	
Burden of grading	(tie)	
Burden of extracurricular activities	x	
Burden of teacher-parent conferences	x	
Burden of record keeping	x	
Burden of retaining credentials		x
Burden of faculty meetings	x	

[a] x denotes the district with the lightest burden.

[33] We have already presented evidence of teacher dissatisfaction with administrators in Chalmers. We have no way of knowing how widespread this situation was at the time of our field work, but, by July 1969, it had made the local paper. See Chalmers Bugle, July 9, 1969.

TABLE 6-16. BURDEN OF EXTRACURRICULAR ACTIVITIES IN
MOSS CITY AND CHALMERS (IN PERCENT)[a]

Degree of Burden	District	
	Moss City	Chalmers
Little burden	59.8 (73)	39.1 (34)
Moderate burden	35.2 (43)	46.0 (40)
Heavy burden	4.9 (6)	14.9 (13)
Totals	100 (122)	100 (87)

[a] $x^2 = 11.36$ with 2 degrees of freedom; significant at .003 level.

TABLE 6-17. BURDEN OF TEACHER-PARENT CONFERENCES IN
MOSS CITY AND CHALMERS (IN PERCENT)[a]

Degree of Burden	District	
	Moss City	Chalmers
Little burden	69.7 (85)	42.5 (37)
Moderate burden	23.0 (28)	46.0 (40)
Heavy burden	7.4 (9)	11.5 (10)
Totals	100 (122)	100 (87)

[a] $x^2 = 15.63$ with 2 degrees of freedom; significant at .0004 level.

TABLE 6-18. BURDEN OF RETAINING CREDENTIALS IN MOSS CITY
AND CHALMERS (IN PERCENT)[a]

Degree of Burden	District	
	Moss City	Chalmers
Little burden	57.4 (70)	69.0 (60)
Moderate burden	33.6 (41)	18.4 (16)
Heavy burden	9.0 (11)	12.6 (11)
Totals	100 (122)	100 (87)

[a] $x^2 = 6.04$ with 2 degrees of freedom; significant at .04 level.

tenure. Therefore, fewer need to worry about credentials. In all
other respects, Moss City teachers are more relaxed than their
counterparts in Chalmers. Again, we can only observe that these
findings can be interpreted either as evidence of the educational
vitality of Chalmers or of poor administrative organization in that

TABLE 6-19. BURDEN OF FACULTY MEETINGS IN MOSS CITY AND
CHALMERS (IN PERCENT)[a]

| | District | |
Degree of Burden	Moss City	Chalmers
Little burden	54.9 (67)	25.3 (22)
Moderate burden	36.1 (44)	57.5 (50)
Heavy burden	9.0 (11)	17.2 (15)
Totals	100 (122)	100 (87)

[a] $x^2 = 18.40$ with 2 degrees of freedom; significant at .0001 level.

district. There seems no easy method of choosing between these
two interpretations, but support for the latter comes from the fact
that, as we have seen, teachers in Chalmers do take a slightly
more jaundiced view of administrators than do teachers in Moss
City. In addition, the student data we have already surveyed indicate that the burdens borne by Chalmers teachers do not pay
off strongly or consistently in the effective socialization of students.
Therefore, whether such burdens are necessary to quality education
is doubtful. That they are not sufficient is certain.

The educational effort put forth by Chalmers does not prevent its teachers from feeling pressure. However, Chalmers teachers
at least appreciate the effort itself. Table 6-20 summarizes scores
on our fourth index of educational climate, teacher perception of
community support for education. The pattern is clear enough, but
only one of the items produced significant differences. Importantly,
however, this was the summary item, number 5, which elicited the
findings in Table 6-21.

Finally, Chalmers teachers score marginally higher than Moss
City teachers on our last index of educational climate—political
participation. Unfortunately, our investigation of this dimension is
less satisfactory than our examination of those other environmental
components about which we have already reported. Only three
questions—each dealing with voting in a different arena—constitute our measure. Nevertheless, Table 6-22 reveals a weak trend.

Virtually all the respondents, regardless of district, vote in
national elections. However, as the span of the electoral arena
narrows, differences between the districts emerge. Ten percent
more of Chalmers than of Moss City teachers vote in every local

TABLE 6-20. PERCEPTION OF COMMUNITY SUPPORT FOR
EDUCATION AMONG MOSS CITY AND CHALMERS TEACHERS

	District[a]	
Item	Moss City	Chalmers
Things community could do for teachers		x
Number of things community could do for teachers		x
Things community could do for schools	(tie)	
Number of things community could do for schools		x
Amount of support community gives education		x

[a] x indicates the district with the highest perception of support.

TABLE 6-21. AMOUNT OF COMMUNITY SUPPORT FOR EDUCATION
AS SEEN BY CHALMERS AND MOSS CITY TEACHERS
(IN PERCENT)[a]

	District		
Amount of support	Moss City		Chalmers
Very little	5.0	(6)	0.0
A moderate amount	69.7	(83)	43.7 (38)
A great deal	25.2	(30)	56.3 (49)
Totals	100	(119)	100 (87)

[a] $x^2 = 22.89$ with 2 degrees of freedom; significant at .00001 level.

election. Of course, none of these items produces statistically significant findings. The trend is, indeed, weak.

SUMMARY AND CONCLUSION

Apparently teachers react only marginally to the educational inputs of administrators and communities. The differences between teachers in the two districts, though favoring Chalmers, are weak and blurred. So indistinct are they that we are reluctant to attribute them to district-related factors. Only if we had discovered a marked and consistent pattern would we have concluded unequivocally that community expenditures and program quality recruit superior, content, unburdened, politically aware teachers capable of effectively socializing their students to democracy. Thus, there is as tenuous a link between educational effort and teacher characteristics as there is between educational inputs and democratic socialization.

What are some possible explanations for the unresponsiveness of teacher recruitment to educational effort? That teaching remains primarily a female profession certainly influences our findings. Female teachers who marry usually discover that their own job preferences must be subordinated to those of their husbands. Consequently, many female teachers cannot respond to the quality of a district or to their own preferences. This occupational pattern obviously limits the capacity of a district such as Chalmers to recruit good teachers.

Parallel considerations reduce the married female teacher's sensitivity to salary differentials. Because the income of such a teacher generally only supplements that of her husband, she is free to concentrate on other than monetary aspects of education.

Of course, a married female teacher may value the educational quality of one district, but this consideration may be outweighed by the proximity of a second district to her home or by the socioeconomic, ethnic, or racial composition of a third district.[34] Thus, educational impacts have a major impact only on certain kinds of teachers.[35]

These factors are reinforced by sex-role norms. Many in the larger society view teaching as only an extension of the maternal, selfless, child-rearing role. Such a perspective militates against the female teacher's attention to such selfish interests as salary. Male teachers, of course, need fear no such cultural sanctions should they make salary a matter of high priority in their selection of a position.

[34] For conservative estimates of the proportion of teachers nationally who take such factors into account, see Coleman *et al., Equality of Educational Opportunity*, p. 170.

[35] See also Ward S. Mason, *The Beginning Teacher* (Washington, D.C.: Government Printing Office, 1961), pp. 74–75.

TABLE 6-22. POLITICAL PARTICIPATION AMONG TEACHERS IN
CHALMERS AND MOSS CITY

	District[a]	
Item	Moss City	Chalmers
Frequency of voting in national elections	(tie)	
Frequency of voting in state elections		x
Frequency of voting in local elections		x

[a] x indicates the district with the greatest frequency.

A last factor that influences the commitment of teachers to a district is geographic mobility. There is no requirement that teachers reside in their district; in fact, many do not. Consequently, quite a few maintain only limited out-of-school contact with their districts or their students. A quick check of the marginals reveals the wide dispersion of the teachers. At the time of the interview, 69 percent of the Chalmers respondents and 53 percent of those in Moss City lived outside their districts. Of course, regardless of where they live, those teachers who are also mothers have little opportunity to stay in the mainstream of their district's activities.

The "absent teacher" is certainly familiar to ghetto dwellers. White teachers enter the ghetto in the morning only to retreat swiftly to suburbia at night. In Los Angeles, this pattern generalizes beyond the ghetto. For one thing, community loyalties are too few to be a hindrance. In addition, freeways speed transportation over the vast expanse of the metropolitan area. If the Los Angeles pattern spreads to other American cities in the years to come, school administrators nationally will find it ever more difficult to recruit dedicated teaching staffs.

Chapter 7
Teacher Differences and Educational Climates

The four purposes of this chapter are (1) to determine the extent and character of differences among teachers, (2) to estimate the incidence of these differences in our districts, (3) to compare the districts once more, this time controlling for relevant teacher variables, and (4) to speculate about some implications our findings have for the interaction of teacher recruitment, educational environment, and the professional structure of teaching. This chapter is an analogue to Chapter 5, where we examined the major effects that variations among students had upon the capacity of our districts to inculcate democratic values. Now we focus on those variations among teachers that condition the relationship of educational inputs to the process of teacher recruitment. In general, differences among teachers loosen the connection between input and recruitment.

Despite the fact that teachers are relatively homogeneous,

there remain some meaningful differences within the teacher population, which fall into a clear pattern. Importantly, this pattern is most distinct in Chalmers and sheds particular light on political socialization in that district.

Many variables could reasonably be expected to distinguish among teachers. Take, for example, tenure. Jennings and Zeigler report that teachers with tenure are not only more conservative educationally than less experienced teachers, but are also more reluctant to introduce politics into the classroom.[1] It is unclear whether Jennings' and Zeigler's finding should be attributed to the age differentials between tenured and nontenured personnel or to varying lengths of exposure to occupational norms. A related possibility, of course, is that tenured teachers may be more sensitive than nontenured teachers to the constraints under which the community permits the schools to operate.

Many observers have cited the sex composition of teaching as another source of differentiation. Of course, large numbers of men now teach, particularly in high schools. Thus, men comprise 57 percent of American high-school teachers, as opposed to only 12 percent of elementary-school teachers. It is not surprising, therefore, that "high school teachers throughout the country are sensitive to the fact that the pronoun 'she' is almost invariably used in discussions about teachers. . . ."[2] We would naturally deduce that sex differences, which Zeigler believes to be central to the political life of American education,[3] should manifest themselves most completely in the secondary school.

Jennings and Zeigler also record substantial differences between teachers whose college major was education and those whose major was not. Education majors not only repress the discussion of political issues in the classroom, but also follow politics less than noneducation majors. In addition, education majors apparently acquiesce to administrative authority more readily than noneducation majors. Finally, education majors are more likely than other teachers to view the school as a custodial institution.[4]

---

[1] M. Kent Jennings and Harmon Zeigler, "Political Expressivism among High School Teachers: The Intersection of Community and Occupational Values," unpublished, 1967, p. 22.

[2] Harmon Zeigler, The Political Life of American Teachers (Englewood Cliffs, N.J.: Prentice-Hall, Inc., 1967), p. 14.

[3] Zeigler, The Political Life of American Teachers, chap. 1.

[4] Jennings and Zeigler, "Political Expressivism among High School Teachers."

We might also hypothesize a relationship between the level of a teacher's college performance and her perspective on teaching. Perhaps teachers who did well in college expect more from themselves and from their students than do other teachers. If so, the gap between hope and accomplishment might be so wide among such teachers as to alienate them from the educational process. Alternatively, we could predict that, because they are unable to perform as well or to obtain as many rewards as their more intelligent colleagues, it is the dull teachers who are the most dissatisfied with the school.

Only multivariate analysis would enable us to examine the effects of all these variables simultaneously. Luckily, however, we need not resort to any such analysis. There are but two major structural differences between teachers: that between elementary- and secondary-school teachers, and that among secondary-school teachers of different fields. The other major source of differentiation, sex, underlies the two structural patterns just mentioned. We have already argued that the varying perspectives of male and female teachers should contribute to divisions between elementary- and secondary-school teachers. In addition, 64 percent of the high-school social-studies teachers in our sample are male, as opposed to only 50 percent of the high-school teachers of other subjects. Therefore, within the high school, it is the social studies teachers who enunciate a distinctly male viewpoint.

Structural differences between high-school and elementary-school teachers, and among high-school teachers apparently summarize differences in the sex composition of teaching. Moreover, differences between those teachers who did the majority of their undergraduate work in education and those who did not also add to elementary-secondary antagonisms. Of the elementary-school teachers, 82 percent had taken the majority of their courses in education. By contrast, only 32 percent of the high-school teachers had done most of their work in education. In keeping with the pattern we are developing, only 23 percent of the high-school social-studies teachers, as opposed to 37 percent of other high-school teachers, had taken a majority of their courses in education. Again, social-studies teachers stand out as a group apart.

Neither grade average nor tenure produces strong or consistent differences among the teachers. We do find many important cleavages between male and female teachers, however, and we also discover some differences among teachers who took varying amounts of education courses. These patterns are interesting in their own right, but our major concern is with the way in which they affect the structure of the school system. Our interests in this study center on the interaction of educational climate and political socialization. Therefore, variations in that climate, as expressed in school structure, will claim the bulk of our attention in this chapter.[5]

PERSPECTIVES OF ELEMENTARY-SCHOOL AND SECONDARY-SCHOOL TEACHERS

We will adhere in this chapter to the format followed in Chapter 6. We will first compare secondary- and elementary-school teachers on our indices of qualifications, morale, perception of burdens, evaluation of community support, and political participation. We will then give special attention to individual items that distinguish most strongly between elementary- and secondary-school teachers.

Our first index of climate is the qualifications of teachers. Table 7-1 suggests that secondary-school teachers are no better prepared than elementary-school teachers. However, secondary-school teachers are more qualified on the one statistically significant item, as indicated in Table 7-2.

It is necessary to reconsider the weak findings reported in Table 7-1. For one thing, many Chalmers elementary-school teachers must take course work in nongraded education to prepare themselves for teaching in their district's two new nongraded elementary schools. We doubt that elementary-school teachers in other districts need to be as active as Chalmers elementary-school teachers. Therefore, we probably ought not to generalize findings on this item beyond the sample districts. In addition, secondary-

---

[5] In short, we are really trying to justify our engaging in a form of spurious correlation. Were we to be statistical purists, we would explain all our findings in this chapter by reference to sex ·differences. Since we are interested primarily in educational structure, however, we believe it warranted to interpret our findings in structural terms, rather than in terms of the sex composition of teaching. It is the effects of sex composition on educational structure that concerns us, not the sex composition itself.

TABLE 7-1. QUALIFICATIONS OF ELEMENTARY- AND SECONDARY-SCHOOL TEACHERS IN MOSS CITY AND CHALMERS[a]

| Item | Teaching level | |
	Elementary	Secondary
Cosmopolitanism of universities		x
Advanced degrees		x
Academic versus educational preparation		x
Quality of colleges	x	
Undergraduate grade average	(tie)	
Current course work	x	
Possession of tenure	x	

[a] x denotes the superior level.

school teachers are not only more cosmopolitan than elementary-school teachers, but more of them also hold advanced degrees and draw upon substantive course work than do elementary-school teachers. Taken together, these findings suggest that secondary-school teachers have a slightly more intellectual bent than elementary teachers. Significantly different proportions of elementary-school and secondary-school teachers have earned advanced degrees. (See Table 7-2.)

TABLE 7-2. PROPORTION OF ELEMENTARY- AND SECONDARY-SCHOOL TEACHERS POSSESSING ADVANCED DEGREES (IN PERCENT)

| Teaching level | Advanced degrees | | Totals |
	Yes	No	
Elementary	20 (16)	80 (62)	100 (78)
Secondary	45 (58)	55 (72)	100 (130)
Totals	36 (74)	64 (134)	100 (208)

Elementary-secondary differences become sharper when we examine morale at the two levels of teaching. As Table 7-3 indicates, secondary-school teachers are consistently more dissatisfied with teaching than are elementary-school teachers.

Many secondary-school teachers complain that they are paid too little and that teaching conditions are poor. Many others have

TABLE 7-3. MORALE AMONG SECONDARY- AND
ELEMENTARY-SCHOOL TEACHERS[b]

	Level taught	
Item	Elementary	Secondary
Views of the salary schedule	x[a] [b]	
Views of teaching conditions	x[a]	
Ratings of own performance	(tie)	
Perception of own effort	(tie)	
Perception of student responsiveness	x	
Perception of own acceptance by students	x[a]	
Perception of cooperativeness of students		x
Perception of students' willingness to work	x[a]	
Number of friends in the district	(tie)	
Closeness of friends in the district	x	
Perception of the extent to which colleagues care about teaching	x	
Perception of extent to which colleagues care about teacher as a person	x[a]	

[a] Items significant at .05 level.
[b] x denotes the superior level.

jaundiced views of their students and are at best skeptical about their colleagues. How can we account for these findings?

Sex differentials are responsible for much of what we find. Each of the five items that produced statistically significant differences between elementary-school and secondary-school teachers also yielded significant and expectable differences between male and female teachers. Men are must less content with teaching than women. But are there any other considerations to be weighed?

We believe that sex differences lay only a motivational foundation for cleavages in teacher orientations. The actual experiences of high-school and elementary-school teachers add motivational superstructures. In fact, teaching is harder at the high-school level than at the elementary-school level. Uncooperative, wily high-school students can make their teachers miserable. Unruly elementary-school children, however, rarely possess the necessary subtlety for consistently aggravating misbehavior. In addition, the innocence and charm that can redeem a troublesome student for his elementary-school teacher have long vanished by adolescence. Moreover, growing cynicism about the school and the upsurge of outside interests—such as cars, sex, and athletics—deflect the high-schooler's attention from education. Small wonder that many high-school teachers find their students burdensome.

As we have indicated, we have reason to believe that high-school teachers are more intellectually aware than elementary-school teachers. If we are right, we would expect the high-school teacher to be especially bitter about the disappointments of teaching. After all, the gap between aspirations and accomplishments should yawn the widest among the more intellectually committed teachers. In addition, their training in substantive fields and their possession of advanced degrees may convince high-school teachers that they deserve autonomy in the classroom. If so, we would expect high-school teachers to be especially resentful of administrative supervision. We probed these hypotheses by utilizing three items. We first asked the respondents to choose between two statements, one of which characterized teaching as unprofessional and unsatisfying, the other of which described teaching as rewarding. Next we asked the teachers to decide whether administrators are skilled professionals doing a useful job or just ex-teachers for whom salary considerations are all-important. Finally, we asked the respondents directly about their relationships with administrators. Tables 7-4, 7-5, and 7-6 report our findings.

TABLE 7-4. PROPORTION OF ELEMENTARY- AND SECONDARY-SCHOOL TEACHERS WHO FEEL TEACHING IS REWARDING VERSUS THOSE WHO FEEL IT IS NOT PROFESSIONAL (IN PERCENT)[a]

| School level | Teaching is: | | Totals |
	Not professional	Rewarding	
Elementary	24 (18)	76 (58)	100 (76)
Secondary	38 (47)	62 (77)	100 (124)
Totals	33 (65)	67 (135)	100 (200)

[a] $x^2 = 3.72$ with 1 degree of freedom; significant at .053.

These confirmatory results are, once again, partly attributable to the sex composition of teaching. Not only are men more critical than women of the rewards in teaching, but men also have fewer successful relationships with administrators than do women. Let

TABLE 7.5. PROPORTION OF ELEMENTARY- AND SECONDARY-
SCHOOL TEACHERS WHO FEEL THAT ADMINISTRATORS
ARE SKILLED PROFESSIONALS VERSUS THOSE WHO
FEEL ADMINISTRATORS ARE MERELY HIGH-
SALARIED EX-TEACHERS (IN PERCENT)

| School level | Administrators are: | | Total |
	High-salaried ex-teachers	Skilled professionals	
Elementary	39 (30)	61 (47)	100 (77)
Secondary	48 (62)	52 (67)	100 (129)
Totals	45 (92)	55 (114)	100 (206)

TABLE 7-6. RELATIONSHIPS OF ELEMENTARY- AND SECONDARY-
SCHOOL TEACHERS WITH ADMINISTRATORS (IN PERCENT)[a]

| School level | Relationship is: | | | Totals |
	Quite satis-factory	Moderately satisfactory	Not satis-factory	
Elementary	86 (67)	12 (9)	2 (2)	100 (78)
Secondary	75 (97)	25 (33)	0	100 (130)
Totals	79 (164)	20 (42)	1 (2)	100 (208)

[a] $x^2 = 8.75$ with 2 degrees of freedom; significant at .01 level.

us not forget, however, that the secondary school provides much ammunition for the alienation that men are prone to feel.

Our third measure of educational climates is the teacher's perception of the burdens the school places upon her. Table 7-7 indicates that elementary-school teachers feel considerably more burdened than do high-school teachers. There are significant differences on two of the seven pressures that high-school and elementary-school teachers are burdened by. Tables 7-8 and 7-9 report these data.

These relationships are again underpinned by the sex composition of elementary-school and secondary-school teaching. In most cases the differences between men and women parallel exactly the differences between high-school and elementary-school teachers.

TABLE 7-7. TEACHING BURDENS AS SEEN BY ELEMENTARY- AND
SECONDARY-SCHOOL TEACHERS

| Item | School level | |
	Elementary	Secondary
Burden of classroom instruction	(tie)	
Burden of grading	x[a]	
Burden of extracurricular activities	x	
Burden of teacher-parent conferences	x	
Burden of record keeping	x	
Burden of retaining credentials	(tie)	
Burden of faculty meetings	x	

[a] x indicates the level experiencing the greater burden.

Paradoxically, elementary-school teachers, who feel comparatively hard-pressed by their work, exhibit higher morale than high-school teachers, who do not feel especially burdened by teaching. In short, to our surprise there is a direct relationship between morale and burdens. How should we interpret this paradox? Perhaps their lesser qualifications persuade elementary-school teachers to expect little from either their own contribution to education or from the educational process itself. However, the well-educated male high-school teacher may exaggerate the minor burdens of his teaching because he wishes to see himself in a position of influence. Each additional demand he experiences, no matter how trivial, reminds him of his lowly status. In addition, his expectations about teaching may be just high enough to result in profound disillusionment when he considers the unglamorous actualities of instruction.

TABLE 7-8. BURDEN OF TEACHER-PARENT CONFERENCES AS SEEN
BY ELEMENTARY- AND SECONDARY-SCHOOL TEACHERS
(IN PERCENT)[a]

| Grade level | Degree of burden | | | |
	Little	Moderate	Heavy	Totals
Elementary	35 (27)	47 (37)	18 (14)	100 (78)
Secondary	73 (95)	24 (31)	3 (5)	100 (131)
Totals	58 (122)	33 (68)	9 (19)	100 (209)

[a] $x^2 = 31.26$ with 2 degrees of freedom; significant at .00001 level.

TABLE 7-9. BURDEN OF FACULTY MEETINGS AS SEEN BY
ELEMENTARY- AND SECONDARY-SCHOOL TEACHERS
(IN PERCENT)

Grade level	Little	Degree of burden Moderate	Heavy	Totals
Elementary	35 (27)	45 (35)	20 (16)	100 (78)
Secondary	47 (62)	45 (59)	8 (10)	100 (131)
Totals	43 (89)	45 (94)	12 (26)	100 (209)

$x^2 = 8.37$ with 2 degrees of freedom; significant at .015 level.

Thus, the psychological effects of teaching burdens in high school may outrun their objective incidence. In so doing, they may lead to the paradoxical disjunction we have observed between morale and burdens.[6]

TABLE 7-10. COMMUNITY SUPPORT OF THE SCHOOLS, AS SEEN BY
ELEMENTARY- AND SECONDARY-SCHOOL TEACHERS[a]

Item	Grade level Elementary	Secondary
Things community could do for teachers	x	
Number of things community could do		(tie)
Things community could do for schools	x	
Number of things community could do for schools	x	
Amount of support community gives education	x	

[a] x denotes teachers perceiving the greater support.

The general pattern we have been sketching reappears, though weakly, in the respondents' views about their community's support for education. High-school teachers are more critical of

[6] Readers will recognize this formulation as deriving largely from reference-group theory. We are suggesting that high-school teachers probably have different reference groups than elementary-school teachers. For an elucidation of reference-group theory, see Herbert H. Hyman and Eleanor Singer (eds.), *Readings in Reference Group Theory and Research* (New York: The Free Press, 1968).

their district than are elementary-school teachers. Table 7-10 summarizes the differences. The trend on this index is unmistakable and entirely consistent with our general findings. However, only one of these items produced statistically significant differences. (See Table 7-11.)

TABLE 7-11. PERCENT OF ELEMENTARY- AND SECONDARY-SCHOOL
TEACHERS WHO BELIEVE THAT THERE ARE THINGS THE
COMMUNITY COULD DO FOR TEACHERS[a]

| Grade level | Could the community do things? | | Totals |
	Yes	No	
Elementary	40 (31)	60 (46)	100 (77)
Secondary	56 (72)	44 (57)	100 (129)
Totals	50 (103)	50 (103)	100 (206)

[a] $x^2 = 4.06$ with 1 degree of freedom; significant at .04 level.

The last of the five educational-climate dimensions, teacher participation in politics, did not discriminate between elementary- and secondary-school teachers. We discovered that all teachers vote with great and equal regularity. Elementary-school teachers report voting in national elections slightly more often than secondary-school teachers, but secondary-school teachers vote more often than elementary-school teachers in state elections. Identical proportions voted in local elections. Thus, our findings on this dimension are inconclusive.

More consistent with our argument is the fact that secondary-school teachers score marginally higher than elementary-school teachers on the two attitudinal dimensions that we investigated—political efficacy[7] and majority rule. The scores are 1.65 and 2.65, respectively, for elementary-school teachers and 1.75 and 2.73 for secondary-school teachers. In addition, elementary-school teachers are more reluctant to discuss political topics in the classroom than are high-school teachers. (See Table 7-12.)

The findings reported in Table 7-12 lead us to predict that high-school students will, in fact, confront more controversial issues

[7] Let us recall that the political-efficacy score is based on the attenuated two-item scale reported in Chapter 6.

TABLE 7-12. WILLINGNESS OF ELEMENTARY- AND SECONDARY-
SCHOOL TEACHERS TO DISCUSS ALL POLITICAL ISSUES
IN THE CLASSROOM (IN PERCENT)[a]

| | *Should all political issues be discussed?* | | |
Level taught	Yes	No	Totals
Elementary	77 (57)	23 (17)	100 (74)
Secondary	88 (113)	12 (16)	100 (129)
Totals	84 (170)	16 (33)	100 (203)

[a] $x^2 = 3.12$ with 1 degree of freedom; significant at .07 level.

in their classes than will elementary-school students. Our hypothesis is confirmed. For example, 79 percent of the high-school teachers had discussed LSD with their classes, as opposed to only 48
percent of the elementary-school teachers. We find comparable
disparities in the frequency of classroom debate about hippies and
about tuition at the University of California. Other topics, either
because—like communism—they appear in the elementary-school
curriculum or because—like riots and Vietnam—they interest students of all ages, are discussed at all levels of the school system.
Thus, as many (71 percent) elementary- as high-school teachers
had considered Vietnam with their students. In general, however,
there appears to be slightly more openness to political discussion
and slightly more support for democratic values among high-school
teachers than among their counterparts in elementary school.

SUBJECT TAUGHT AND TEACHER PERSPECTIVES

We have isolated contrasting teaching climates in elementary and
secondary schools. Now we shall demonstrate that social-studies
teachers in high school exaggerate the pattern of low morale, high
qualifications, light burdens, diminished sense of community support, and distinctively high levels of political discussion and democratic attitudes that is characteristic of their high-school colleagues.
(Because most elementary-school teachers teach whole grades
rather than particular subjects,[8] we have excluded them for the
following comparisons.)

[8] There is some indication, however, that teaching specializations are beginning to disperse downward into the elementary school.

Let us first compare the qualifications of social-studies teachers with those of teachers of the humanities and teachers of other subjects. The number of social-studies teachers is too small to prevent our findings from being tentative. Nonetheless, as Table 7-13 suggests, we still find consistent differences between the three groups of respondents.

TABLE 7-13. QUALIFICATIONS OF HUMANITIES, SOCIAL-STUDIES, AND OTHER HIGH-SCHOOL TEACHERS[a]

Item	Social studies	Subject taught Humanities	Other
Cosmopolitanism of universities	x		x (tie)
Advanced degrees	x		
Academic versus education preparation	x		
Quality of college	x		
Undergraduate grade average	x		
Current course work			x
Possession of tenure	x		x (tie)

[a] x denotes teachers with the highest qualifications.

Of all the respondents, those who teach social studies are clearly the most qualified and those who teach humanities the least qualified. Differences on most of these items are small, but, as Table 7-14 reveals, considerably more social-studies teachers than other teachers possess advanced degrees.

TABLE 7-14. PROPORTION OF HIGH-SCHOOL HUMANITIES, SOCIAL-STUDIES, AND OTHER TEACHERS WHO HOLD ADVANCED DEGREES (IN PERCENT)[a]

Subject taught	Possession of advanced degrees Yes	No	Totals
Social studies	64 (14)	36 (8)	100 (22)
Humanities	44 (21)	56 (27)	100 (48)
Other	38 (23)	62 (37)	100 (60)
Totals	44 (58)	56 (72)	100 (130)

[a] $x^2 = 15.58$ with 3 degrees of freedom; significant at .08 level.

Social-studies teachers have all the qualifications that, if our hypothesis is correct, should produce low morale. Thus, we can employ the morale scores of the social-studies respondents to test the interpretation we set forth while discussing the differences between elementary-school and secondary-school teaching climates. Unfortunately, Table 7-15, which reports the morale items, lends our interpretation little comfort.

TABLE 7-15. MORALE AMONG HUMANITIES, SOCIAL-STUDIES, AND OTHER HIGH-SCHOOL TEACHERS[a]

Item	Social studies	Subject taught Humanities	Other
Views of the salary schedule		x	
Views of teaching conditions		x	
Ratings of own performance		x	x (tie)
Perception of own effort	x		
Perception of student responsiveness		x	
Perception of own acceptance by students	x	x	x (tie)
Perception of cooperativeness of students	x		
Perception of students' willingness to work		x	
Number of friends in district	x		x (tie)
Closeness of friends	x	x (tie)	
Perception of the extent to which colleagues care about teaching			x
Perception of extent to which colleagues care about teacher as a person	x	x	x (tie)

[a] x denotes teachers with the highest morale.

The inconclusiveness of these findings does little to strengthen our argument; however, let us notice that not one item in the morale index produces statistically significant findings. Therefore, let us at least reserve judgment on our hypothesis until we explore further.

The hypothesis does predict correctly that social-studies teachers will be skeptical about the teaching career. Thus, Table

7-16 reports marked differences between the judgments of social-studies teachers and other teachers about the status of teaching.

TABLE 7-16. PROPORTION OF HUMANITIES, SOCIAL-STUDIES, AND OTHER TEACHERS WHO FEEL TEACHING IS REWARDING VERSUS THOSE WHO FEEL IT IS NOT PROFESSIONAL (IN PERCENT)[a]

Subject taught	Response Not professional	Rewarding	Totals	
Social studies	65 (13)	35 (7)	100	(20)
Humanities	20 (9)	80 (36)	100	(45)
Other	37 (22)	63 (37)	100	(59)
Totals	35 (44)	65 (80)	100	(124)

[a] $x^2 = 14.12$ with 3 degrees of freedom; significant at .002 level.

Social-studies teachers object to the lack of prestige in the teaching career. By contrast, other high-school teachers find little in their situation to lament. Furthermore, though percentile differences are weak, we find that social-studies teachers are, of all teachers, the least satisfied with administrators. Again our interpretation gains support.

Table 7-17 summarizes the respondents' perceptions of the

TABLE 7-17. INSTRUCTIONAL BURDENS AS VIEWED BY HUMANITIES, SOCIAL-STUDIES, AND OTHER HIGH-SCHOOL TEACHERS[b]

Item	Subject taught Social studies	Humanities	Other
Burden of classroom instruction			x
Burden of grading			x[a]
Burden of extracurricular activities			x
Burden of teacher-parent conferences	x		
Burden of record keeping	x		
Burden of retaining credentials	x	x (tie)	
Burden of faculty meetings	x		

[a] Statistically significant.
[b] x denotes that group of teachers perceiving the lowest burdens.

burdens they bear. It is consistent with our interpretation that so-cial-studies teachers feel the lightest burdens.

The pattern revealed by Table 7-17 conforms generally to our argument. Humanities teachers, who manifest the highest levels of morale, suffer under the greatest teaching burdens. Social-studies teachers, who are relatively demoralized, enjoy the lightest burdens. The pattern is identical to that observed among elementary-school and secondary-school teachers and may be explained by reference to the considerations advanced in the earlier case.

Our interpretation predicts that social-studies teachers will view their community's support of education skeptically; humani-ties teachers, however, should be most pleased with their com-munities. Table 7-18 supports this hypothesis, though again differences on individual items are not significant.

TABLE 7-18. COMMUNITY SUPPORT OF THE SCHOOLS AS SEEN BY HUMANITIES, SOCIAL-STUDIES, AND OTHER HIGH-SCHOOL TEACHERS[a]

Item	Social studies	Subject taught Humanities	Other
Things community could do for teachers		x	
Numbers of things community could do		x	
Things community could do for schools			x
Number of things community could do	x	x	x (tie)
Amount of support community gives education			x

[a] x denotes that group of teachers perceiving the greatest support.

Teachers of the humanities and of other subjects are equally uncritical of their communities; social-studies teachers are, how-ever, quite critical. On only one item, that which assessed the vol-ume of criticism about the communities' school support, did the unhappiness of humanities teachers and of other teachers rise to the level regularly manifested by social-studies teachers.

As might be expected, the social-studies teachers vote more

regularly than either of the other two groups of teachers. Ninety-five percent of the social-studies teachers cast ballots in all national elections, as opposed to only 79 percent of the teachers of other subjects and 90 percent of the humanities teachers. The gap between these teacher groups held steady for state elections, but widened for local elections. Eighty-two percent of the social-studies teachers reported always voting in local elections, whereas only 50 percent of the other two groups combined claimed this high a level of voting.

Table 7-19 indicates that, consistent with our interpretation, social-studies teachers score high on the two measures of democratic attitudes. The teachers of other subjects, however, fare equally well. Again, it is the humanities teachers who lag behind.

TABLE 7-19. BELIEF IN MAJORITY RULE AND LEVEL OF POLITICAL EFFICACY AMONG HIGH-SCHOOL TEACHERS OF DIFFERENT SUBJECTS

| Subject taught | Dimension | |
	Majority rule	Political efficacy
Social studies	2.78 (22)	1.86 (21)
Humanities	2.63 (46)	1.73 (45)
Other	2.96 (51)	1.74 (51)
Totals	2.73 (119)	1.75 (117)

Finally, it is no surprise that, of all the respondents, social-studies teachers are the most open to political debate. Every social-studies teacher agreed that no political issue should be barred from a hearing in the classroom. Of the rest of the high-school teachers, only 86 percent were willing to discuss any political topic in class that might arise.

For this reason, as well as because political issues are the very stuff of social studies, actual political controversy occurs most often in social-studies classes. Ninety-six percent of the social-studies respondents had discussed Vietnam in class, while only 73 percent and 55 percent, respectively, of the humanities teachers and those of other high-school subjects had dealt with this bitterly contested issue. Findings such as these are clearly at odds with Jennings' and Zeigler's assertion that social-studies teachers are too timid to undertake the discussion of controversial matters.[9] The treatment of poltical issues is, however, more comprehensive than it may at first appear. Thus, majorities of the three high-school teacher groups had confronted all but two of the controversial issues, the sole exceptions being communism and tuition at the University of California.

Can the distinctiveness of the social-studies contingent be accounted for by its predominantly male composition? Earlier we showed that sex composition paralleled exactly the divergent educational climates of elementary- and secondary-school teachers. Does the same pattern apply to educational climates based on subject matter? The answer is only partially affirmative. Most humanities teachers are women and, as we have seen, humanities teachers exhibit the familiar pattern of high morale, heavy burdens, satisfaction with teaching, and political quiescence. Nevertheless, there are proportionately as many male teachers in the third, residual, category of teachers as there are male social-studies teachers. Yet, social-studies teachers and teachers of other subjects manifest substantially different orientations. We therefore conclude that something beyond sex ratios, something in the very process of social-studies teaching, creates disaffection from the high school.

To summarize, those teachers who are the best qualified, the most interested in politics, and the least burdened, are the most critical of the school, the community, and the administration of education. The pattern, in other words, is one of strain between competent teachers and their schools. The most alienated teachers are men, the majority of whom, as high-school instructors, deal with relatively mature students and, in many cases, specialize in the social studies.

Among all high-school teachers, those charged with the inculcation of democratic values are most discontent with their position. We can only speculate about the consequences of this situation for the school and for political socialization. Perhaps what little motivation to political activity the social studies convey is partially offset by the occasionally visible unhappiness of social-studies teachers. The disparity between teacher and student political values

[9] Jennings and Zeigler, "Political Expressivism among High School Teachers," p. 6.

intrudes itself once more at this point. Earlier, when we compared the political-efficacy and majority-rule scores of teachers and twelfth-graders, we observed a sizable gap. But this gap widens to a chasm separating social-studies teachers from twelfth-graders. Social-studies teachers may be more democratic than other teachers, but their belief in democracy apparently does not convey itself to their studies. The alienation of social-studies teachers may be both cause and consequence of this condition.

The next task concerns the influence the school districts exert upon the patterns we have observed. Do high-school teachers in Chalmers report higher morale, superior qualifications, more respect for their district, more dedication to political participation, a more democratic set of values, and lighter burdens than high-school teachers in Moss City? How do social-studies teachers in Chalmers react to their district's attempt to attain quality education? In short, does the educational effort expanded by Chalmers reduce the alienation of its high-school teachers generally and its social-studies teachers particularly?

There are several hypotheses. We might first argue that Chalmers' exertions ought to have precisely the reduction effect we have predicted, especially if, as we suggested earlier, Chalmers' educational superiority is concentrated at the high-school level. In this connection, let us recall the marked pro-democratic shift among Chalmers students during the secondary-school years. Thus, any evidence that Chalmers high-school teachers generally and social-studies teachers particularly are less alienated than their counterparts in Moss City would not only support the present hypothesis, but would also strengthen our argument that the Chalmers schools do, in fact, produce compensatory political socialization. However, should we discover no parallelism between the pro-democratic attitude change among Chalmers high-school students and the educational climate in the Chalmers secondary schools, both hypotheses would suffer.

We should not be surprised, however, if we discover a quite different pattern. Perhaps a district that attempts to create quality education attracts well-qualified, eager high-school teachers who bring with them unrealistically high expectations about the schools, the students, the administration, and the community. Such teachers, as we have seen, are the most prone to disillusionment. Thus, we may find substantial alienation among high-school and social-studies teachers in Chalmers.[10] Let us see which of the two patterns fits the data.

HIGH-SCHOOL AND SOCIAL-STUDIES TEACHERS IN MOSS CITY AND CHALMERS

The necessity of placing two controls simultaneously on our teacher data prevents decisive conclusions about the hypotheses. Nonetheless, as we will see, both high-school teachers in general and social-studies instructors in particular are less alienated in Chalmers than in Moss City. Tables 7-20 through 7-24 provide the data for our high school sample.

TABLE 7-20. QUALIFICATIONS OF SECONDARY-SCHOOL TEACHERS IN CHALMERS AND MOSS CITY[a]

| | District | |
Item	Moss City	Chalmers
Cosmopolitanism of universities	x	
Advanced degrees		x
Academic versus education preparation		x
Quality of colleges		x
Undergraduate grade average		x
Current course work	x	
Possession of tenure		x

[a] x denotes the district with the better qualified teachers.

These findings indicate that the Chalmers secondary-school teaching environment is clearly superior to that of Moss City. High-school teachers in Chalmers are better qualified, possess higher morale, perceive greater community support for their activities, and vote more regularly than do their counterparts in Moss City. Only on the burdens dimension, which has always favored

[10] I recognize that the use of the term "alienation" is not entirely warranted in this context. Alienation signifies far more extreme disengagement than we have uncovered in our study. For elucidation of the concept, see Robert Blauner, *Alienation and Freedom* (Chicago: University of Chicago Press, 1964). chap. 2.

TABLE 7-21. MORALE OF SECONDARY-SCHOOL TEACHERS IN
CHALMERS AND MOSS CITY[a]

Item	District Moss City	Chalmers
Views of salary schedule		x
Views of teaching conditions	(tie)	
Ratings of own performance	(tie)	
Perception of own effort		x
Perception of student responsiveness	x	
Perception of acceptance by students		x
Perception of cooperativeness of students	(tie)	
Perception of students' willingness to work		x
Number of friends in district		x
Closeness of friends		x
Perception of extent to which colleagues care about teaching	(tie)	
Perception of extent to which colleagues care about teacher as a person	(tie)	

[a] x denotes the district whose teachers have the higher morale.

TABLE 7-22. TEACHING BURDENS AMONG SECONDARY-SCHOOL
TEACHERS IN CHALMERS AND MOSS CITY[a]

Item	District Moss City	Chalmers
Burden of classroom instruction	x	
Burden of grading	(tie)	
Burden of extracurricular activities	x	
Burden of teacher-parent conferences	x	
Burden of record keeping	(tie)	
Burden of retaining credentials		x
Burden of faculty meetings	x	

[a] x denotes the district whose secondary-school teachers perceive least burden.

Moss City, does the pattern not hold. Thus Chalmers' superior educational input does reduce the alienation of its secondary-school teachers; conversely, Moss City's minimal effort can produce no such reduction.

Earlier we argued that the secondary school provides com-

TABLE 7-23. COMMUNITY SUPPORT OF THE SCHOOL, AS SEEN BY
SECONDARY-SCHOOL TEACHERS IN CHALMERS AND MOSS CITY[a]

	District	
Item	Moss City	Chalmers
Things community could do for teachers	(tie)	
Number of things community could do		x
Things community could do for schools		x
Number of things community could do for schools		x
Amount of support community gives education		x

[a] x denotes the district whose teachers perceive greater support.

TABLE 7-24. POLITICAL PARTICIPATION AMONG SECONDARY-
SCHOOL TEACHERS IN CHALMERS AND MOSS CITY[a]

	District	
Item	Moss City	Chalmers
Voting at national level		x
Voting at state level		x
Voting at local level		x

[a] x denotes the district whose teachers participate most.

pensatory democratic socialization for Chalmers students. If we
were correct, we ought to expect support for democratic values to
run high among high-school teachers in Chalmers. Our expectation
is, however, disappointed. Chalmers secondary-school teachers
scored only 1.71 on political efficacy, as opposed to the 1.78 score
of Moss City secondary-school instructors. Furthermore, the Chalmers high-school teachers were no more favorably inclined toward
majority rule than were their counterparts in Moss City. The scores
for the two groups were, respectively, 2.72 and 2.74.

But is a comparison between teachers in the two district all
that is relevant at this point? Not necessarily. We are equally interested in comparing the attitude changes of students with the values
of elementary-school and secondary-school teachers *within* districts. These latter comparisons have important implications. For
example, we discover that Chalmers secondary-school teachers are

considerably more efficacious and majoritarian than are elementary teachers in that district. The political-efficacy and majority-rule scores are 1.49 and 2.48 for Chalmers elementary-school teachers, as opposed to 1.71 and 2.72 for Chalmers secondary-school teachers. Thus, the pattern of democratic values among teachers in Chalmers mirrors the attitude changes found among Chalmers students. Just as elementary-school students in Chalmers are much less democratic than high-schoolers in that district, so also are Chalmers elementary-school teachers much less democratic than Chalmers high-school teachers.

We find additional parallelism between teachers and students in Moss City. There is little difference between the democratic support levels of Moss City secondary- and elementary-school teachers. The elementary-school teachers in Moss City scored 1.81 and 2.81, respectively, on political efficacy and majority rule; Moss City high-school teachers scored only 1.78 and 2.74 on the same dimensions. This value similarly mirrors exactly the minimal pro-democratic attitude changes among Moss City students.

Finally, more Chalmers than Moss City secondary-school teachers discuss controversial political topics. There are marked interdistrict disparities in attention to tuition at the University of California, riots, and hippies. Equal proportions of secondary-school teachers had discussed Vietnam and LSD, but on no issue were Moss City secondary-school teachers more vocal than their counterparts in Chalmers. Unfortunately, however, when we compare elementary-school teachers in Chalmers with elementary-school teachers in Moss City, we find the former proportionately even more talkative about controversial topics than are Chalmers secondary-school teachers. Interdistrict differences on some items are substantial. For example, only 38 percent (15) of the Moss City elementary-school teachers had discussed LSD, as opposed to 60 percent (22) of the Chalmers elementary-school teachers. These findings do not reflect value shifts among students in the two districts and therefore conflict with our interpretation. Nonetheless, the weight of the evidence does point to student-teacher parallelism across the grade span.

Tables 7-25 through 7-27 reveal the extent to which social-studies teachers in Chalmers differ from their counterparts in Moss City. Disparities involving this specialized and crucial cadre of teachers not only surpass those for high-school teachers as a group, but also demonstrate clearly the superiority of the social-studies teaching climate in Chalmers.

Table 7-27 shows that Chalmers' attempt to produce quality education affects social-studies teachers even in the previously troublesome area of teaching burdens. Whereas other teachers in

TABLE 7-25. QUALIFICATIONS OF SOCIAL-STUDIES TEACHERS IN CHALMERS AND MOSS CITY[a]

| | District | |
Item	Moss City	Chalmers
Cosmopolitanism of universities	x	
Advanced degrees		x
Academic versus education preparation		x
Quality of colleges	x	
Undergraduate grade average		x
Current course work		x
Possession of tenure		x

[a] x denotes teachers with superior qualifications.

TABLE 7-26. MORALE OF SOCIAL-STUDIES TEACHERS IN CHALMERS AND MOSS CITY[a]

| | District | |
Item	Moss City	Chalmers
Views of the salary schedule	(tie)	
Views of teaching conditions		x
Ratings of own performance		x
Perception of own effort		x
Perception of student responsiveness		x
Perception of acceptance by students		x
Perception of cooperativeness of students	x	
Perception of student willingness to work		x
Number of friends in district		x
Closeness of friends		x
Perception of extent to which colleagues care about teaching		x
Perception of extent to which colleagues care about teacher as a person	x	

[a] x denotes teachers with superior morale.

TABLE 7-27. INSTRUCTIONAL BURDENS AMONG SOCIAL-STUDIES
TEACHERS IN CHALMERS AND MOSS CITY[a]

| | District | |
Item	Moss City	Chalmers
Burden of classroom instruction	x	
Burden of grading	(tie)	
Burden of extracurricular activities		x
Burden of teacher-parent conferences	x	
Burden of record keeping	x	
Burden of retaining credentials		x
Burden of faculty meetings		x

[a] x denotes teachers feeling least burden.

Chalmers consistently complain about the burdens of teaching,
Chalmers social-studies teachers are no more unhappy about their
instructional loads than are Moss City social-studies teachers. This
is not to say that Chalmers has wiped out alienation among its
social-studies teachers. On the contrary, social-studies teachers in
Chalmers are every bit as displeased with their administrative relationships as are other Chalmers high-school teachers, nor are they
convinced that teaching is a professional or rewarding occupation.
In fact, 83 percent (5) describe their job as unprofessional; by
contrast, the comparable figure in Moss City is only 57 percent
(8). Similarly, 71 percent (5) agree with the proposition that administrators are primarily ex-teachers who possess no special skills;
in Moss City only 47 percent (7) of the social-studies teachers take
this jaundiced view.

Chalmers social-studies teachers do agree that the people of
their district give great support to education. Table 7-28 portrays
the strength of this feeling.

Moreover, as Table 7-29 indicates, social-studies teachers in
Chalmers vote more regularly than do their counterparts in Moss
City.

The Chalmers social-studies environment is superior to that
in Moss City on four of the five dimensions of climate. Given the
small number of social-studies teachers in our sample, we believe
that the patterns in the data are exceptionally clear. Do these
differences reappear in the political values of social-studies teachers

TABLE 7-28. COMMUNITY SUPPORT OF THE SCHOOLS, AS SEEN BY
SOCIAL-STUDIES TEACHERS IN CHALMERS AND MOSS CITY[a]

Item	District	
	Moss City	*Chalmers*
Things community could do for teachers	x	
Number of things community could do		x
Things community could do for schools		x
Number of things community could do for schools		x
Amount of support community gives education		x

[a] *x* denotes those teachers perceiving highest support.

TABLE 7-29. VOTING PARTICIPATION OF SOCIAL-STUDIES TEACHERS
IN MOSS CITY AND CHALMERS[a]

Item	District	
	Moss City	*Chalmers*
Voting at national level		x
Voting at state level		x
Voting at local level		x

[a] *x* denotes those teachers who vote most.

and in the frequency of political controversy in social-studies
classes? The answer to the first part of this question is "No," but
to the second part, "Yes."

Chalmers social-studies teachers are more majoritarian than
their Moss City counterparts. The scores of the two groups, respectively, on majority rule are 3.00 and 2.64. However, social-studies
teachers in Chalmers are somewhat less efficacious than their colleagues in Moss City. Chalmers social-studies teachers do rank high
on the two dimensions of democracy when compared to the other
high-school teachers in their district. Social-studies teachers in
Moss City, on the other hand, are considerably less majoritarian
than the rest of the Moss City secondary-school teachers. Table
7-30 reveals the complicated pattern of the data.

Finally, more social-studies teachers in Chalmers than in
Moss City had discussed five of the six controversial political issues.

TABLE 7-30. BELIEF IN MAJORITY RULE AND LEVEL OF POLITICAL EFFICACY AMONG HIGH-SCHOOL TEACHERS OF VARIOUS SUBJECTS IN MOSS CITY AND CHALMERS

District	Subject taught	Majority rule	Political efficacy
Moss City	Social studies	2.64 (14)	1.93 (14)
	Humanities	2.83 (31)	1.80 (31)
	Other	2.93 (29)	1.75 (29)
Chalmers	Social studies	3.00 (9)	1.71 (9)
	Humanities	2.20 (15)	1.63 (15)
	Other	3.00 (22)	1.73 (22)

The sole exception is rioting, which every social-studies teacher in both districts had confronted. The differences separating the districts are small on individual items, but the overall pattern clearly favors Chalmers.

TEACHER RECRUITMENT AND EDUCATIONAL QUALITY

Any school district that desires to improve its quality must recruit superior teachers. Such a district will attempt to lure prospective teachers with a variety of incentives,[11] such as generous salaries, advanced facilities, innovative programs, flexible administrators, and exciting students. The success of these incentives depends upon three factors: (1) the composition of the recruitment pool from which teachers are to be drawn, (2) the impact of the incentives on that pool, and (3) the quality control devices that a district can apply. These factors in tandem generally weaken the connection between district effort and teacher quality. Hence, despite its efforts, Chalmers has not recruited quite as distinctive a teaching staff as administrators in that district might desire. Why?

The first explanation involves teacher supply. A district can choose its teachers only from those applicants offered it either by universities or by other districts. Not only the size, but also the

[11] For a theoretical consideration of incentives in the context of organization theory, see Peter B. Clark and James A. Wilson, "Incentive Systems: A Theory of Organization," *Administrative Science Quarterly*, 6, No. 2 (September 1961), pp. 129–167.

quality of this recruitment pool is limited. A crucial factor that contributes to this situation is the nature of teacher education. Graduates with education degrees are generally not the most accomplished of students.[12] Therefore, districts such as Chalmers must fish in a recruitment pool stocked with few potentially superior teachers. Furthermore, in many states certification requirements bar promising noneducation majors from teaching in public schools.[13] Many of our best college students, who would undoubtedly welcome the chance to teach, refuse to give up valuable substantive course work in favor of education credits. Thus, certification requirements that incorporate teacher-education courses may deter many potentially superior instructors from a teaching career. Although these requirements may do little harm to most districts, they do penalize the few that are striving to attain educational quality.

Schools of education also reduce creative political diversity among teachers.[14] So anxious are teachers' colleges to keep the schools out of politics that they reinforce the passive attitudinal propensities of their predominantly female clientele. In turn, by reducing value diversity and initiative among teachers, schools of education penalize districts that, like Chalmers, are interested in recruiting an elite teaching corps.

The incentives that Chalmers can offer are insufficient to upgrade markedly the quality of its teaching staff. There are, after all, two aspects of the salary incentive. The first is the position of a district's salary schedule in relation to those of other districts. We have already seen that Chalmers does well in this respect. The second, however, is the relationship between the salaries paid by even a beneficent district such as Chalmers and the salaries other occupations can offer those qualified to teach. Even superior teacher salaries cannot compete with average salaries in private

---

[12] Educators have become increasingly sensitive to this problem. See, for example, T. M. Stinnett and Albert J. Huggett, *Professional Problems of Teachers*, 2d ed. (New York: Crowell-Collier and Macmillan, Inc., 1963), p. 35.

[13] See James B. Conant, *The Education of American Teachers* (New York: McGraw-Hill, Inc., 1963), chap. 3.

[14] Egon G. Guba, Philip W. Jackson, and Charles E. Bidwell, "Occupational Choice and the Teaching Career," in W. W. Charters, Jr., and A. L. Gage (eds.), *Readings in the Social Psychology of Education* (Boston: Allyn and Bacon, Inc., 1963), pp. 271–278.

industry. Therefore, Chalmers' salaries, although attractive to the existing recruitment pool, do little to alter the form or character of the pool itself.

Here we confront a paradox. Local control, which permits individual school districts to make special efforts in education, also weakens those efforts once they are made. The resources that localities can channel into education rarely permit a district to distinguish itself. Community financing assures that only a few educational innovations will be undertaken at any one time and that only relatively insignificant salary differentials will be maintained. Consequently, most communities exert little control over the kinds of teachers they recruit.[15]

Much that I have been saying appears inconsistent with contemporary efforts in the politics and economics of education. I seem to be lamenting the fact that the current structure of teacher recruitment prevents gross educational inequalities; I am apparently implying that inequalities in educational opportunity have their value. I support no such extreme position. Equality of *good* education is a goal to which I eagerly subscribe; at the moment, however, such a goal is beyond reach. Today's public education, whether equal or unequal, is poor. Worse yet, most districts can do little to raise themselves above this dead level. Thus, it is only within the currently limited opportunity structure of education that I find Chalmers' dilemma regrettable.

My argument should not be taken as an unconditional brief for the nationalization of public education. A national program that did not create minimum *quality* education everywhere or that did not encourage local educational diversity, fitted to local needs, would probably be as unsatisfying as the present system of generally ineffective, but occasionally exciting education.[16]

---

[15] This formulation constitutes an implicit criticism of the effectiveness of incremental policy making. Incrementalism often assumes that slow and disjointed movements toward a goal are sufficiently effective for most situations. On the other hand, when goals cannot be reached incrementally, and when incrementalism does not prevent even current expectations from going unmet, one can hardly sanction it as a method. For elucidation of incrementalist theory, see Charles E. Lindblom, *The Intelligence of Democracy* (New York: The Free Press, 1965).

[16] For a review of arguments for and against nationization of public education, see Frank J. Munger and Richard F. Fenno, Jr., *National Politics and Federal Aid to Education* (Syracuse, N.Y.: Syracuse University Press, 1962), chap. 3.

Neither the composition of the teacher recruitment pool nor the volume of local incentives brings ambitious districts such as Chalmers a handsome return on their educational investments. Let us then turn to our third contributing factor, the absence of intra-district controls over teacher quality. The existence of this situation may be traced partly to the fact that the financial demands of education have distracted educational policy makers from developing the necessary tools to measure teaching quality. As Raymond Callahan puts it, "the emphasis on the business and mechanical aspects of education and the neglect of the instructional side . . . is still with us in the sixties."[17] Consequently, administrators and laymen alike rarely know what they have in their teachers or what they are getting from them.

The school's dependence on a problematic financial base is not the sole reason for its failure to develop methods of evaluating instruction. Teachers themselves wish to escape evaluation. Partly through their strenuous efforts, the use of rating and merit plans actually declined until recently. In 1922 nearly 60 percent of the public schools applied teacher evaluation schemes; in 1967 only 8 percent did.[18] Most school districts can only hope that their financial exertions will recruit good teachers, for they can neither assess the competence of teachers when they are first hired nor can they weed out teachers who have become incompetent.

The absence of acceptable teacher-evaluation techniques is linked to the absence of comprehensive student evaluation against national standards of achievement.[19] How can the efforts of teachers be measured against nonexistent student achievement norms? Even where standardized tests are employed, differential levels of student performance are usually attributed to the backgrounds of students rather than to the practices of teachers. We have already argued that meaningful teacher evaluation is still possible despite these problems, but there is no gainsaying the political difficulties involved.

[17] Raymond E. Callahan, *Education and the Cult of Efficiency* (Chicago: University of Chicago Press, 1964), p. 254.

[18] Willard R. Lane *et al., Foundations of Educational Administration: A Behavioral Analysis* (New York: Crowell-Collier and Macmillan, Inc., 1967), p. 344.

[19] Francis Keppel, *The Necessary Revolution in American Education* (Harper & Row, Publishers, 1966), pp. 109–110.

Students ought to be tested before and after a course of study in order to measure accomplishment. Change over time can measure both teacher competence and student achievement. However, because different teachers handle the same pupils at the same time and, occasionally, in the same subjects, it is difficult to single out the contributions of particular teachers, nor will such assessments circumvent the problem of setting differential student norms.

These are only a few of the reasons that school districts find it difficult to recruit and retain superior teachers. This lack of articulation between district effort and teacher quality, in turn, reduces the relationship between educational inputs and political socialization.

Chapter 8

The Public School and the Public Weal: On Putting the Pieces Together

Some years ago Samuel Stouffer closed his inquiry into American attitudes towards civil liberties by speculating about "what the answers to some of these questions mean for people who can do something about them."[1] Stouffer thought that the scholar should not shrink from recommendations to the policy maker about subjects that concerned them jointly. Few contemporary American political scientists feel similarly free to explore in depth the normative import of their empirical findings. Yet, we need not eschew judicious recommendation, particularly when the context of normative discussion permits us to review our findings and to place them in a useful theoretical perspective. So long as we take care to reveal our premises and to practice the elemental canons of fairness, we

[1] Samuel A. Stouffer, *Communism, Conformity, and Civil Liberties* (Gloucester, Mass.: Peter Smith, 1963), chap. 9.

have earned the right not only to recommend, but also to attempt a reconciliation between the role of scholar and the role of citizen.

THE SCHOOL AS AN INTERCEPTING INSTITUTION

Every social institution may be pictured as a channel through which rush the streams of its clients' behavior. Each such institution attempts to extract from its clients enough loyalty, support, and dedication to maintain itself and to fulfill the function that society has assigned it. Public education provides a good example of this process. The school intercepts and houses the careers of three groups of people: its students, its staff, and its policy makers. Each of these three groups is, in varying measure, interested in perpetuating the school as an institution; however, each group also wishes to use the school for its own benefit. Thus, at some times the interests of these three groups coincide, while at other times they are at odds.

No social institution can completely coordinate large, disparate groups of people confronted intermittently. Only total, residential institutions, such as mental hospitals, prisons, and monasteries, can so regulate the life of the inmate as to have an overpowering effect on him.[2] Indeed, occasionally even the prisoner can summon personal resources to counter the effects of the prison. Thus, the high recidivism rate attests to the resistance of inmates to the goals of the penal system.[3]

The school faces unique problems in attempting to intercept, shape, and reshape the careers of its clienteles. Two of its clientele groups are only minimally involved with it. The student comes to school involuntarily, matches his values against the school's, and eventually leaves for good.[4] This situation places severe strains

[2] For the seminal study of total institutions, see Erving Goffman, "On the Characteristics of Total Institutions" in Goffman, *Asylums* (New York: Doubleday and Company, Inc., Anchor Books, 1961), chap. 1.

[3] For elucidation and statistics, see Donald R. Tuft and Ralph W. England, Jr., *Criminology*, 4th ed. (New York: Crowell-Collier and Macmillan, Inc., 1964), pp. 502–506.

[4] This formulation borrows heavily from Burton R. Clark, "Sociology of Education," in Robert E. L. Faris (ed.), *Handbook of Modern Sociology* (Skokie, Ill.: Rand McNally and Company, 1964), pp. 734–770.

upon the educational staff, for, as David Riesman writes, ". . . the superintendent of schools must, if he lasts that long, educate a new group of constituents every few years. . . ."[5]

Nor are the policy makers who control allocations to the school continually involved with educational policy. State legislators count education as only one of their many concerns. The local school board, which has direct operating responsibility for the school, is staffed by private citizens whose major commitments lie beyond the educational system and who consider themselves to be volunteers shouldering their share of the civic load.

Consequently, as Dawson and Prewitt correctly note, there is no central agency that supervises political socialization in the United States.[6] The public school would logically be such an agency, but its enervating struggle to gain and retain the support of its clienteles prevents it from becoming more than an unusually loosely structured intercepting institution. Let us use the school to illustrate some of the characterizing features of intercepting institutions.

First, an intercepting institution attempts to coordinate processes that take place at different levels of the social structure. The school, for example, is involved at the psychological level when it imposes itself on the maturation of its first clientele, students. The school is involved, at the sociological level, when it recruits its teachers and administrators. Finally, the school is involved at the political level when it competes with other institutions and groups for a portion of society's scarce resources.

Second, an intercepting institution coordinates its diverse clienteles only tangentially. Groups in the intercepting institution cooperate just enough to preserve the institution, but not enough to endanger their own autonomy. Thus, as we have seen, the effect of teachers on students is limited and compensatory. Similarly, the impact of policy makers on the recruitment of teachers is marginal. Finally, the effect of political allocations on the socialization of students is reduced by the difficulties of providing a quality educational environment and by the resistances that children are able to mount.

[5] David Riesman, *Constraint and Variety in American Education* (New York: Doubleday and Company, Inc., Anchor Books, 1958), p. 123.
[6] Richard E. Dawson and Kenneth Prewitt, *Political Socialization* (Boston: Little, Brown and Company, 1969), p. 30.

Third, the diverse processes that the intercepting institution mediates and the many perspectives brought to the institution by its clienteles frustrate and complicate the setting of institutional goals. The periodic attempts of schoolmen to articulate an overall set of purposes for public education bear witness to this problem.[7] Educators do share some goals, such as the creation of a literate public, but there remain sizable disagreements, some of which Coleman describes in his analysis of educational change and the Black Revolution.[8]

Finally, their inability to articulate a set of goals makes it difficult for intercepting institutions to establish criteria for acceptable performance. Thus, we have already had more than enough occasion throughout this study to lament inadequate student achievement measures and ambiguous indices of educational quality. It is the school's lack of common objectives that allows its clientele groups, particularly teachers, to escape meaningful assessment.

All political systems contain some intercepting institutions, but such institutions are especially prevalent in democracies. This is true for two reasons. First, the technological development necessary to sustain democratic systems requires both mass education and the upgrading of specialized occupations.[9] Therefore, democracies produce a plethora of sophisticated occupational interest groups, able and willing to advance their own interests. These groups discover that they can protect their interests only by paying careful attention to the operations of institutions. Thus, democratic institutions find themselves constantly at the mercy of raiding clientele groups, most of which are well-organized, well-financed, and legally secure.[10]

Second, democracies attempt to disperse political power in

[7] For one such important statement, see *General Education in a Free Society*, Report of the Harvard Committee (Cambridge, Mass.: Harvard University Press, 1945).

[8] James S. Coleman, "The Concept of Equality of Educational Opportunity," *Harvard Educational Review, Equal Educational Opportunity* (Cambridge, Mass.: Harvard University Press, 1969), pp. 9–25.

[9] For a good statement, see Winston White, *Beyond Conformity* (New York: The Free Press, 1961), chaps. 6–8.

[10] For a good description of occupational interest groups, see Corinne Lathrop Gilb, *Hidden Hierarchies: The Professions and Government* (New York: Harper & Row, Publishers, 1966); a more analytical statement is

order to prevent particular groups or institutions from gaining exclusive control over vital functions. Indeed, fragmented authority is part of what we mean by democratic pluralism. The consequence of these efforts toward fragmentation is that there exists no operational dictum in the American system that legitimizes government control over political socialization, or, indeed, over any other area of social activity. The intercepting institution rarely confronts the power of government.[11]

The intercepting character of the school places a peculiar light on our speculations about political socialization in the United States. We must realize that only if we can secure the cooperation of the many groups that share control over the school can we improve socialization to democracy through the school. In short, the relationships among educators, students, and policy makers—the three principal clientele groups of the school—must be tightened. Analogously, the processes of child development, teacher recruitment, and educational policy making must be more thoroughly integrated. This formulation suggests our strategy for the remainder of this chapter. We will first approach our findings from the point of view of the psychologist who is interested in understanding human maturation more fully and in making the schools more effective socialization agencies. Next, we will look at our findings through the eyes of the educator, concerned with improving the teaching of democratic values. We will then view our findings as would the policy maker, struggling to articulate a public policy for education.

To simplify our discussion, we will take each of these three viewpoints in turn. We will also couch our conclusions in a series of recommendations to those educators, policy makers, and psychologists who are interested in improving the school as an agency of democratic socialization. This procedure follows Stouffer's strategy closely. Only in summation will we speak more generally to larger questions about the assumptions that have guided our study.

Theodore Lowi, "The Public Philosophy: Interest Group Liberalism," *American Political Science Review*, 61, No. 1 (March 1967), pp. 5–25.

[11] Theodore Lowi, *The End of Liberalism* (New York: W. W. Norton and Company, Inc., 1969), chaps. 4–5.

RECOMMENDATIONS TO PSYCHOLOGISTS

1. *We must learn more about thought and intelligence over the grade span.*

Psychologists should address two complementary segments of this problem. The first involves the symbolic character of childish thought and the second, the nature of abstract reasoning.

Early in his educational experience the child integrates such democratic symbols as the vote and political efficacy. Presently educational quality sustains support for democratic symbolism. Of course, attachment to the symbols of democracy is a prerequisite to the persistence of democratic systems; however, ultimately, democracies require that a good portion of citizens understand and apply abstract democratic principles. Thus, the psychologist can aid the process of democratic political socialization if he can explain the widespread survival of symbolic thought past childhood.

In this connection, the psychologist should examine two competing hypotheses. The first, which derives from psychoanalytic theory, states that symbolic thought after childhood stems from neurotic repression.[12] The second, suggested by Lidz, argues that much adult communication with children confirms a natural childish propensity to symbolic thought.[13] These two hypotheses have differing emphases. The first places symbolic thought in the context of abnormal parent-child relationships. The second explains symbolic thought as the outcome of common cultural and class practices. Evidence and theory regarding the first hypothesis are no doubt already familiar to the reader; however, considerations relevant to the second, being less well-known though highly suggestive, deserve brief review.

It seems clear that the cognitive and linguistic styles of children are class-related. Hess and Shipman demonstrate that lower-class parents transmit a unidimensional, impoverished vocabulary to their children. This vocabulary walls off the child from sophisti-

[12] See, for example, Charles Odier, *Anxiety and Magic Thinking*, trans. Marie-Louise Schoelly and Mary Jane Sherfey (New York: International Universities Press, Inc., 1956).

[13] Theodore Lidz, *The Person* (New York: Basic Books, Inc., 1969), pp. 199–200.

cated, analytical thought.[14] Moreover, Roger Brown maintains that young children need not always speak and think in concrete, highly personalistic, or symbolic terms. According to Brown, the linguistic modes and conceptual capacities of the child depend primarily on the language habits of his parents.[15] Thus, we should not automatically assume that genetic immaturity requires children to reason symbolically.

It is, of course, unlikely that symbolic, personalistic support for democracy would be erased by different methods of childrearing or by different patterns of parental communication with children. We have no wish to fall into the errors with which Bruner's influential theories of learning have been charged.[16] Some people may simply be intellectually incapable of anything but symbolic reasoning. Still, should psychologists discover no insurmountable barriers to the early teaching of abstract thought, the character and effectiveness of political socialization in the schools might well be altered.

Concomitant with our desire to understand the course of symbolic thought is a complementary interest in conceptually sophisticated, abstract thinking. Piaget and his associates have already elaborated a general paradigm for the emergence of formal reasoning.[17] We feel that further work in this area should take place within Piagetian parameters. Moreover, an equally important task for the psychologist is the translation of his knowledge about abstract thought into formulations suitable for classroom application. So far this translation has eluded us.

[14] Robert D. Hess and Virginia C. Shipman, "Early Experience and the Socialization of Cognitive Modes in Children," in Robert J. Havighust, Bernice L. Neugarten, and Jacqueline M. Falk (eds.), *Society and Education* (Boston: Allyn and Bacon, Inc., 1967), pp. 74–86.

[15] Roger Brown, "How Shall a Thing Be Called?" in Robert J. C. Harper *et al., The Cognitive Process: Readings* (Englewood Cliffs, N.J.: Prentice-Hall, Inc., 1964), pp. 647–655. Much of the criticism cited here is, implicitly, a critique of Piaget's theories of childhood thought. For elucidation, see Leonard Berkowitz, *The Development of Motives and Values in the Child* (New York: Basic Books, Inc., 1964), chap. 3.

[16] For a brief description of Bruner's theories, see W. H. Denton, "Problem-solving as a Theory of Learning and Teaching," *High School Journal*, 49, No. 8 (May 1960), pp. 382–390.

[17] See especially Barbel Inhelder and Jean Piaget, *The Growth of Logical Thinking*, trans. Anne Parsons and Stanley Milgram (New York: Basic Books, Inc., 1958).

We do not mean to ignore Gage's argument that "the need for theories of teaching stems . . . from the insufficiency *in principle* [italics his] of theories of learning. Theories of learning deal with what the learner does. But changes in education must depend in large part upon what the teacher does."[18] Insufficiency "in principle" may not be insufficiency in practice, however. Surely Gage does not contend that the teacher should practice in ignorance of what her students are likely to enjoy and assimilate? Were a teacher to behave in so bizarre a fashion, she could well be accused of dereliction of duty. Once this point is granted, all that it becomes necessary to note is that it is the psychologist's responsibility to formulate for the teacher some usable description of her students' cognitive boundaries. Such a description cannot but aid and encourage the development of a theory of teaching.

2. *The psychologist should undertake a more precise and thorough study of adolescence.* Our findings suggest several reasons for such a project. The most important is the paradox that emerges from the disparity between the developmental crises[19] that fill adolescence and the only moderate amounts of pro-democratic movement in our student sample. The psychologist should address himself to understanding why the vicissitudes of adolescence are reflected so weakly in the student's political evolution.

In addition, as we have seen, many adolescents are able to conceptualize such important values as political efficacy, liberalism-conservatism, and rules of the game. Thus, it becomes important to understand why some adolescents can conceptualize and others cannot. It is equally important to discover why some values are conceptualized more easily than others. Any such study should test two contradictory hypotheses about adolescent conceptual ability. The first hypothesis suggests that the adolescent's capacity to intellectualize depends almost entirely on his inherited cognitive tools.

[18] N. L. Gage, "Theories of Teaching," in Ernest R. Hilgard (ed.), *Theories of Learning and Instruction*, 63d Yearbook of the National Society for the Study of Education, pt. 1 (Chicago: University of Chicago Press, 1964), p. 271.

[19] The notion of an adolescent development crisis is explained most effectively by Erik Erikson. See, for the seminal statement, Erik H. Erikson, *Young Man Luther* (New York: W. W. Norton and Company, Inc., 1962), pp. 254–259; for a recent reformulation, see Erikson, *Identity: Youth and Crisis* (New York: W. W. Norton and Company, Inc., 1968), chap. 3.

The second hypothesis refers adolescent conceptualization to the inner turmoil of adolescence itself. As Lidz puts it, "The adolescent . . . utilizes his capacity to think and reason in order to control his impulses, not necessarily by reasoning out rational solutions of his problems, but through diverting his interests into intellectual channels."[20] Whether the adolescent's capacity to intellectualize grows from purely cognitive sources or from ego-defensive reactions against unacceptable impulses can have a bearing not only on teaching strategies, but also on the school's ability to reach different kinds of students.

Finally, we need more investigation of adolescents because, as Jennings and Niemi hint and as our own data make clear, the adolescent experience does not produce a stable, democratic political ideology.[21] The twelfth-grader possesses only moderate comprehension of and support for the norms of democracy. The psychologist should aim at telling us how adolescent political equivocation serves adolescent turbulence. He should also direct his energies to exploring the modalities of adolescent thought; such an effort would increase the chances that instruction in democratic values will stand on firm motivational ground.

3. *The psychologist should direct his attention to the identification and validation of achievement motivation. Furthermore, efforts should be undertaken to link achievement motivation to political socialization.* We have already observed marked and persistent political differences between high-achieving and low-achieving students. We have also described the distinctiveness of our "A" students, whose levels of democratic support rise rapidly early in the educational cycle, only to level off sharply by twelfth grade. These findings all suggest the centrality of achievement motivation to differences in the political socialization of various groups of students.

Despite the interest that many psychologists have taken in achievement motivation, the concept remains insufficiently developed for fruitful incorporation into research on political socializa-

[20] Lidz, *The Person*, pp. 340–341.
[21] M. Kent Jennings and Richard G. Niemi, "The Transmission of Political Values from Parent to Child," *American Political Science Review*, 62, No. 1 (March 1968), pp. 169–185; see also Jennings and Niemi, "Patterns of Political Learning," *Harvard Educational Review*, 38, No. 3 (Summer 1968), pp. 443–468.

tion.[22] The psychologist should prepare achievement motivation for interdisciplinary exploitation. Two tasks in particular require completion.

The first involves validation and measurement. At present, there are only minimal correlations between projective and questionnaire assessments of achievement motivation.[23] Such extreme sensitivity to measurement technique weakens one's confidence about just what, in fact, is being measured. Assuming a reliable measure can be developed, achievement motivation must then be related to the academic performance of different social groups. It seems obvious that identical amounts of achievement motivation will have different effects on the socialization of ghetto blacks as opposed to suburban whites. Only when such differences have been revealed can we assess the generality of the concept's utility.

Underlying our observations in this area is our belief that the causal chain linking academic performance to support for democratic values must be explicated. Perhaps the talented seem democratic only because they have the desire and ability to offer the "proper" responses to survey questions. But a more genuine process may be involved. Can it be that the intellectual flexibility necessary for academic success and the sense of self-confidence and accomplishment bred by success constitute the intellectual preconditions for early democratic support?

Finally, any investigation of achievement motivation should include an inquiry into what might be called the "tuning-in–shutting-off syndrome." This term describes the paradox that, just as duller students begin to assimilate democratic values in high school, their brighter compatriots become skeptical about democracy. Are the gaps between bright and dull students so vast that they dictate opposed reactions to the same material?

4. *The psychologist should undertake a more thorough investigation of sex-role socialization.* Two considerations prompt

---

[22] For a recent collection that surveys the theoretical status of the field, see John W. Atkinson and Norman T. Feather (eds.), *A Theory of Achievement Motivation* (New York: John Wiley and Sons, Inc., 1966).

[23] Vaughn J. Crandall, "Achievement," in Harold Stevenson (ed.), *Child Psychology*, 62d Yearbook of the National Society for the Study of Education, pt. 1 (Chicago: University of Chicago Press, 1963), p. 421; see also Berkowitz, *The Development of Motives and Values in the Child*, pp. 11–19.

this recommendation. The first is our discovery that, if anything, girls are slightly more democratic than boys.[24] Strong sex differences in socialization are apparently confined to participation-related variables. The second springs from the sex-related developmental differences reported by Adelson and Douvan. Apparently, girls never internalize their values as completely as boys.[25]

These two considerations present us with an interesting problem. Our survey methods described student attitudes in only the grossest terms. We employed no techniques to uncover the depth or the salience of political commitments. Adelson and Douvan's findings suggest the possibility that our girls may not have internalized their democratic values as completely as boys. If so, we would no longer be warranted in concluding that boys and girls are equally democratic, for the operational significance of female political values would be less than that of male values.

5. *The psychologist should investigate the relationship between personality and political socialization.* The independent variables employed in our study are familiar sociological categories—such as social class, sex, and scholastic achievement. As our explanatory regression analysis indicated, these variables, while useful in predicting levels of political information, are of limited help in accounting for differences in democratic support. Therefore, a renewed study of personality and politics might increase our predictive power.

I am aware of the modest disrepute into which the psychologizing of politics has fallen.[26] However, the reasons for such disrepute can be traced mainly to the elaborate, unverifiable, and unnecessary hypotheses that an earlier generation of psychologists offered to explain otherwise explicable political behavior. By contrast, our findings demand psychologizing because so much variance remains unexplained by conventional indicators and theories.

---

[24] Our findings are not inconsistent with those of Langton, who finds that wives are currently at least as influential in the socialization process as husbands. Our findings and his in tandem suggest sharp changes in the political status and values of women. See Kenneth P. Langton, *Political Socialization* (New York: Oxford University Press, 1969), chap. 3.

[25] Elizabeth Douvan and Joseph Adelson, *The Adolescent Experience* (New York: John Wiley and Sons, Inc., 1966), chap. 7.

[26] For a careful reconsideration of the problem, see Fred I. Greenstein, *Personality and Politics* (Chicago: Markham Publishing Co., 1969), chap. 3.

SUGGESTIONS FOR EDUCATORS

1. *More should be done to increase the allegiance of high-school teachers to their occupation. Special efforts should be directed at the teachers of social studies.* Our findings have shown that it is among high-school and, particularly, social-studies instructors that the greatest alienation from teaching may be found. We have also seen that high-school teachers are crucial to the educational enterprise because they encounter many students who are only just gaining the capacity to conceptualize abstractions and are at the same time beginning to question some of the political assumptions to which they have repeatedly been exposed. The high-school teacher must be aided in his efforts to meet the adolescent challenge.

We believe that unhappiness among high-school teachers can be traced to the predominantly male composition of the high school, to the aspiration-achievement gap felt by male teachers, and, perhaps, to the sensitivity of high-school teachers to administrative supervision. Furthermore, as Riesman points out, high-school teachers have recently lost "relative status," because the general public is increasingly composed of people with high-school or college educations themselves.[27] These well-educated parents often claim to know as much about the social studies as do social-studies teachers. Unfortunately, the social-studies teacher cannot use the prestige accorded him by a set of technical, verified theories to isolate himself from the public. In this sense, he suffers in comparison with his natural-science colleagues.

It is obviously easier to offer these general observations than to prescribe specific remedies. Nonetheless, two suggestions come to mind. One possible method for ameliorating the "relative status" problem is increased employment of sophisticated social-science theorizing and reasoning in the high-school classroom.[28] Prospective teachers should be exposed to the social sciences not only for

[27] Riesman, *Constraint and Variety in American Education*, p. 126.
[28] This suggestion seems to fit the prescriptions of educators interested in upgrading the quality of social-science teaching. For example, see Byron G. Massialas (ed.), *New Challenges in the Social Studies* (Belmont, Calif.: Wadsworth, 1966); see also Donald W. Oliver and James P. Shaver, *Teaching Public Issues in the High School* (Boston: Houghton Mifflin Company, 1966).

their applicability to social-studies instruction, but also for their status-conveying side effects. That teachers presently assimilate all too little of this material seems abundantly evident.

Efforts to transmit the social sciences to teachers should not be haphazard, piecemeal, or ad hoc. Hastily assembled NDEA summer institutes for teachers already on the job are insufficient. Instead, relevant instruction should become an expected part of the curriculum followed by *prospective* teachers. Such instruction might be organized along lines suggested by the Conant analysis of teacher education.[29]

Ultimately, however, the alienation of high-school teachers generally and social-studies teachers particularly can be reduced only when teaching becomes a genuinely exciting experience. This observation leads us to our next recommendation.

2. *The social studies must become more interesting for both students and teachers.* Carr writes, "Research has shown, quite consistently, that the [social studies] field is not popular with students and that this discontent—or even active dislike—begins as early as the fifth grade, about the time subjects begin to replace centers of interest which are close to the child."[30] Why are the social studies an object of distaste?

According to Patterson, the school has remained committed to repetitive, rote learning about American history and government.[31] This approach, particularly if adhered to throughout the grade span, soon becomes tedious for students and teachers alike. Indeed, many students actually encounter identical aspects of American government at three different points in their public-school careers. Such students can hardly be blamed for a lack of enthusiasm. In addition, because the social studies differ from the natural sciences, where basic understandings provide a foundation for complex theories, the social studies all too easily degenerate into repetitiveness.

Thus, the social-studies curriculum must be reevaluated. Its

[29] James B. Conant, *The Education of American Teachers* (New York: McGraw-Hill, Inc., 1963).

[30] Edwin R. Carr, *The Social Studies* (New York: The Center for Applied Research in Education, 1965), p. 51.

[31] Franklin Patterson, "Citizenship and the High School: Representative Current Practices," in Franklin Patterson *et al., The Adolescent Citizen* (New York: The Free Press, 1960), pp. 100–173.

current logic leads from the child's experience with close-at-hand manifestations of government to the larger issues of state, nation, and world. This is not an unsound set of premises.[32] It is unsound, however, to delay the consideration of social problems long after the child becomes aware of such problems. Today, unlike in times past, the mass media impress the concerns of the great society on even the young child. Consequently, these concerns must be related to the child's experience much earlier than was necessary for an earlier generation of children. Otherwise the child will, in all likelihood, come to disassociate the social studies from their seminal concerns.

We do not mean to imply that because today's child is well informed, he is sophisticated. Quite the contrary. In fact, the large gap between information and debate on the one hand and conceptual sophistication on the other accounts for much that is mindless in youthful politics. The mass media can stimulate political awareness and convey political information, but the school must provide political perspective.

The school has slowly begun to adjust. Our data show that high-school teachers are immersed in the discussion of controversial issues with their students. Furthermore, there is promise in the inquiry and discovery methods of instruction, both of which aim toward the teaching of conceptual strategies rather than repetitive histories.[33] However, whether such strategies involve and engage the student remains to be seen.

Educational innovations like the inquiry and discovery methods may enliven social-studies teaching. They cannot succeed, however, unless they are actually implemented. This consideration leads us to our next recommendation.

3. *Educators should analyze and apply the process of successful educational innovation.* Educational innovation is one of the least understood but most vital components of social change. Nonetheless, there are a few empirical findings and theoretical considerations that may contribute to an understanding of the process.

According to Gross, the principal is the key personage in the

[32] Indeed, it accords well with much of what we know about the child's usual learning process.

[33] For descriptions of these procedures, see Byron G. Massialas and C. Benjamin Cox, *Inquiry in Social Studies* (New York: McGraw-Hill, Inc., 1966); see also Oliver and Shaver, *Teaching Public Issues in the High School.*

initiation and implementation of educational change.[34] Not only must the principal encourage and monitor innovation, but he must also protect the innovating teachers. Gross offers a host of propositions about successful educational innovation, of which perhaps the most important is his conclusion that principals innovate most effectively only when they have a hand in recruiting teachers.[35] Educators wishing to innovate should, therefore, pay special attention to the commitment and freedom of principals.

There is also evidence that successful innovation requires integration into a professional community able to supply information and resources quickly. Without a link to such a community, potential educational innovators at the local level may have difficulty gaining outside support for or even internal knowledge about educational innovations.

Campbell and Bunnell's study of the diffusion process in science and mathematics innovation illustrates the importance of local ties to the larger professional community.[36] Campbell and Bunnell demonstrate how unevenly these nationally sponsored innovative programs spread across the country. Only wealthy urban and suburban school districts have fully exploited such programs. These findings can be partly understood by the fact that wealthy districts maintain close ties to national innovative agencies and are, therefore, in a position to act as pacemakers for less fortunate districts.

It therefore behooves all school districts intending to innovate to cultivate the national educational community. Even attendance at professional meetings can help, as Coleman, Katz, and Menzel discovered in their study of medical innovation.[37]

4. *Educators must formulate, adopt, and implement reliable teacher evaluation methods.* That new teacher evaluation methods are needed becomes obvious, not only from a perusal of our findings, but also from an examination of what educators themselves say. For example, Medley and Mitzel contend that current evalua-

[34] Neal Gross *et al.*, "National Principalship Study," No. 3, U.S. Office of Education, Contract #853 (SAE–8702), 1965.

[35] Gross, "National Principalship Study," chap. 7, p. 13.

[36] Roald F. Campbell and Robert A. Bunnell, "Differential Impact of National Programs on Secondary Schools," in Havighurst, Neugarten, and Falk (eds.), *Society and Education*, pp. 180–185.

[37] James S. Coleman, Elihu Katz, and Herbert Menzel, *Medical Innovation: A Diffusion Study* (Indianapolis: The Bobbs-Merrill Company, Inc., 1966), pp. 42–45.

tion techniques are useless because they rely on perceptions of teacher effectiveness rather than on "a direct measure of the effects on pupils of the teachers studied."[38] The "teacher rating" method has numerous shortcomings, as indexed by the closer correlation between subject personality and rated efficiency than between subject performance in college and rated efficiency.[39] Apparently the superficial characterizing marks of competence impress more raters than does the actual classroom performance of the teacher. Not surprisingly, therefore, ". . . a teacher whose pupils learn almost nothing from him is just about as likely to be rated highly effective as one whose pupils learn a great deal. A characteristic highly correlated with 'effectiveness' as judged by a supervisor or other trained person is no more likely to be correlated with measured effectiveness than any other."[40]

We have already considered some barriers to proper teacher evaluation. The political hindrances to setting student achievement norms are matched by the reluctance of teachers to accept invidious comparison. Nonetheless, these are not insurmountable problems. Three requirements underlie reliable teacher evaluation. First, we must be able to measure how much a student has learned. This requirement can only be met by systematic testing before and after a student has taken a course. Such a testing program should be mandatory in all schools. Second, we must be able to assign the responsibility for student performance to individual teachers. This requirement can be met only by assigning individual teachers to specific units of course material. Where team teaching is practiced, whole teams should be compared with each other. However, every teacher should do some individual teaching, for evaluative purposes if for no other. Third, we must assume teacher compliance with evaluation by utilizing a system of incentives. Teachers who do not perform well should not be rewarded; teachers who perform exceptionally well should receive enhanced rewards.

---

[38] Donald M. Medley and Harold E. Mitzel, "The Scientific Study of Teacher Behavior," in Arno A. Bellack (ed.), *Theory and Research in Teaching* (New York: Columbia University, Teachers College, 1963), p. 83.

[39] Willard R. Lane *et al., Foundations of Educational Administration: A Behavioral Analysis* (New York: Crowell-Collier and Macmillan, Inc., 1967), p. 345.

[40] Medley and Mitzel, "The Scientific Study of Teacher Behavior," p. 84.

Let us try to anticipate some objections to teacher evaluations. Some critics might claim that our views reflect an unduly limited conception of teaching, a conception that considers instruction a mechanical process in which prefabricated ideas are spoonfed to students. We admit to no such view of education. We realize that some kinds of ideas and talents escape proper measurement. We also agree that at times the enthusiasm a teacher conveys may be just as important as her transmission of subject matter. But our recommendations are not at odds with these observations. We urge only that those facets of teaching that *are* measurable be measured, and that the resulting evaluations of teaching play some, but not the only, role in teacher selection and promotion.

Other critics might predict that the adoption and application of effective teacher evaluation would destroy teacher morale. We would not deny the possibility of teacher unhappiness. Indeed, it would be useless to do so, for Willard Lane has documented instances of it.[41] However, competition among teachers has its healthy side as well. What such teachers may lose in the sense of closeness they formerly enjoyed, the system may gain from their increased attention to and creativity in instruction.[42]

Nothing we have said resolves the problems associated with setting different achievement norms for students from different backgrounds. This problem is not surmountable. Nonetheless, administrators and teachers familiar with a district can informally agree upon differential student achievement standards. Lest this practice sound both anti-democratic and morally suspect, we hasten to assert its current prevalence. It is folly to believe that those most knowledgeable about the problems of teaching different groups of students will simply disregard those problems when evaluating teachers. Nor does such a practice require invidious distinctions between the capacities of various groups. We ask only that teachers who function predominantly in one ethnic environment be compared with others performing in that same environment. Such comparisons need not involve judgments about the ultimate potential of any group.

---

[41] Lane, *Foundation of Educational Administration*, p. 345.

[42] We are aware of one last objection to our approach. Some teachers may "teach to the test," in the process turning the classroom into a highly stereotyped mechanism. Whether teaching to the test is harmful, however, depends upon the quality of the test and not the practices of the teacher.

SUGGESTIONS FOR POLICY MAKERS CONCERNED WITH EDUCATION

1. *Public education requires more financial support.* This suggestion is neither original nor profound; nonetheless, it is as important as any other single observation made in this chapter. How, in fact, can more money be raised for the schools? Let us briefly explore some possibilities.

The first alternative involves restructuring the educational tax base. It is by now obvious to all that continued reliance on the property tax is unfeasible. The middle-income property owners who supply the bulk of property taxes are increasingly unwilling to shoulder the load. Indeed, even if it operated properly, the property tax would never provide anywhere near the funding capacity today's schools demand.[43]

Conclusions such as that advanced above usually have been followed by an appeal to the federal or state government for support. However, we feel that the unique place of the public school in American life dictates some continued effort to keep educational control local. Urban policy makers are already urgently investigating new local tax sources for various local programs. Perhaps such sources, including, for example, business inventories, can take up some of the slack.

Underlying the funding problem, however, is a need for political leaders to make a profound commitment to public education. Specifically, policy makers must not cast public education as the scapegoat for long-festering political and social ills. The schools deserve no more castigation for the social problems of our time than do other institutions. Politicians who capitalize upon "turmoil in the schools" for the enhancement of their own political careers do education no service. Such officials must realize that the viability of mass education in a democracy takes priority over the vicissitudes of public schooling itself. Any withdrawal of political support for the school can only perpetuate the very conditions that politicians and voters alike deplore.

2. *Policy makers must concern themselves with quality con-*

---

[43] For a good description of the educational economics of property taxation, see Jesse Burkhead, *State and Local Taxes for Public Education* (Syracuse, N.Y.: Syracuse University Press, 1963).

trol devices in the school. As we have seen, schools need more than money. Even Chalmers could not consistently elevate the level of its students' socialization to democracy. Thus, educational policy makers must find ways to reward efficiency and effectiveness. In particular, they should take three obvious steps.

The first is the acceleration of school-district consolidation. Numerous studies show that students perform best in consolidated schools.[44] In other words, consolidation is a good educational investment. The reasons for the relationship between student performance and school consolidation are simple. Only schools of reasonable size can support the educational innovations that lead to better student performance. Put another way, consolidated schools benefit from economics of scale. In addition, teachers gravitate to consolidated districts, where the pay scale is high.[45] Consolidation thus has the side benefit of upgrading the teacher recruitment pool.

But advocating school consolidation is no longer of much utility. The consolidation movement is by now so widespread that many of its advantages have already been realized. However, policy makers can adopt two other helpful programs. State legislatures can modify the foundation programs to reward enterprising school districts. In addition, policy makers at all levels can make funds available for the evaluation and encouragement of good teaching.

It is a truism that in politics efforts follow incentives. Educators who are assured state financial support for their initiatives will gain the chance to upgrade education in their localities markedly and rapidly. Hence, once formulas have been devised to control for differences in community capacity to support education—and Bailey *et al.* believe such methods exist[46]—adjustment of state-aid guidelines to reward innovation should become a high-priority item for educational policy makers.

We have already said enough about the need to reward good teaching. Now we need only observe the obvious: that effort in this direction can proceed only if educational policy makers pro-

---

[44] See, for example, William Inman and Donald Rushing, "Process and Product in School Consolidation," *Journal of State School Systems Development*, vol. 1, No. 3, (Fall 1967), pp. 173–180; see also Leslie L. Chisholm, *School District Reorganization* (Chicago: Midwest Administration Center, ca. 1958).
[45] Chisholm, *School District Reorganization*, p. 77.
[46] Stephen K. Bailey *et al., Schoolmen and Politics* (Syracuse, N.Y.: Syracuse University Press, 1962).

vide the financial and political "muscle" to enforce newly adopted evaluation procedures.

3. *Policy makers must shield social-studies teachers from extremists in the community.* We have shown that most teachers do not directly experience political pressures. Instead, local displeasure is funneled through school administrators and educational policy makers. Thus, if the policy maker wishes to protect the teacher, he must be willing to interpose himself between community and school.

No one need doubt the difficulty of such a decision. The tradition of local control testifies to the magnitude of pressures that policy makers may sustain when they choose to defend social-studies teachers who have transgressed the boundaries that the community has, often unconsciously, erected. In addition, the normal public apathy about school affairs often creates a vacuum into which the most intemperate critics of the schools move without hindrance. In many cases, therefore, extremists have an impact out of proportion to their numbers.

There is no foolproof method by which policy makers can be imbued with a desire to protect social-studies teachers. We do know that in those districts where school politics is structured, organized, and competitive, teachers and politicians alike are relatively free from community intimidation.[47] Within such districts, policy makers can brace themselves against party or caucus organizations to resist extremist pressures. One obvious conclusion, therefore, is that politicians interested in promoting the educational experience should concentrate on building their own political organizations. This conclusion is a particularly happy one because it is symbiotic with the goals of politicians themselves.[48]

We realize that our recommendations to policy makers have been both general and familiar. They are, nonetheless, important, because, as our findings indicate, within limits the school *can* socialize to democracy. In other words, our study should convince politicians that their conformity to our suggestions can pay off in more successful democratic socialization.

[47] David W. Minar, "The Community Basis of Conflict in School Politics," *American Sociological Review*, 31, No. 4 (December 1966), pp. 822–835.
[48] Increasingly, as a number of studies indicate, local politicians are attempting to build personal followings outside the party machinery. See, for example, James Q. Wilson, *The Amateur Democrat* (Chicago: University of Chicago Press, 1962).

CRITIQUE AND ENVOI

This book has conceived political socialization to be the outcome of three processes—child development, acculturation, and policy making. Most of this study has treated these processes empirically. However, our recommendations for the improvement of the school as a socialization agent have been predicated on a normative assumption: that the school's conveyance of democratic norms is a worthy enterprise. It is now time to question this assumption.

A case can be made that any more pervasive educational influence in political socialization would actually constitute a hindrance to democracy. We have argued that enhancing the influence of the school would better harness child development, acculturation, and policy making in the service of democracy. But some might say that discontinuity in these three socialization processes has positive as well as negative aspects. Certainly the intercepting character of the school currently assures that a citizen's commitment to democracy cannot be engineered by government. Instead, such commitment arises from the most intimate circumstances of man's life—his experience on the job, with his peers, or with the political system itself. This form of belief in democracy transcends mere intellectual assent to a set of principles. Instead, it springs from the roots of individual experience. Certainly those philosophers who focus upon the authenticity and autonomy of choice would argue that real commitment to democracy is inconsistent with external coercion from the educational system.[49] Would the acceptance of our recommendations turn valid democratic commitment into mindless assent to democratic principles?

Other critics might note that the many lukewarm democrats in our midst present opportunities as well as dangers to the system. The discontented will always submit democracy to test. In turn, testing permits democracies to learn from their people. Perhaps those who withhold support from the system provide it with the criticism it needs to protect itself and to grow.[50] In this view, the challenge to democracy is to profit from but not to fall prey to discontinuities in socialization.

[49] I have in mind the philosophers of existentialism, particularly Sartre.
[50] This view borrows heavily from the sociological theories of Lewis Coser. See, particularly, Lewis A. Coser, *Continuities in the Study of Social Conflict* (New York: The Free Press, 1967), chap. 3.

Is it inconsistent for us to advocate improvement in democratic socialization and yet to avow a belief in the utility of socialization discontinuities? Not really. We are concerned only that there be enough democrats in the American system to permit it to learn from but not to succumb to dissidence. We would differ from our hypothetical critics only in striking the balance between socialized commitment and creative discontinuity.

Other critics might argue that our recommendations smack of a conservative bias. Certainly much empirical democratic theory and some research into political socialization does appear to emphasize and even advocate political stability above all else.[51] It might seem that because our study focuses upon the inculcation of traditional democratic norms, it is ripe for this same criticism.

But we have not slighted the analysis of revitalizing change. On the contrary, we have described the limited capacity that formal education brings to the system's struggle to maintain itself. Our study also uncovers such precursors of youthful instability as low levels of partisanship and high rates of support for political participation beyond the vote. In addition, we have shown that student understanding of and commitment to democracy grows only moderately during adolescence. High school thus ends with the promise of substantial flexibility in the political behavior of the young. In short, social change breeds in the many interstices of the school. Our recommendations are intended not to prevent, but to manage this change.

So much for criticisms of the approach we have taken, the conclusions we have derived, and the recommendations we have offered. Our final thoughts return to the school. Though many political theorists have speculated on the contribution that the school brings to democracy, none, with the possible exception of John Dewey, has articulated a philosophy of democratic education.[52] This failure of vision is reflected in the bitter fruits that our schools are currently reaping. Public education today serves as a lightning rod, attracting the diverse and clamorous forces that have

[51] It is precisely this tendency that Dennis and Easton attempt to thwart. See Jack Dennis and David Easton, *Children in the Political System* (New York: McGraw-Hill, Inc., 1969), pt. 1.

[52] See, for example, John Dewey, *The Child and the Curriculum* (Chicago: University of Chicago Press, 1959); see also John Dewey, *Democracy and Education* (New York: Crowell-Collier and Macmillan, Inc., 1916).

produced a crisis in democracy. It is not rhetoric alone that suggests that the viability of the school mirrors, in microcosm, the viability of the democratic system. Thus, we can think of no more opportune time to reconsider the political theory of democratic education.

The school will continue to perform indifferently until educators and the lay public agree upon and aim toward meeting the legitimate goals of schooling. Education cannot serve the public weal until the public serves education. That the extremes of occupational and cultural specialization in the age of technology present formidable barriers to any consensus on education does not alter this point. Should the schools fail to socialize, the democratic system will stand at the mercy of powerful forces over which it has only indirect and limited control. We have shown that the efforts of policy makers to improve education can have strategic, though restrained, positive effects on democratic socialization. Whether such efforts will be forthcoming is a question that no study—but only the people—can answer.

Appendix A
The Methodology of the Study

This appendix provides some details pertinent to the conduct of the study. We could not include every relevant piece of information, but we do treat salient factors involving sample, administration, field procedures, and methodological decisions.

THE STUDENT STUDY

We undertook two pretests of the student questionnaire. The first occurred during the early summer of 1967. This pretest covered one hundred summer school ninth- and twelfth-graders in Chalmers. None of these pretested respondents made his way into the main study the following fall. We ran a second pretest on thirty-five sixth-graders at the UCLA Elementary School. In both cases, we were mainly concerned to eliminate ambiguous items from the questionnaire. We included a Question-Unclear option in the final schedule to control ambiguous items still further. Naturally, more sixth-graders than ninth- or twelfth-graders found questions unclear. However, in the case of only one item did as many as 20 percent of the sixth-graders report that they did not understand the question. Missing data on the attitudinal items were assigned the relevant mean scores for the dimension. This procedure allowed us to retain many respondents in the sample.

The student field work lasted approximately six weeks during the late fall and early winter of 1967. We determined from conversations with school officials that it would be impossible to select a random sample of individual students. To administrators, the problems associated with administering questionnaires to some students but not to others in a class seemed insurmountable. We therefore decided to sample whole classes. We selected the sample classes with the cooperation of school principals, each of whom was told that we desired no unrepresentative extremes of intelligence, accomplishment, or motivations to be included in our study. Our findings lead us to believe that we have a good sample, although the high proportion of "A" students among sixth-graders gives us pause. Unfortunately, the requirement of student anonymity prevented us from assessing parts of this problem.

We constructed the questionnaires to occupy the average sixth-grader no more than one class period (approximately fifty minutes). In practice, most students at all grade levels found it easy enough to complete the questionnaires in forty minutes or less.

We sampled sixth-graders in each of Chalmers' seven elementary schools; in all, we looked at ten classes. The imbalance occurs because of the size of individual schools. We also sampled nine classes of ninth-graders and seven of twelfth-graders from Chalmers Junior High School and Chalmers High School. We have data from approximately 40 percent of the sixth-, ninth-, and twelfth-graders in Chalmers. In Moss City, the much more populous of the two districts, we selected nine classes from each of nine elementary schools. At least two of these nine schools were in each high-school attendance area. This practice assured us an accurate geographical representation of the district. We followed a similar procedure with our high-school sample. Each of the four Moss City High Schools provided two ninth-grade classes and two twelfth-grade classes. In all, we sampled approximately 10 percent of the sixth-, ninth-, and twelfth-graders in Moss City.

The unequal sample percentages in the two districts can be easily explained. We wanted to assure not only a representative sample from the districts, but also a sample large enough for the sort of statistical manipulations we anticipated. A much greater proportion of Chalmers than of Moss City students was needed to meet this requirement.

We decided early that we would ask home-room teachers to administer our questionnaires. This is an unusual procedure and requires explanation. Our pretesting experience convinced us that outsiders soliciting information while assuring students of anonymity produced among some respondents both levity and deliberate sabotage of the testing procedure. We hoped that the combination of familiar teachers handling the questionnaire administration, assurances to students that their identities were protected, and re-iteration that the study had no bearing on school work would retain the desirable degree of student seriousness without biasing our findings. We are convinced in retrospect that our procedure was sound.

We provided each teacher with a preliminary explanatory statement to be read to the class. In this way we kept administration uniform. In addition, teachers were themselves oriented before they administered the questionnaires.

Each teacher, upon collecting the questionnaires, publicly sealed them in an envelope and, shortly thereafter, conveyed them to her principal. Our observations of the testing period suggested that most students found the procedure a relaxing and interesting break from school routine. Almost all were serious and diligent. A number of teachers said that, once the questionnaires were collected, they had used some of the items as a take-off for class discussion.

THE TEACHER STUDY

We undertook the teacher field work during the spring of 1968, after selecting a random sample of each district's instructors from personnel records supplied by the districts. Proceeding alphabetically, we chose every third Chalmers teacher and every tenth Moss City teacher. The administrators in each district had informed their teachers that the project was authorized; consequently, few teachers who were selected refused to be interviewed. We interviewed approximately one-third of Chalmers' teachers and one-tenth of Moss City's teachers.

The percentile imbalance in the sample can again be explained by reference to the size of the districts. Only by interviewing one-third of the Chalmers staff could we be assured of a large enough sample for our analytic purposes. The same criterion could be met in Moss City with only a 10-percent sample.

Trained interviewers at the UCLA Survey Research Center conducted the interviews. Interviewers first contacted teachers by phone, told them of the purposes of the study, and assured them of their district's cooperativeness and of their own anonymity. Many respondents were already familiar with the student phase of the study. Most interviews took place at the school where the instructor taught. This procedure, while not optimal from our point of view, proved acceptable. We had hoped that all interviews could be conducted at teachers' residences. In this way, we hoped to avoid any halo or intimidation effect that might come from school surroundings. Unfortunately, most teachers were understandably anxious to enhance the convenience of their participation by fitting the interview into their school day. Furthermore, it proved financially more desirable for interviewers to see several teachers in the course of the day at a particular school, rather than to seek out individual teachers throughout the huge metropolitan Los Angeles area.

Most interviews took place during the teacher's free period or lunch break; others took place after school. The teacher usually spoke with the interviewer in relative privacy, most often in the teachers' lounge. Interviewers reported that almost all teachers seemed relaxed and unconcerned about their surroundings as they talked. Interviews usually lasted between thirty-five and fifty minutes, depending upon circumstances, interruptions, and the enthusiasm shown by the respondent.

A NOTE ON TESTS OF STATISTICAL SIGNIFICANCE

We have not dwelt on tests of statistical significance in this study for two reasons. The first is that such tests are useful principally for assessing whether findings can be generalized beyond the sample to some larger population. In our case, generalization goes *only to the districts involved*. As our description should have made clear, our samples were deliberately selected so that we could be reasonably sure that they accurately represent their districts. Hence, we have used statistical tests mainly for illustrative purposes.

Second, our student sample is so large that tests of statistical significance can add little to our student analysis. Significance tests are most useful when sample sizes are so small that the law of large numbers and the normal distribution cannot be assumed to be operating. We have thus confined most of our tests of significance to our teacher sample.

For elucidation of these problems from a perspective similar to our own, see Edward R. Tufte, "Improving Data Analysis in Political Science," *World Politics*, 21, No. 4 (July 1969), pp. 641–655; and Hannan C. Selvin, "A Critique of Tests of Significance in Survey Research," *American Sociological Review*, 22, No. 4 (October 1957), pp. 519–527.

Appendix B
The Instruments of the Study

[Both instruments are included for perusal. The code in parentheses following each question in Section I of the student questionnaire signifies the value dimension in which the question was grouped. The codes and dimensions are identified at the end of Section I of the questionnaire. (Obviously, such codes and dimension names did not appear on the student's questionnaire.)]

THE STUDENT QUESTIONNAIRE

These are some questions about government and current events. We are interested in the way students think about government. *You should not sign your name on this questionnaire. We do not need to know your name.* This is not a test and has nothing to do with your schoolwork. However, these questions *are important.* Many children in Los Angeles are helping us by answering them.

Therefore, please answer these questions as honestly and completely as you can.

Section I

First, we want to find out how you *feel* about the following things. Tell us if you *agree* or *disagree* with the following statements.

1. An election doesn't mean much unless the persons running disagree about some important things. (EFE)
   ____ I agree   ____ no opinion
   ____ I disagree   ____ question unclear

2. When you have elections, the vote of an important person should count for more than the vote of an average man. (MAR)
   ____ I agree   ____ no opinion
   ____ I disagree   ____ question unclear

3. The government should see to it that every American has enough money to live on. (LIC)
   ____ I agree   ____ no opinion
   ____ I disagree   ____ question unclear

4. When people don't like what is going on, they should try to change things by voting instead of using force. (RUG for sixth and ninth grades)
   ____ I agree   ____ no opinion
   ____ I disagree   ____ question unclear

5. The poor person should be helped to take part in politics, because he doesn't have as good a chance as the rich man. (OPP for sixth and ninth grades, POE for twelfth grade)
   ____ I agree   ____ no opinion
   ____ I disagree   ____ question unclear

6. What happens in the government will happen no matter what people do. It is like the weather; there is nothing people can do about it. (POE for sixth grade)
   ____ I agree   ____ no opinion
   ____ I disagree   ____ question unclear

7. If we let just a few people run things, our way of life would be in danger. (MIR)
   ____ I agree   ____ no opinion
   ____ I disagree   ____ question unclear

8. People in the government care about what people like my parents think. (POE for ninth and twelfth grade, VOTE for sixth grade)

___ I agree   ___ no opinion
___ I disagree   ___ question unclear

9. In addition to letting people vote, we should help them to take part in politics in other ways. (OPP for ninth and twelfth grades)

___ I agree   ___ no opinion
___ I disagree   ___ question unclear

10. A person who disagrees with almost everybody should still be allowed to talk. (MIR)

___ I agree   ___ no opinion
___ I disagree   ___ question unclear

11. Unless we have elections every so often, our democracy will not last. (EFE)

___ I agree   ___ no opinion
___ I disagree   ___ question unclear

12. Elections are silly, since most people don't know what they are voting for anyway. (PEC)

___ I agree   ___ no opinion
___ I disagree   ___ question unclear

13. A country is not really free until every person can vote. (VOTE)

___ I agree   ___ no opinion
___ I disagree   ___ question unclear

14. Democracy does not really mean that most of the people should run things. (MAR)

___ I agree   ___ no opinion
___ I disagree   ___ question unclear

15. I believe everyone should be able to speak out no matter what his ideas are. (FRS)

___ I agree   ___ no opinion
___ I disagree   ___ question unclear

16. I don't mind how a politician does his job as long as he gets the right things done. (RUG)

___ I agree   ___ no opinion
___ I disagree   ___ question unclear

17. A book that has wrong political ideas should not be printed. (FRS, RUG for twelfth grade)
    ____ I agree   ____ no opinion
    ____ I disagree   ____ question unclear

18. If those who disagree with most other people do not use force, they have every right to talk about their ideas. (MIR)
    ____ I agree   ____ no opinion
    ____ I disagree   ____ question unclear

19. The government has no business encouraging people to vote. (Not used)
    ____ I agree   ____ no opinion
    ____ I disagree   ____ question unclear

20. It is not up to government to make sure that all Americans have jobs. (LIC)
    ____ I agree   ____ no opinion
    ____ I disagree   ____ question unclear

21. People must be told when there is to be an election so that they can find out about the people running for office. (EFE)
    ____ I agree   ____ no opinion
    ____ I disagree   ____ question unclear

22. The government must have some say in what businessmen can do. (Not used)
    ____ I agree   ____ no opinion
    ____ I disagree   ____ question unclear

23. If people will not listen to and give in some to those who disagree with them, our government will be in real danger. (Not used)
    ____ I agree   ____ no opinion
    ____ I disagree   ____ question unclear

24. If too many people take part in politics, it will only lead to more disagreements. (OPP)
    ____ I agree   ____ no opinion
    ____ I disagree   ____ question unclear

25. It is all right to get around the law if you don't actually break it. (RUG)
    ____ I agree   ____ no opinion
    ____ I disagree   ____ question unclear

26. The government should see to it that schools in need get money. (Not used)
    ___ I agree   ___ no opinion
    ___ I disagree   ___ question unclear

27. The government ought to make sure that all people can vote. (VOTE)
    ___ I agree   ___ no opinion
    ___ I disagree   ___ question unclear

28. Most people are smart enough to know what is right or wrong in politics. (MAR)
    ___ I agree   ___ no opinion
    ___ I disagree   ___ question unclear

29. Government ought to see to it that old and poor people get good medical care. (LIC)
    ___ I agree   ___ no opinion
    ___ I disagree   ___ question unclear

30. Sometimes elections should not be held, because they may divide our people and help our enemies. (EFE)
    ___ I agree   ___ no opinion
    ___ I disagree   ___ question unclear

31. If the government would stay out of the way, private business would solve most of the country's problems. (Not used)
    ___ I agree   ___ no opinion
    ___ I disagree   ___ question unclear

32. In a democracy like ours, all our ideas must be open to change and discussion. (Not used)
    ___ I agree   ___ no opinion
    ___ I disagree   ___ question unclear

33. The real American way of life is dying so fast that we may have to use force to save it. (RUG for sixth grade, POE for ninth grade)
    ___ I agree   ___ no opinion
    ___ I disagree   ___ question unclear

34. In America only the people should be allowed to decide if a government leader is good or bad. (MAR)
    ___ I agree   ___ no opinion
    ___ I disagree   ___ question unclear

35. No matter what a person's political ideas are, he should have the same legal rights as anyone else. (RUG for sixth and ninth grades)
    ____ I agree   ____ no opinion
    ____ I disagree   ____ question unclear

36. It is just as important to allow people to take an active part in politics as it is to let them vote. (OPP)
    ____ I agree   ____ no opinion
    ____ I disagree   ____ question unclear

37. Unless all points of view can be discussed, there is little chance that the truth can ever be known. (FRS)
    ____ I agree   ____ no opinion
    ____ I disagree   ____ question unclear

38. Although the few must be allowed to say what they think, we cannot let them run things. (MIR)
    ____ I agree   ____ no opinion
    ____ I disagree   ____ question unclear

39. No matter who people vote for in elections, things go on pretty much the same. (POE for sixth grade)
    ____ I agree   ____ no opinion
    ____ I disagree   ____ question unclear

40. Many local elections aren't important enough to bother with. (PEC)
    ____ I agree   ____ no opinion
    ____ I disagree   ____ question unclear

41. If a person doesn't care how an election comes out, he shouldn't vote in it. (PEC)
    ____ I agree   ____ no opinion
    ____ I disagree   ____ question unclear

42. The whole government is run by a few big, powerful men and they don't care about us ordinary people. (POE)
    ____ I agree   ____ no opinion
    ____ I disagree   ____ question unclear

43. If people are not allowed to vote, they may use force to get their way. Therefore, we must make sure they can vote. (VOTE for ninth and twelfth grades)
    ____ I agree   ____ no opinion
    ____ I disagree   ____ question unclear

44. It isn't important to vote when the man you like doesn't have a chance to win. (PEC)

_____ I agree   _____ no opinion
_____ I disagree   _____ question unclear

Key to Dimension Value Code

VOTE—Support for the vote

POE—Political efficacy

RUG—Rules of the game

OPP—Opportunity to participate

FRS—Freedom of speech

MAR—Majority rule

EFE—Importance of elections

LIC—Liberalism

MIR—Minority rights

PEC—Sense of civic obligation

Section II

Now we want to see how much you _know_ about government. Please check the right answer to each question. If you don't know the answer to a question, don't worry. This is _not_ a school test. Just mark "don't know" and go on to the next question.

1. What type of government does the city of Los Angeles have?
   _____ city manager
   _____ weak mayor-council
   _____ strong mayor-council
   _____ commission
   _____ commission-council
   _____ don't know

2. The two branches of the California State Legislature are called
   _____ the Assembly, the House of Representatives
   _____ the Assembly of Representatives, the State Senate
   _____ the State Senate, the House of Representatives
   _____ the State Senate, the Assembly
   _____ the Congress, the State Senate
   _____ don't know

3. The Governor of the state of California is
   _____ Edmund G. ("Pat") Brown
   _____ Jesse Unruh
   _____ George Murphy
   _____ Ronald Reagan
   _____ Thomas Kuchel
   _____ don't know

4. Which is a power the states share with the national (federal) government?
   _____ coining money
   _____ making treaties
   _____ declaring war
   _____ issuing stamps
   _____ amending the United States Constitution
   _____ don't know

5. The number of United States Supreme Court Justices is
   _____ twelve
   _____ nine
   _____ five
   _____ ten
   _____ fifteen
   _____ don't know

6. The President of the United States is elected for a term of
   _____ four years
   _____ six years
   _____ two years
   _____ five years
   _____ one year
   _____ don't know

7. The three branches of the United States government are
   _____ Congress, the Supreme Court, the President
   _____ House of Representatives, Supreme Court, President
   _____ Senate, Supreme Court, President
   _____ Senate, House of Representatives, President
   _____ Congress, the Cabinet, the President
   _____ don't know

8. In the United States House of Representatives, the number of representatives for a state is
   _____ based on the geographical area of the state
   _____ based on the state's population

_____ equal to the number in every other state
_____ based upon the number of voters in the state
_____ decided by the governor of the state
_____ don't know

9. The Mayor of the city of Los Angeles is
_____ George Murphy
_____ George Christopher
_____ Thomas Kuchel
_____ Sam Yorty
_____ Alan Cranston
_____ don't know

10. A United States senator from the state of California is
_____ Max Rafferty
_____ Sam Yorty
_____ Thomas Kuchel
_____ Mark Hatfield
_____ Everett Dirksen
_____ don't know

11. Alexei Kosygin is a political leader of
_____ Hungary
_____ Soviet Union (Russia)
_____ Poland
_____ Bulgaria
_____ Rumania
_____ don't know

12. The Attorney General of the state of California is
_____ Robert H. Finch
_____ Alan Cranston
_____ Max Rafferty
_____ Frank M. Jordan
_____ Thomas C. Lynch
_____ don't know

13. The Secretary of the United States Department of Health, Education, and Welfare is
_____ John W. Gardner
_____ Henry H. Fowler
_____ Stewart L. Udall
_____ Orville Freeman
_____ Donald F. Hornig
_____ don't know

14. The Majority Leader of the United States Senate is
     ___ Thomas Dodd
     ___ Dean Rusk
     ___ Mike Mansfield
     ___ Everett Dirksen
     ___ Gerald Ford
     ___ don't know

15. The British Prime Minister is
     ___ Harold Wilson
     ___ Peter Griffiths
     ___ Harold Holt
     ___ George Brown
     ___ Lester Pearson
     ___ don't know

16. Mao Tse-tung is the leader of
     ___ Cuba
     ___ Philippines
     ___ Thailand
     ___ Communist China
     ___ Russia
     ___ don't know

Section III

Now, here are some questions about you as a person and what
you do. (Please check the correct answer.)

1. What does your father do for a living? What is his job? (If
   he is retired or no longer living, what did he do for a living?)
   Please give a full answer—for example, "salesman in a department store," "puts in phones for the telephone company,"
   and so forth. _____

2. How far did your parents go in school?

Father	Mother	
_____	_____	less than high school
_____	_____	some high school (9–11 years)
_____	_____	completed high school (12 years)
_____	_____	some college
_____	_____	completed college
_____	_____	went beyond college
_____	_____	don't know

3. In what country (countries) were your parents born? _____
   _____

4. In what country (countries) were your grandparents born?
   _____

5. I am _____ a boy _____ a girl

6. How many years have you been going to school in Moss City?
   _____

7. What is your grade average?
   _____ A   _____ B—
   _____ A—   _____ C+
   _____ B+   _____ C
   _____ B   _____ C—
            _____ D+ or below

8. Do you read newspapers?   _____ yes   _____ no
   What newspapers do you read? _____
   About how often do you read newspapers?
   _____ most days   _____ about every other day
   _____ hardly ever

9. In any one week during the school year, about how many
   hours of television do you watch?
   _____ 0 to 5   _____ 5 to 10   _____ 10 to 15
   _____ 15 to 20   _____ 20 or more

10. In addition to your schoolwork, do you read books for fun?
    (If no, please go on to question 11.)
    _____ yes   _____ no
    Which kind of books do you read most of the time?
    _____ fiction (for example, novels)
    _____ nonfiction (for example, history)
    During the last school year, about how many books did you
    read outside of your schoolwork?
    _____ 0 to 3   _____ 3 to 6   _____ 6 to 9
    _____ 9 to 12   _____ 12 or more

11. Do you go to the movies?   _____ yes   _____ no   (If
    no, please go on to question 12.)
    In any one month during the school year, about how many
    movies do you go to see?
    _____ 0 to 2   _____ 2 to 4   _____ 4 to 6
    _____ 6 to 8   _____ 8 or more

12. Do you read magazines? ____ yes ____ no (If no, please go on to question 13.)
    Which magazines do you read? _____

13. Here are some questions about your activity in school affairs. Have you:

    a. run for any office in school
       (such as student council)? ____ yes ____ no
    b. worked for a school political
       candidate? ____ yes ____ no
    c. discussed school elections with
       your friends? ____ yes ____ no
    d. been a member of any school
       organizations? ____ yes ____ no
       If yes, what organizations? _____
       _____
    e. let your class representative know
       what you think about a school
       problem? ____ yes ____ no
    f. let your teacher or principal know
       what you think about a school
       problem? ____ yes ____ no

14. Here are some questions about your participation in the community. Have you:

    a. worked for a community political
       candidate? ____ yes ____ no
    b. discussed elections with your
       friends? ____ yes ____ no
    c. been a member of any community
       organizations? (Boy Scouts,
       church groups, Little League) ____ yes ____ no
       If yes, how many?
       ____ 1   ____ 4
       ____ 2   ____ 5
       ____ 3
    d. let your congressman know what
       you think about a community
       issue? ____ yes ____ no
    e. ever written your congressman for
       any reason? ____ yes ____ no

15. Here are some questions about your future activity in community and political affairs. How likely do you think it is that you will:

a. run for public office?

___ not very likely   ___ somewhat likely
          ___ very likely

b. vote in national elections?

___ not very likely   ___ somewhat likely
          ___ very likely

c. vote in local elections?

___ not very likely   ___ somewhat likely
          ___ very likely

d. work for a political candidate?

___ not very likely   ___ somewhat likely
          ___ very likely

e. join a community-service organization? (for example, Chamber of Commerce, League of Women Voters, Kiwanis, etc.)

___ not very likely   ___ somewhat likely
          ___ very likely

f. join a political organization? (for example, Young Democrats, Young Republicans, etc.)

___ not very likely   ___ somewhat likely
          ___ very likely

g. let your congressman know what you think about a public issue?

___ not very likely   ___ somewhat likely
          ___ very likely

h. run for office in a community-service organization? (for example, Lion's Club, League of Women Voters, Kiwanis)

___ not very likely   ___ somewhat likely
          ___ very likely

16. Would you like, someday, to run for political office?

___ yes   ___ no

17. Which of these are you?

___ a Republican
___ a Democrat
___ an Independent
___ other   (If other, which party? ___)
___ don't know

18. Is there anything you like about the Democratic party?
    ___ yes   ___ no
    If you said yes, what do you like? _____

19. Is there anything you like about the Republican party?
    ___ yes   ___ no
    If you said yes, what do you like? _____

20. Is there anything you dislike about the Democratic party?
    ___ yes   ___ no
    If you said yes, what do you dislike? _____

21. Is there anything you dislike about the Republican party?
    ___ yes   ___ no
    If you said yes, what do you dislike? _____

THANK YOU FOR YOUR COOPERATION

THE TEACHER QUESTIONNAIRE

Introduction

Good morning (afternoon, evening) I am _____ from the
Survey Research Center at UCLA. As I mentioned when we set
up this appointment, Professor Merelman of the Civic Education Committee is conducting a study of the school's influence on
the development of students' democratic ideals. Your name was
chosen as part of a probability sample of teachers from the
_____ Unified School District. Your answers will be held
in strict confidence and at no time in the analysis of the data will
your name be connected with any answer that you may give. May
we begin?

Let's start by talking about your teaching background.

1. Where did you attend college? _____

2. What degrees do you hold?
    ___ AA   ___ AB   ___ BS
    ___ MA   ___ MS   ___ Ph.D.
    ___ B.Ed.   ___ M.Ed.   ___ Ed.D.

3. From what institutions did you receive degrees? _____

4. What were your major fields in college? _____

_____

5. Did you do most of your work in education or in other fields?
   ____ education   ____ other fields

6. a. What was your overall grade-point average as an under-
      graduate? _____
   b. What was your overall grade-point average as a graduate?

_____

7. Are you presently participating in any in-service training program in your district?
   ____ yes   ____ no

8. Are you still taking formal college course work as part of
   your teaching career?
   ____ yes   ____ no
   IF R ANSWERS YES, PROBE: What courses? _____

_____

9. How many years have you been teaching in your district?

_____

10. Do you have tenure?
    ____ yes   ____ no

11. What subjects do you teach? _____

12. Are you presently teaching courses that you were trained to
    teach?
    ____ yes   ____ no

13. What grade level do you generally teach? _____

Now let's talk about your present teaching situation.

14. As things stand now, how many years do you plan to con-
    tinue teaching? _____

    IF R PLANS TO LEAVE WITHIN THREE YEARS, ASK REASON AND
    THEN SKIP TO 16

    IF R PLANS TO STAY BEYOND THREE YEARS, PROBE BY ASKING:
    What about your present district? Do you plan to stay in it?

_____

15. Why do you plan to (stay, leave, undecided)? _____

_____

16. How much have you enjoyed teaching in your district? Would you say it had been
    ____ very enjoyable?   ____ somewhat enjoyable?
    ____ not very enjoyable?

17. What do you like best about teaching in your district? _____
    _____

18. How do you feel about the salary schedule of your district? In your opinion is it
    ____ unsatisfactory?   ____ satisfactory?   ____ superior?

19. What do you think about the teaching conditions in your district? Are they
    ____ superior?   ____ satisfactory?   ____ unsatisfactory?

20. How about your extracurricular duties? Are they
    ____ burdensome?   ____ moderate?   ____ light?

21. How would you rate your own performance as a teacher? Would you say it was
    ____ superior?   ____ satisfactory?   ____ unsatisfactory?

22. Would you say that you tried as hard as you could as a teacher
    ____ none of the time?   ____ a little of the time?
    ____ half the time?   ____ most of the time?
    ____ all of the time?
    Let's talk for a moment about your students and colleagues.

23. How responsive are your students as a whole? Would you say they were
    ____ not very responsive?   ____ moderately responsive?
    ____ quite responsive?

24. How do the students feel about you as a teacher? Would you say they like you
    ____ very much?   ____ moderately?   ____ not very much?

25. How cooperative are your students? Would you say they were
    ____ quite uncooperative?   ____ moderately cooperative?
    ____ quite cooperative?

26. How much effort do your students put into their schoolwork? Would you say they try
    ____ very hard?   ____ moderately hard?   ____ not very hard?

27. Shifting the subject momentarily, about how many good friends do you have among other teachers in your district?

_____

IF R SAYS "NO FRIENDS," SKIP TO QUESTION 29

28. How close would you say these friends are? Are they
____ very close?   ____ moderately close?
____ not very close?

29. Are your fellow teachers interesting people?
____ yes   ____ no
IF R SAYS YES, CONTINUE TO #30. IF R SAYS NO, SKIP TO #31.

30. In what way are they interesting? _____

31. How much do your fellow colleagues care about your teaching ability and overall professional performance? Do they care
____ very much?   ____ somewhat?   ____ not very much?

32. Which of the statements on this card best characterizes your feelings about the people you teach with?
SHOW R CARD
____ a.   ____ b.   ____ c.

33. How much do your fellow teachers care about you as a person? Do they care
____ very little?   ____ somewhat?
____ very much?   ____ don't know?   (DON'T READ)

Now let's talk about some other aspects of your teaching. In the following sets of statements will you please tell me which statement you are most likely to agree with.

34. Here is the first set:
    a. Teaching is far more rewarding and satisfying than I had ever believed it would be. ____
    b. My experience in education convinces me that teaching, at the present time, does not enjoy professional status. ____

35. Which of these would you be more likely to agree with?
    a. Administrators are skilled and experienced former teachers who play an integral role in the instruction of the young. ____

    b. Administrators are ex-teachers who have sought their present positions primarily because of salary considerations. ____

36. And what about these?
    a. Classroom instruction is the most important form of educational activity. ____
    b. Classroom instruction is important, but administration and counseling probably contribute more to the overall educational program. ____

37. In general, how would you characterize your relationships with the school administrative authorities? Would you say these relationships were
    ____ quite satisfactory?   ____ moderately satisfactory?
    ____ not satisfactory?

38. Now I am going to read you a list of several aspects of your job. Will you please tell me if you consider each aspect as being little or no burden, a moderate burden, or a heavy burden.

The first aspect is:	class-room instruc-tion	Is it:	little or no burden ____	a mod-erate burden ____	a heavy burden ____
The next aspect is:	grading	Is it:	little or no burden ____	a mod-erate burden ____	a heavy burden ____
The next aspect is:	extra-curric-ular activi-ties	Is it:	little or no burden ____	a mod-erate burden ____	a heavy burden ____
The next aspect is:	teacher-parent confer-ences	Is it:	little or no burden ____	a mod-erate burden ____	a heavy burden ____
The next aspect is:	record keeping	Is it:	little or no burden ____	a mod-erate burden ____	a heavy burden ____

| The next aspect is: | retaining and improving credentials | Is it: | little or no burden ____ | a moderate burden ____ | a heavy burden ____ |
| The last aspect is: | faculty and committee meetings | Is it: | little or no burden ____ | a moderate burden ____ | a heavy burden ____ |

39. All things considered and knowing what you now know, if you had it to do over again, how likely is it you would go into teaching? Is it
    ____ quite likely?   ____ somewhat likely?
    ____ not very likely?

No doubt you have some opinions about the community you teach in and of your superiors. Let's talk a little about this.

40. I am going to read you a list of groups. Will you please indicate if you have ever received suggestions from any of these groups designed to improve or change your teaching.
    a. The first is your superiors (principals, and so forth)
       ____ yes   ____ no
       IF R INDICATES YES, THEN PROBE: What sorts of suggestions? _____
    b. The next is parents
       ____ yes   ____ no
       IF R INDICATES YES, THEN PROBE: What sorts of suggestions? _____
    c. The next is other teachers
       ____ yes   ____ no
       IF R INDICATES YES, THEN PROBE: What sorts of suggestions? _____
    d. The next is community groups
       ____ yes   ____ no
       IF R INDICATES YES, THEN PROBE: What sorts of suggestions? _____

41. How helpful, in general, have these suggestions been? Have they been
    ____ quite helpful?   ____ moderately helpful?
    ____ not helpful?

42. What kinds of community support to the general educational program (for instance, favorable publicity about the schools by a local newspaper) are unique to your district? _____
_____

43. Are there things that the community could do for its teachers in your district that it is not now doing?
____ yes   ____ no
IF R ANSWERS YES, THEN PROBE: What specifically could the community do? _____

44. Are there any things that the community could do for its schools that it is not now doing?
____ yes   ____ no
IF R ANSWERS YES, THEN PROBE: What specifically could the community do? _____

45. How much support would you say that the community gives to public education as a whole? Would you say the community gives
____ very little support?   ____ moderate support?
____ a great deal of support?

46. What groups (political, business, religious) in the community affect the conduct of education most in your district? _____
_____

47. What groups are the major supporters of public education in your district? _____

48. Are there any groups critical of public education in your district?
____ yes   ____ no
IF R ANSWERS YES PROBE: Who are they? _____

Now we'd like to obtain your response to several questions about government and politics. Most of the questions I'm going to ask may sound rather simple to an adult. Some were designed for youngsters. Please try to ignore their lack of sophistication and answer as frankly as possible. Tell me if you agree or disagree with each item as I read it.

49. When you have elections, the votes of an important person should count for more than the vote of an average man. Do you
____ agree?   ____ disagree?   ____no opinion (DON'T READ)

50. What happens in the government will happen no matter what people do. It is like the weather, there is nothing people can do about it. Do you

     ___ agree?   ___ disagree?   ——no opinion (DON'T READ)

51. People in the government care about what people like me think. Do you

     ___ agree?   ___ disagree?   ——no opinion (DON'T READ)

52. A person who disagrees with almost everybody should still be allowed to talk. Do you

     ___ agree?   ___ disagree?   ——no opinion (DON'T READ)

53. Democracy does not really mean that most of the people should run things. Do you

     ___ agree?   ___ disagree?   ——no opinion (DON'T READ)

54. If those who disagree with most others do not use force, they have every right to talk about their ideas. Do you

     ___ agree?   ___ disagree?   ——no opinion (DON'T READ)

55. Most people are smart enough to know what is right or wrong in politics. Do you

     ___ agree?   ___ disagree?   ——no opinion (DON'T READ)

56. In America only the people should be allowed to decide if a government leader is good or bad. Do you

     ___ agree?   ___ disagree?   ——no opinion (DON'T READ)

57. Although the few must be allowed to criticize, we cannot let them rule. Do you

     ___ agree?   ___ disagree?   ——no opinion (DON'T READ)

58. No matter who people vote for in elections, things go on pretty much the same. Do you

     ___ agree?   ___ disagree?   ——no opinion (DON'T READ)

59. There are some powerful men who are running the whole government and they do not care about us ordinary people. Do you

     ___ agree?   ___ disagree?   ——no opinion (DON'T READ)

And now for some general questions.

60. How often do you vote in national elections? Do you vote

     ___ all of the time?   ___ most of the time?
     ___ half of the time?   ___ infrequently?   ___ never?

61. How often do you vote in state elections? Do you vote
    ___ all of the time?   ___ most of the time?
    ___ half of the time?   ___ infrequently?   ___ never?

62. How often do you vote in local elections? Do you vote
    ___ all of the time?   ___ most of the time?
    ___ half of the time?   ___ infrequently?   ___ never?

63. Are there any political or social issues that you think should not be discussed in the classroom?
    ___ yes   ___ no
    IF R ANSWERS YES, PROBE: Which issues, specifically? ___
    _____

    IF R GAVE EXAMPLES OF ISSUES, ASK: Why shouldn't these issues be discussed? _____

64. Which, if any, of these subjects have you discussed with your students in the past school year in class?
    a. Vietnam?   ___ yes   ___ no
    b. narcotics and LSD?   ___ yes   ___ no
    c. tuition at the University of
       California?   ___ yes   ___ no
    d. rioting in U.S. cities?   ___ yes   ___ no
    e. the hippie phenomenon?   ___ yes   ___ no
    f. communism?   ___ yes   ___ no

65. Would you say that you were:
    ___ a Republican?
    ___ a Democrat?
    ___ an independent?
    ___ a member of another party?
    ___ no party identification? (DON'T READ)
    IF R ANSWERED EITHER REPUBLICAN OR DEMOCRAT, ASK:
    Do you think of yourself as a strong or not-so-strong party partisan?
    ___ strong Democrat
    ___ weak Democrat
    ___ strong Republican
    ___ weak Republican

66. What is your religious preference?
    ___ Protestant
    ___ Roman Catholic

_____ Jewish
_____ Buddhist
_____ Greek Orthodox
_____ other
_____ none

67. INTERVIEWER: NOTE SEX OF R
_____ male
_____ female

Thank you for your time.

Index